DISCOVERING CANADIAN ART
Learning the Language

Bryan Bennett
Constance P. Hall

Prentice-Hall Canada Inc.,
Scarborough, Ontario

Cover: *Swing Home*, Robert Sinclair
1980, acrylic on canvas, 185.4 cm
x 100.9 cm, superimposed on a detail
from the same painting.

Prentice-Hall Inc., Englewood Cliffs, New Jersey
Prentice-Hall International, Inc., London
Prentice-Hall of Australia, Pty., Ltd., Sydney
Prentice-Hall of India, Pvt., Ltd., New Delhi
Prentice-Hall of Japan, Inc., Tokyo
Prentice-Hall of Southeast Asia (Pte) Ltd., Singapore
Editora Prentice-Hall do Brasil Ltda., Rio de Janeiro

Canadian Cataloguing in Publication Data
Bennett, Bryan, 1947-
Discovering Canadian art : learning the language

For use in schools.
ISBN 0-13-215310-6 (pbk)
ISBN 0-13-215203-7 (bound)

1. Art appreciation - Juvenile literature.
2. Composition (Art) - Juvenile literature.
I. Hall, Constance P. (Constance Purmal), 1944-
II. Title.

N85.B46 1984 701'.1 C84-098170-8

Production Editor: Wilda Lossing
Design: Michael van Elsen Design Inc.
Illustrations: Victoria Birta
Production: Barbara Almos
Colour Separation: Colourgraph Reproduction Systems Inc.
Composition: Compeer Typographic Services Ltd.
Manufactured in Canada by Bryant Press
For use in schools.
ISBN 0-13-215310-6 (pbk) ISBN 0-13-215203-7 (bound)

4 5 6 BP 89 88 87

Contents

To David Ian,
David and Scott

Acknowledgements

The authors are deeply grateful to the many people who have helped to make this book possible and to all the artists, artisans, galleries and museums who generously allowed work to be included.

Special thanks to Susan Campbell, National Gallery of Canada; Paulette Charette, The Canada Council Art Bank; Brian Stratton and Sandy Cook, McMichael Canadian Collection; Maia Sutnik, Art Gallery of Ontario; Sandy Dunn, Ontario Crafts Council; Dr. Margaret Travis, C.S.E.A. Canadian Young People's Art Collection; Scott Turner, Haakon Bakken, Robin King, Jacqui Allen, Sheridan College of Visual Arts/School of Crafts and Design; Marie McDonald, Creative Source, Wilcord Publications Ltd.; Linda Goodwin, Ontario Ministry of Tourism and Recreation.

Also, special appreciation to Joanne Bennett for typing, filing and correspondence.

In addition, thanks to Marlene Fletcher and Deana Maynard, Faculty of Science, McMaster University, for word processing.

At Prentice-Hall Canada Inc. we also wish to thank Henry Cunha and Lois Rock for their editorial assistance.

YOU AND ART

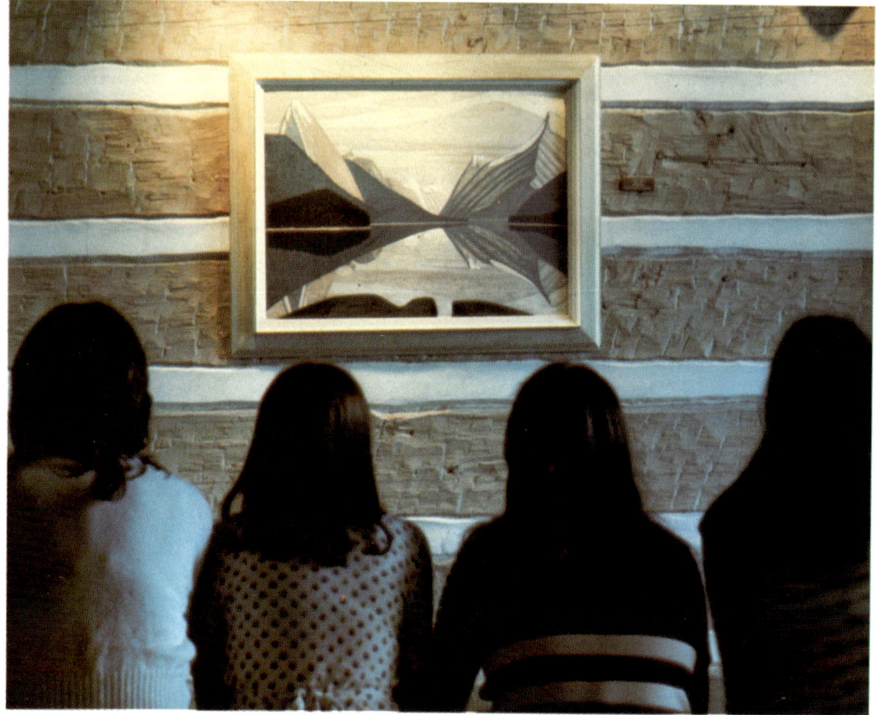

1-1 Viewing art, McMichael Canadian Collection, Kleinburg

1. What Is Art?

Imagine a world without art! What would you have to take away? The fine paintings that hang in art galleries? Sculpture in public places? The dancing fountains and the colourful wall designs in shopping malls? The eye-catching window displays and posters? What would be left of the stately old churches once the stone carvings, the wood carvings and the stained glass windows were removed? What would be left of buildings themselves? What would become of the objects around you and even the clothes that you are wearing? What would be left? Look around and you will see how artists, craftspeople and designers all produce work that make your world more interesting.

Art is made by individuals from selected materials and is seen by others. The artist–viewer relationship in art may be compared to that of the speaker and the listener in a conversation. *Art is humanity's visual language*. Art may be straightforward and easy to understand or it may be complex. In either case, knowing how the language of art works can help you to understand and appreciate more of your visual world.

This book aims to teach you the basics of the art language. It focuses on Canadian art, because that makes up so much of the art around you. As you read this book, you will become more aware of your visual world, what you see and how you see it. You will see how *design* elements and principles are the words and grammar of the language of art. You will recognize the *media* commonly used by the artists. Finally, you will discover how the meanings of art become clearer after considering *subject matter* and *style*.

Generally, words that appear in *italic* type are key words in art. They are defined in the glossary at the back of the book.

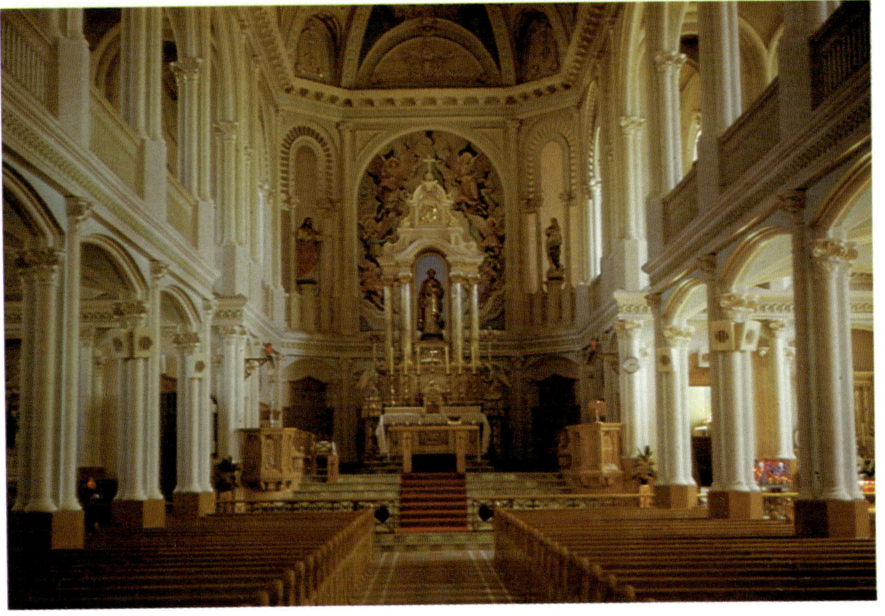

1-2 St. Peter's Church (interior) Cheticamp, Nova Scotia

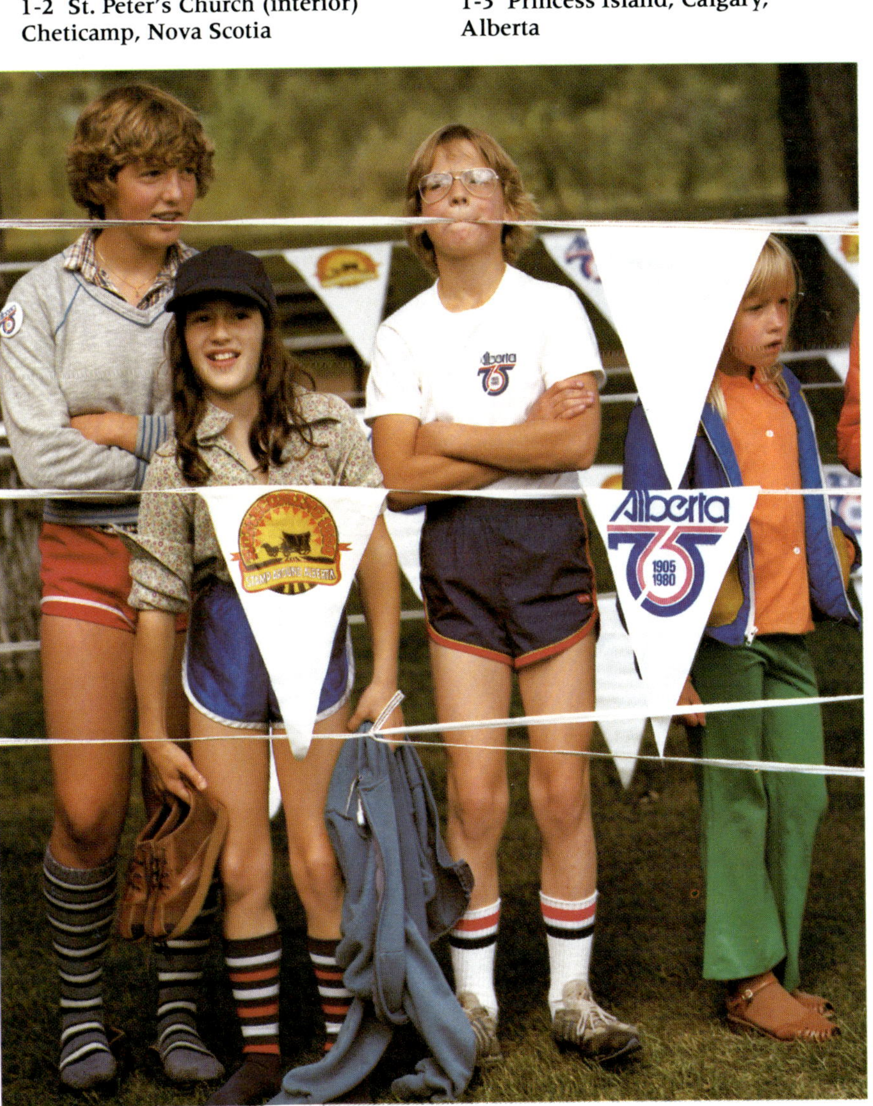

1-3 Princess Island, Calgary, Alberta

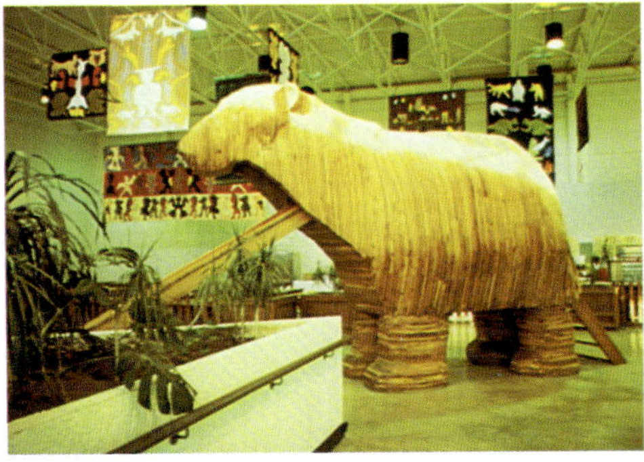

1-4 Polar bear sculpture slide, Town Complex, Churchill, Manitoba

Art is everywhere! Art is so much a part of your life that you can easily take it for granted.

Look Again

- Search through the pictures in this book for examples of the type of art that you see in your everyday life.
- On your way to school tomorrow make a list of the art that you see.

2. Why People Make Art

A lot of people make art to support the needs of business and industry. Such art, called *commercial art*, includes book illustrations, advertisements in magazines, and posters. It also includes the design of products, such as cars and telephones, and the design of packages for many different items. Commercial artists possess the special interests and artistic skills that the commercial world needs to produce and promote its goods and services.

Other art is made for a variety of reasons. It may be used for self-expression – to share personal thoughts and feelings with other people. It may be used to share the beliefs of a group of people, such as a protest group, or a nation. It may be made to brighten up a dull environment. The types of people who make art are just as varied. Students make art as part of a course. Many people – including students – make art as an enjoyable hobby. For other people, making art is the most important part of their lives – whether or not it is their regular job – and they put a lot of effort into developing their skills.

This book aims to show you a sample of the work of artists from across Canada. It includes some "famous" art, of the type you see in galleries. In addition, it includes examples of commercial art, student art, and crafts. The aim is to help you to discover some basic ideas in art. This art is made by young people and by adults, by men and by women. It includes art made by Canada's Native peoples as well as other Canadians whose families have come from many different parts of the world. All of them use the same language: the language of art.

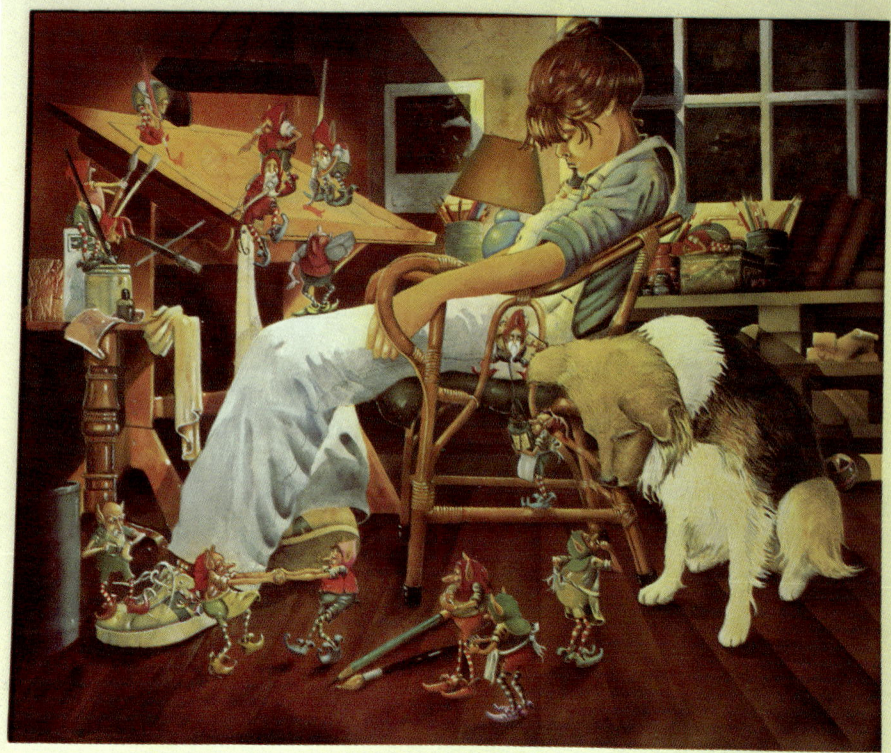

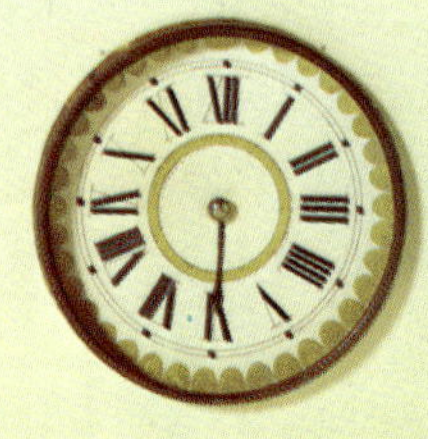

2-1 *Why do they all call at once?*
Maryann Kovalski
Maryann Kovalski is a commercial artist. Her illustrations are commissioned works of art. Here she has illustrated herself at her work place. The picture is called *Why do they all call at once?* What do you think she is trying to say in this picture? What particular parts of the picture give you that message?

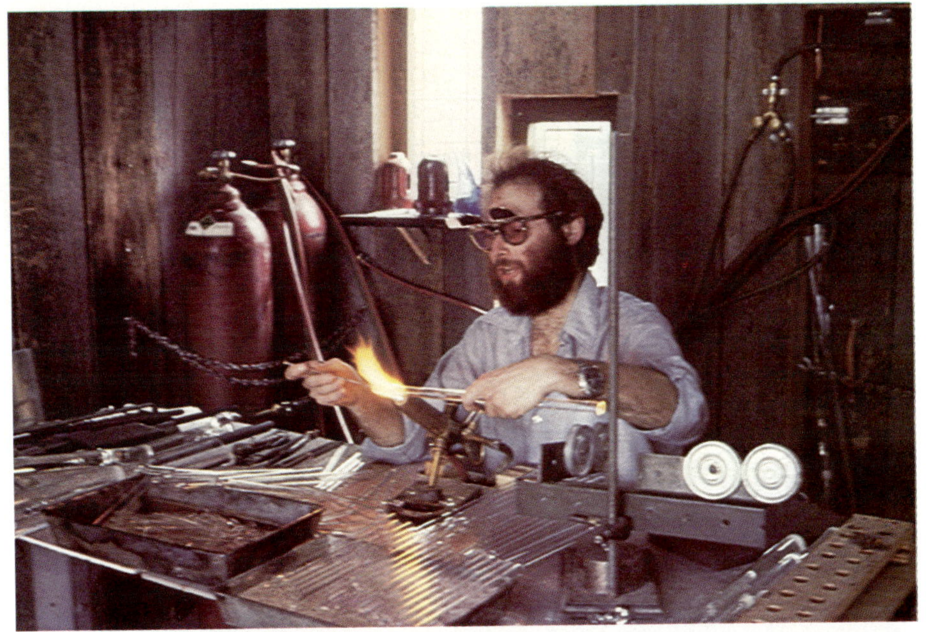

2-2 Glass sculptor at work
Winnipeg artisan Len Chodirker is a sculptor in glass. His studio is different because of the materials he uses. An example of his work may be seen in Chapter 27.

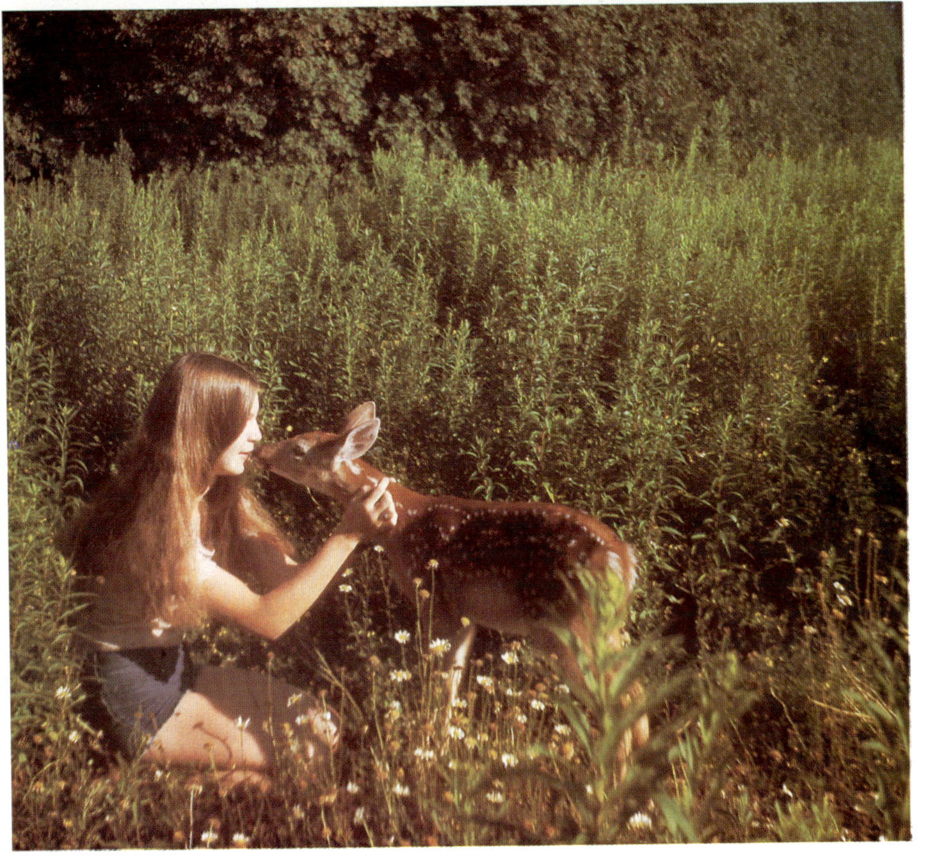

2-3 Wildlife artist with fawn
Judy Robinson-Oldfield is a wildlife artist. Here we see Judy with Felix, a fawn she raised by hand. Felix is a favourite subject for Judy's art work and may be seen again in Chapter 32. Why do you think Judy has chosen wildlife as the subject of her art?

Look Again

- Make a list of the reasons why *you* make art.
- Now read the text and see if your reasons are mentioned.
- Are there other reasons for making art than the ones you chose? If there are, write them down as part of your list.

- Look through Section Three of this book, and try to find at least one example of art that has been made for each reason on your list.

- Do you ever think that it would be glamorous to be an artist? Look again at Maryann Kovalski's studio, and the studio of Len Chodirker. Did you think that an artist's studio would look so much like a workshop? If not, what did you think it would look like?
- What do you think a fashion designer's studio would look like? What about the studio of a person who photographs famous people?
- What kind of studio would you like to work in?

3. Forms of Art

Art can take many forms. This book can only show you a small sample. It includes the following forms:

There is painting, sculpture and architecture. These forms are sometimes called the *fine arts*. There are also forms known as *applied arts*. This book includes several of them: drawing, printmaking, graphic arts, crafts, and photography.

An important classification of forms of art concerns dimension. Some forms of art are *two-dimensional*. The two dimensions are length and width. Two-dimensional art is flat. Paintings, drawings, prints and photographs are two-dimensional. Other forms of art are *three-dimensional*. The third dimension is depth. Sculpture, architecture and some crafts are three-dimensional. Two-dimensional art is meant to be viewed from the front only. Three-dimensional art can be looked at from a variety of angles.

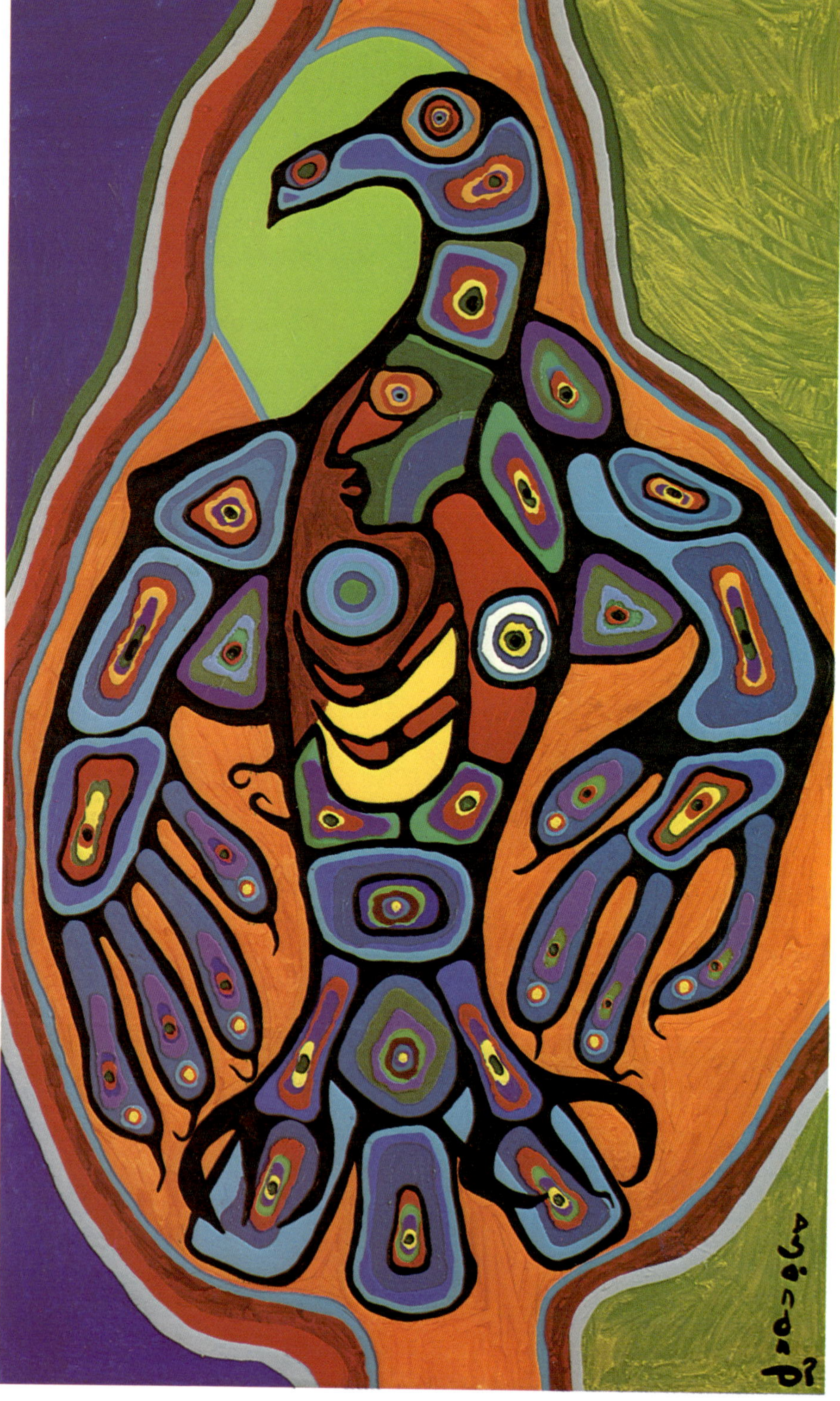

3-1 *Thunderbird with Inner Spirit*, **Norval Morrisseau**
Painting and drawing are familiar art forms. Norval Morrisseau's *Thunderbird with Inner Spirit* reflects his Ojibwa heritage in the modern medium of acrylic paint.

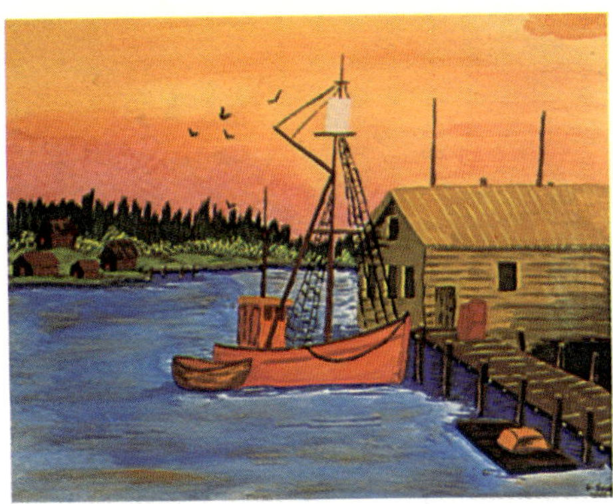

3-2 ***The Old Harbour, Powell River B.C.*****, Sandra Scott**
The Old Harbour, Powell River B.C. is an example of art created by students like you. The Canadian Society for Education through Art has contributed to this book many fine examples of student art from across Canada.

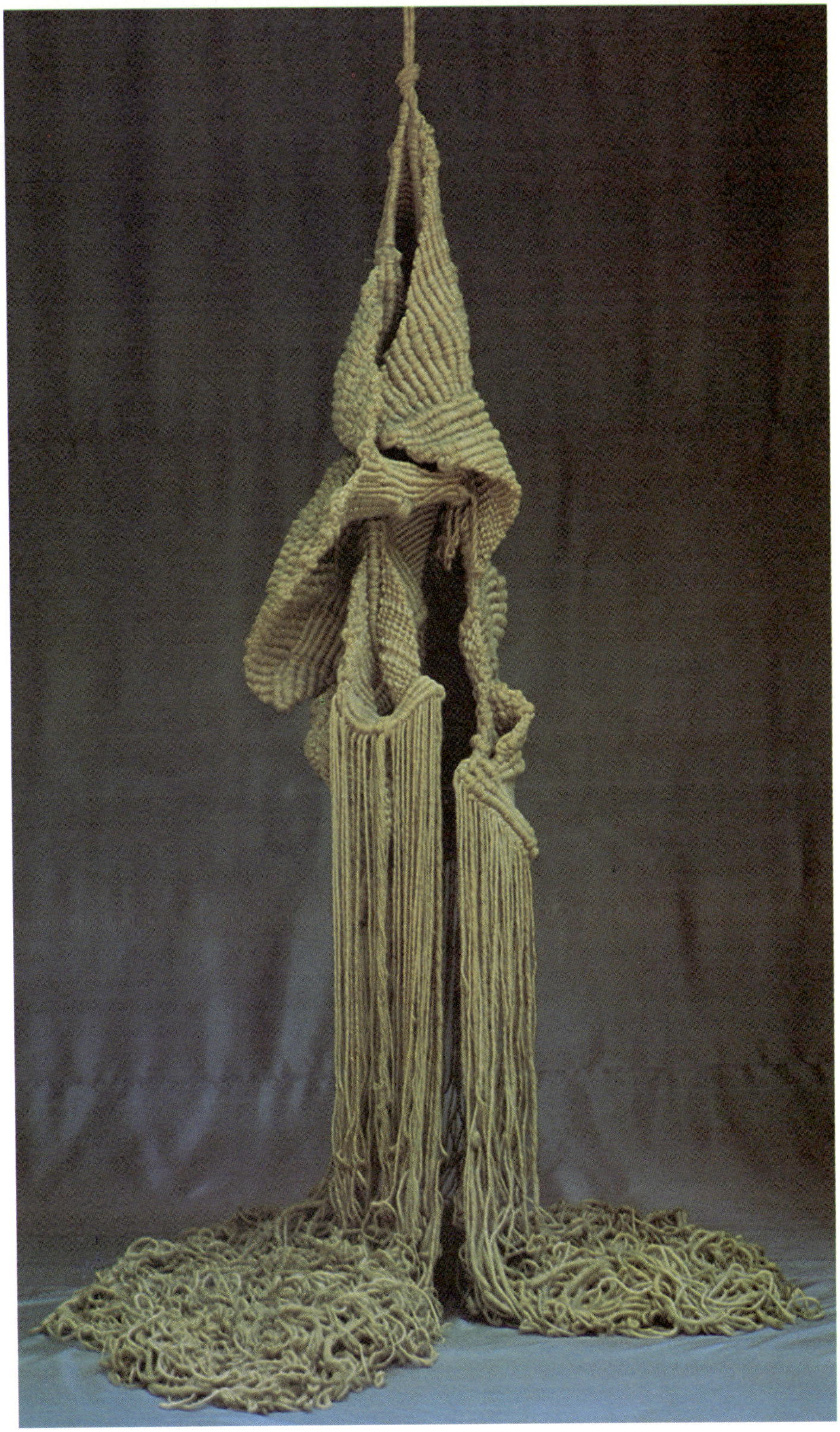

Look Again

- The caption to 3-1 tells you that the artist uses a modern medium to say something about his traditional Indian heritage. What things in this picture recall the traditional past?
- Why do you think Norval Morrisseau uses modern paint for a traditional painting?

- Art is created in many forms. While only fine art (painting), student art, and crafts have been shown here, examples of other forms appear elsewhere. The titles of Chapters 20-27 tell you which forms of art appear in this book. Try to find examples of all those forms in other chapters!

- Of the images shown here, which are two-dimensional and which are three-dimensional art forms?

3-3 ***Elizabethan Study, No. 1*****, Frauke Voss**
Knotting is only one of the many craft forms presented in this text. Other examples of crafts appear in Chapter 27 and elsewhere in this book.

4-1 Dragon Fyre poster for Canada's Wonderland, Cliff Kearns
Posters are used to catch your attention. Cliff Kearns' poster is intended to attract you to an exciting amusement park ride.

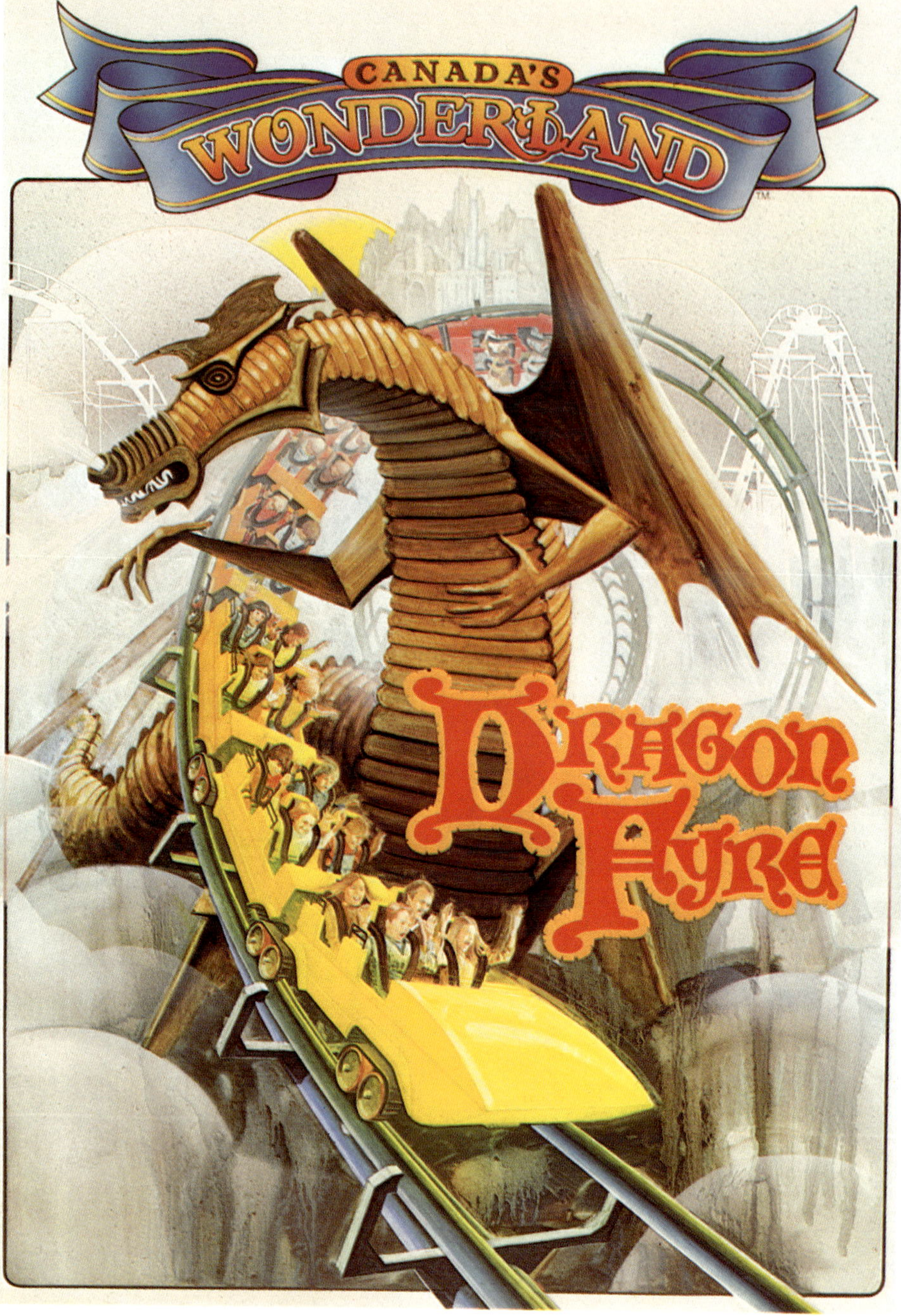

4. The Messages Sent by Art

An artist who creates a work of art creates a new visual image. This visual image carries a message to people who view it. As you become more aware of your role as a viewer, you become more aware of the variety of messages sent by art. These messages can be separated into three categories.

First, *art can be used to send all the messages for which words are commonly used*. Like written and spoken language, the visual language of art can tell stories and relay facts. For example, many historical events and facts about ancient cultures, including those of Canada's own Native peoples, have been recorded through art rather than writing. Today, as in the past, statues and paintings honour important people and commemorate great deeds. Advertising posters catch your attention and persuade you in the way that radio commercials do. The cartoon section of your newspaper, on the other hand, may amuse or entertain you as much as any joke you hear.

Second, *art can often be better at expressing messages for which words seem inadequate*. The stained glass windows of a church colour the light inside the building and make it seem special and holy. Illustrations and carefully composed photographs on greeting cards help send emotional messages of love, joy and grief that are hard to put into words.

Third, *art can simply ask the viewer to enjoy its appearance*. The images created by artists add to the quality of life. The lines, shapes, colours and textures of works of art may be created to give visual pleasure.

Some images are made to decorate. Jewellery adorns people and banners bring places to life. Meanwhile, the designers of our world make useful things pleasing to look at. Fashion designs in clothing, product designs of cars and lamps, for example, have a visual role as well as a practical role.

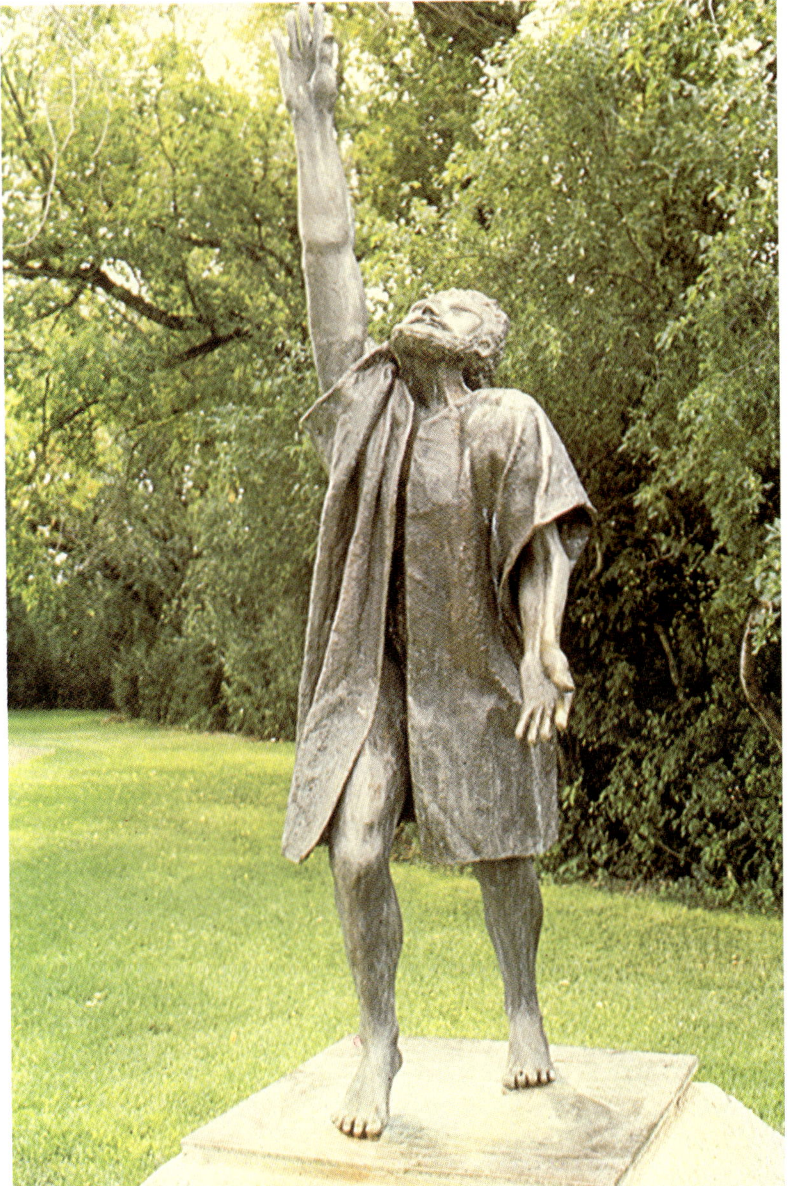

4-2 ***Louis Riel, Métis leader*****, John Nugent, Wascana Centre, Regina**
Louis Riel led the Métis people in the Red River Rebellion of 1869 to protect the rights and culture of the Métis people. In 1885, Riel was hanged.

Look Again

- Could Cliff Kearns' poster persuade you to ride the Dragon Fyre?
- What sort of ride do you think it would be? Relaxing or exciting? Slow or fast? Make a list of all the words you can think of to describe the ride.
- What images in the picture made you think of those words?

- What feeling is portrayed by the Louis Riel statue?
- Look elsewhere in this book for a piece of art that makes you feel happy.

- Imagine you could choose any piece of art from Section Four of this book to put in your own room. Which one would you choose, and why?

- Think about three types of messages sent by art. What other example of these types of messages can you think of?

- Does art ever send more than one type of message? Think of examples.

Look for three general areas in each work of art: subject matter, form and message (artists sometimes call the message "expressive content"). The subject in each illustration is a person. The form of one is a drawing, the other is sculpture. Both express sadness as the message to the viewer.

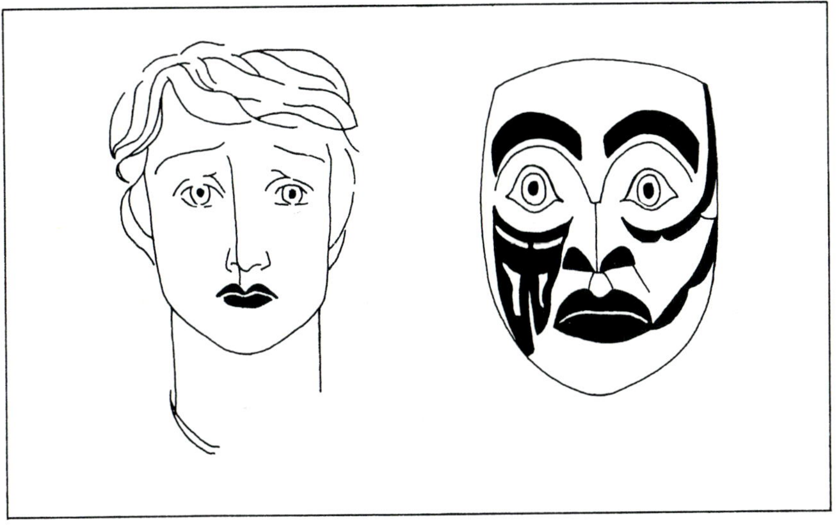

YOU AND THE VISUAL PROCESS

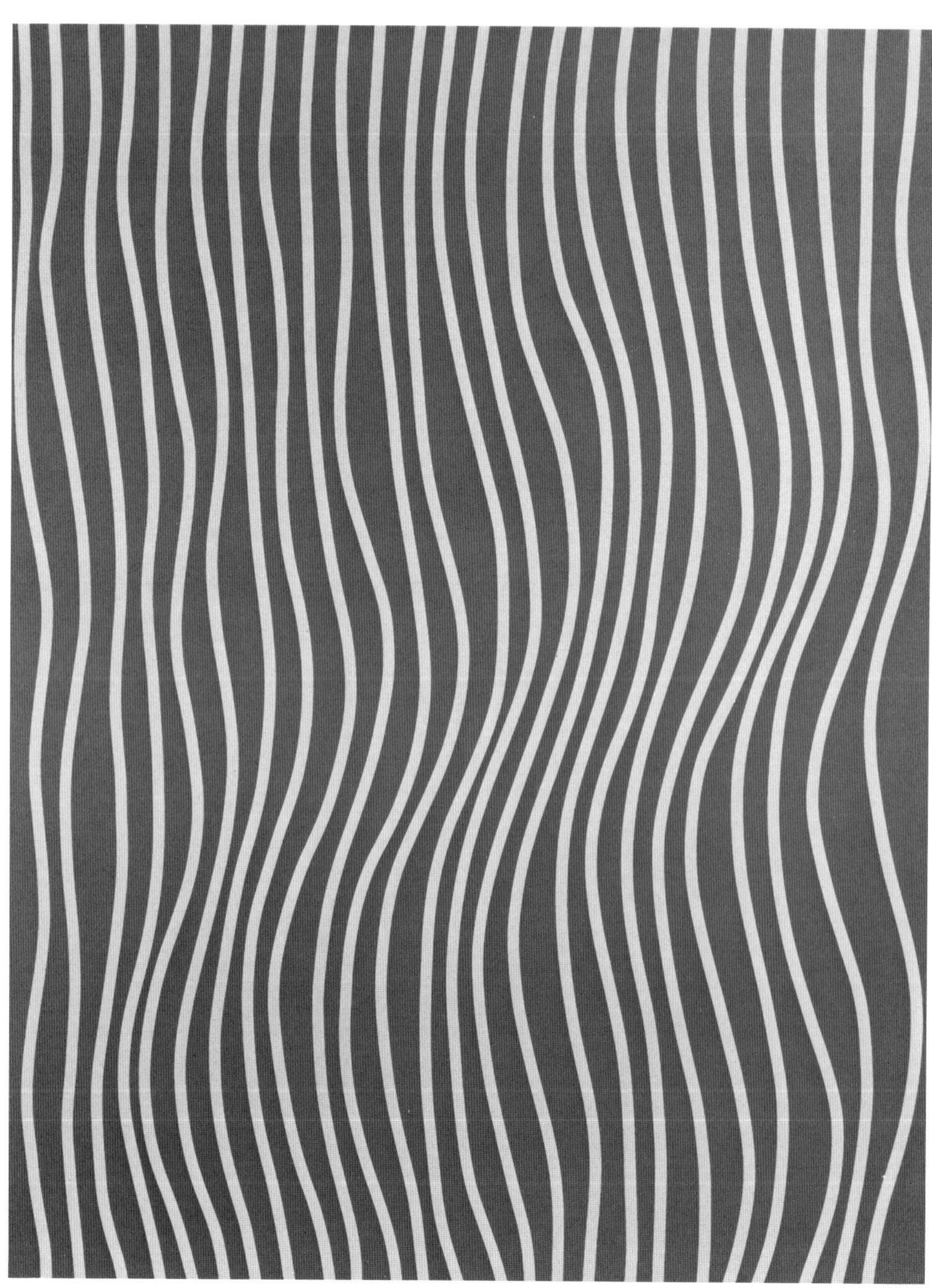

5. What Do You See?

There are more visual images in today's world than in any other time. You are surrounded by images in many forms: television, video games, neon signs, billboards, movies, magazines, newspapers. Then there are the millions of designed articles made available to the modern world because of new materials and mass production methods. You are constantly picking up information from what your eyes see.

Your eyes work automatically, searching for visual meanings that you can use. With all the visual images to choose from, what causes your eyes to select the ones that they do? Here are some basic causes.

Familiarity with objects affects what you see. If you look around the room that you are in, you will notice that you automatically focus on some objects but not on others. For example, in the art room your eyes may focus momentarily on the sink that you use regularly. However, an unfamiliar object

5-1 *Lower St. Lawrence*, Marcel Barbeau
Art that deals with optical effects is often called Op art. (Optical means "having to do with sight.") What optical effect does this picture create?

would immediately catch your eye because of your previous knowledge of the room.

Your particular aim also determines what you perceive. If you walk down a busy city sidewalk on the way to a particular movie theatre, you may not notice a huge sign announcing "30% off" in a store window on your left. You may also miss the trash container at the curb side. These images will not help you get to the theatre. But you will notice the two other movie theatres on that street and the street signs that tell you which block you are on. Why? Quite simply, because this information will help you find the right movie theatre. You see what you need to see.

What you like affects what you see. When you are shopping your eyes scan the displays. They focus on items whose lines, shapes or colours attract you. After all, you know what you like and you are quick to spot it.

The way you look at things is also important. If you tilt your head, you will see images from unusual angles. Some previously unnoticed shapes may take on a new appearance. Try looking through a rolled up piece of paper or look through a small rectangular hole in a piece of cardboard. You may find that your perceptions of familiar objects change.

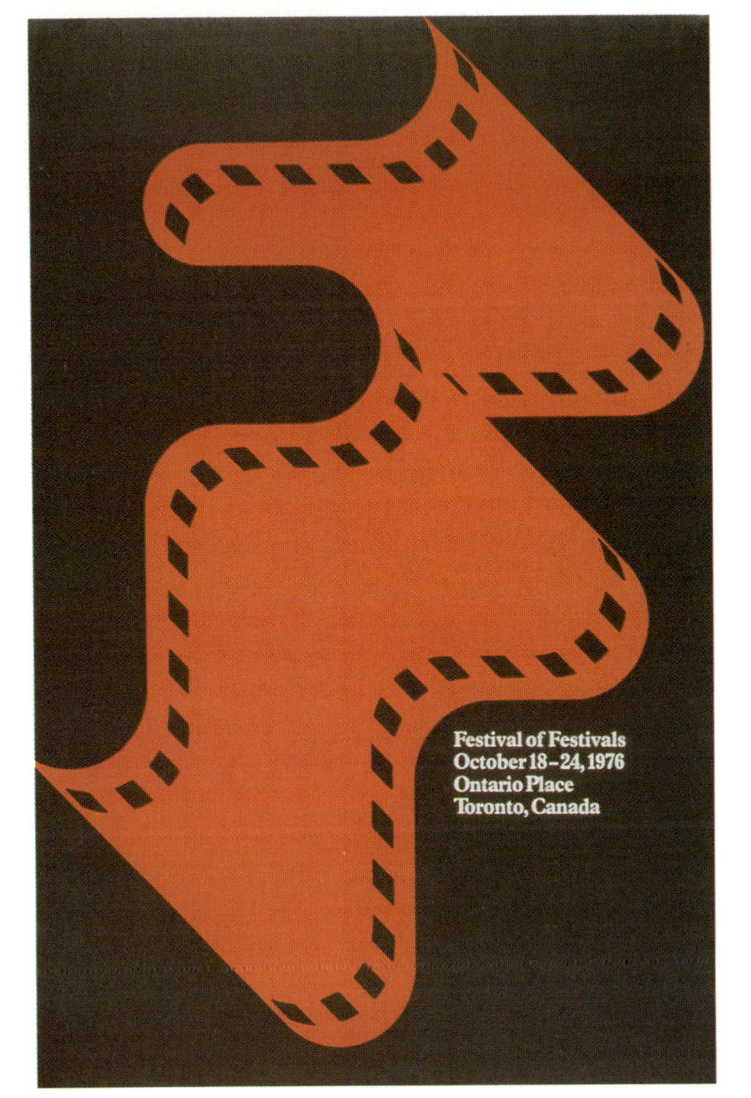

5-2 *Festival of Festivals*, Robert Burns
Commercial artists use their knowledge of visual perception to create images that attract your attention. Where are the two F's in this logo for the Festival of Festivals?

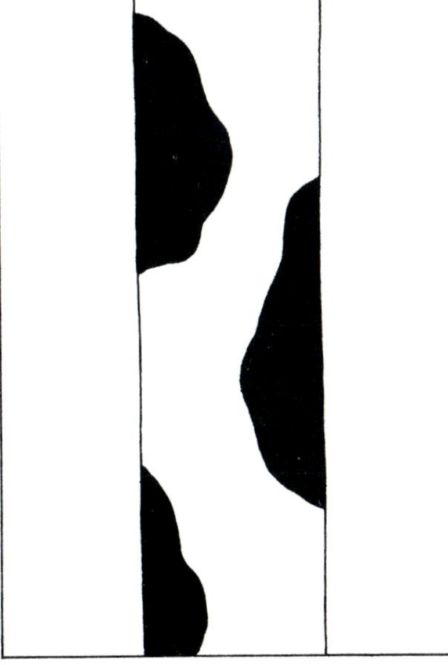

Picture riddles like this one were very popular in the 1950s. What do you think this picture riddle represents? Being stumped by a picture riddle shows you how much you need to make sense out of what you see. The answer to this riddle is "a giraffe passing by a window." You think images like this one are funny because you feel a release of tension when you discover or are told the simple image.

Look Again

- Close you eyes and visualize the room you are in. What familiar objects can you name?
- Look at 5-1. What other optical effects could you imagine?

6. Seeing More of Your World

Now that you know something about the visual process, you will probably experiment with your new ways of seeing. Instead of ignoring images that are not useful, you may try to see what you have been missing. If you do, you will become much more aware of the lines, shapes, colours and textures of the world around you. Visual awareness involves looking closely at images that you might otherwise not notice.

Set different goals each day: lines one day, textures the next. Note also that visual awareness is heightened by awareness of other sensations, such as smells and sounds. Close your eyes and make mental images of aromas you smell and sounds you hear. Become more aware of your world.

When you make a visual discovery, such as the fact that many different greens are seen in the leaves of a tree, you suddenly see the effect everywhere and in different places. This is much like learning a new word. Suddenly the word that you never noticed before seems to be used everywhere. One awareness discovery often leads to another. You never stop learning from your visual perception.

Remember, art is a visual language. Practice increases your ability to understand. Practise being more aware of the images around you. The discoveries that you make about the lines, shapes, colours and textures of the world in which you live will help you to understand the lines, shapes, colours and textures of the art that you see.

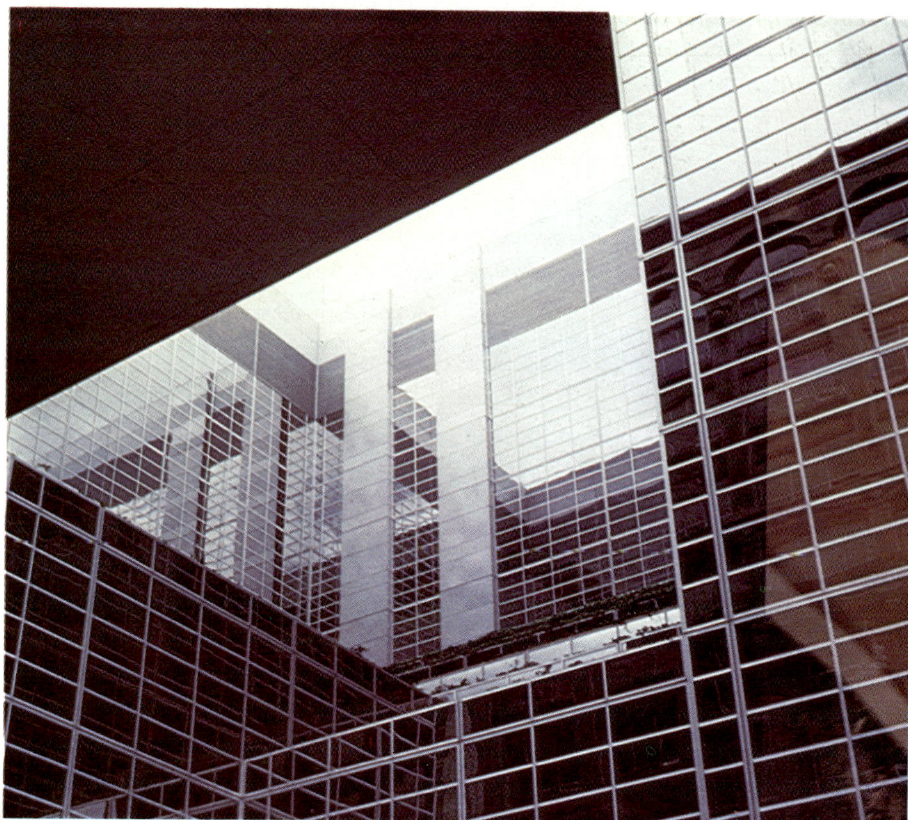

6-1 Royal Bank Building, Ottawa
Be aware of the lines around you. Discover for yourself how lines created by people are different from the lines seen in nature.

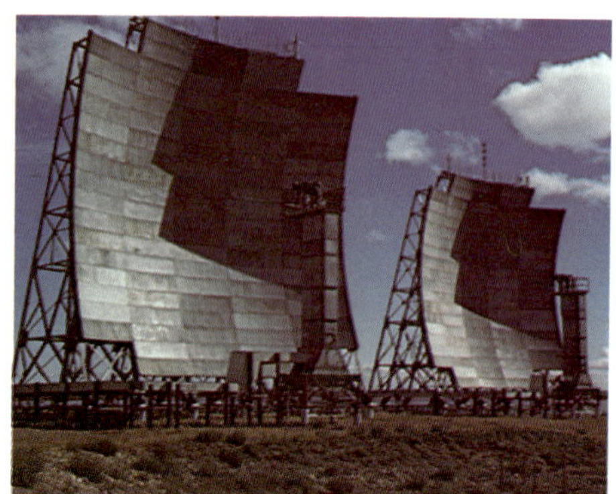

6-2 Dew Line radar dishes, Tuktoyaktuk, N.W.T.
Simple shapes can sometimes be overwhelming. The Dew Line radar dishes at Tuktoyaktuk, N.W.T. contrast dramatically with a barren Arctic coastline.

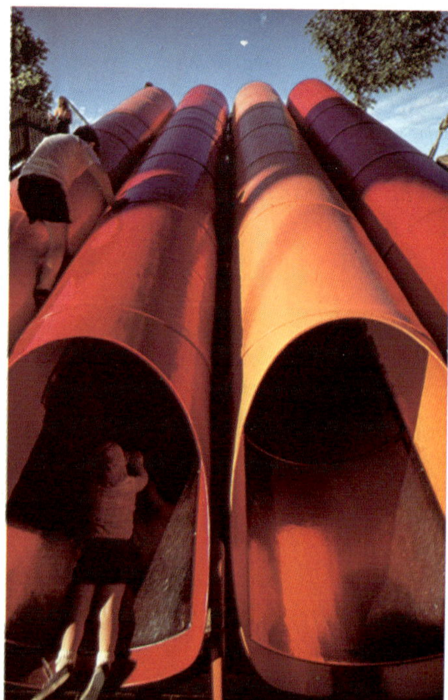

6-3 Tube slide, Ontario Place
Colour is often used to create a certain mood. Notice how the colour of the tube slides add to the excitement of Ontario Place.

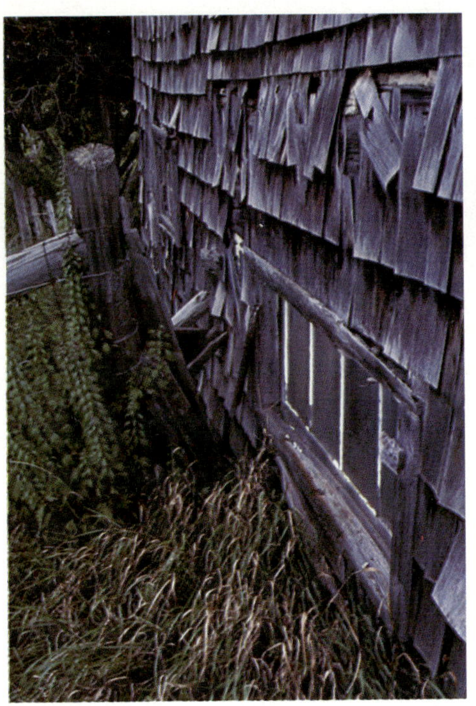

6-4 Weathered shingles
Rough and smooth textured surfaces offer yet another source of visual interest.

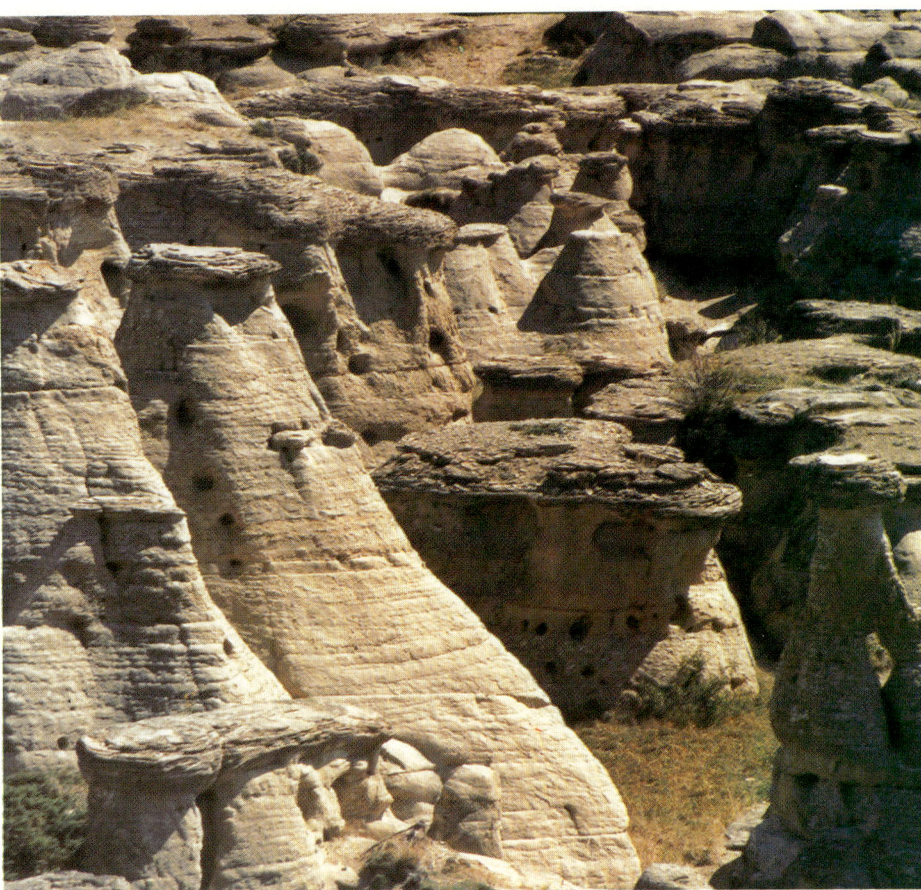

6-6 Hoodoos Badlands, Drumheller, Alberta
Light falling on three-dimensional forms creates many light and dark tones of the colour. Here the Hoodoos Badlands of Drumheller, Alberta are made more dramatic by strong sunlight. Become aware of the way light affects the world you see.

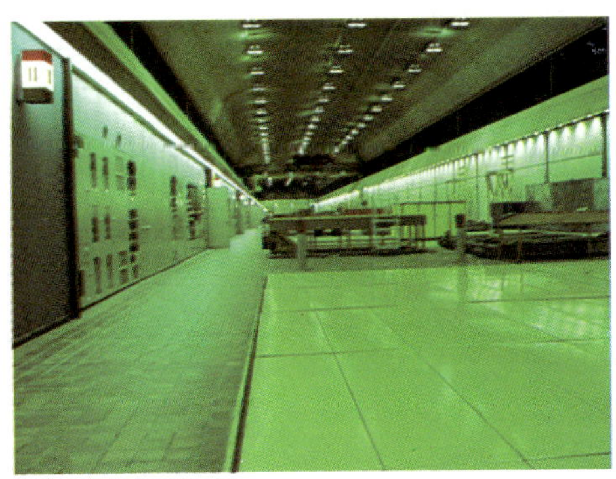

6-5 Underground powerhouse, Churchill Falls, Labrador
The main powerhouse room at Churchill Falls, Labrador is more than three hundred metres underground. Notice how the unbroken lines of this room create a sensational feeling of space.

Look Again

- Learn to observe the environment. It will enable you to view art with the same curiosity and patience. Here are some ideas to get you started:
- Look for a natural object that is perfectly round.
- Look for something edible that is blue.
- Look for a fabric that is furry, and another that is glossy.
- Look for the horizon when you go to a downtown area.
- Look for line patterns in brickwork.
- Look for aeroplane lights in the night sky. How can you tell that the lights are so much closer than the stars?

YOU AND THE LANGUAGE OF ART

7. The Elements Work Together

Line, shape, colour, texture and space are the elements of design. They often have been compared to the words used in language. The artist uses the elements together to send a visual message. They help to depict the subject matter in a way that expresses the artist's meaning. In this section each element will be looked at in turn. Knowing about the physical properties of each element will help you to recognize how each one is used in the works of art you see.

8. Line

A *line* begins with a dot and creates a track or path as it moves. Not all lines are the same. They may be long or short, wide or narrow. Lines can vary in direction. They may be straight or curved, diagonal, vertical or horizontal. Changes in direction may be graceful or abrupt. Lines may appear to have different moods – gentle, harsh, delicate, rough – depending on their physical characteristics.

Line is related to other elements of design. For example, it is related to space. A single line can act as a track to lead your eye to an important part of a picture. A horizontal line can appear to lie in front of you as you look at a picture, but a diagonal line can seem to move into the distance like a road. This quality of line creates the appearance of space on a flat surface such as paper or canvas.

Line is also related to texture. Repeated lines may be used to draw the texture of fur or the bark of a tree.

Line also relates to the depiction of light and dark, which is known as *value*. Different values can be drawn by placing lines nearer or farther apart. Parallel lines grouped close together form areas that appear to be dark. Lighter areas are created when more space is left between each line.

Line is a basic element in art. Look for it in many compositions. It can describe the subject matter or express an emotion. It may appear as a code – as letters or symbols. In all these ways it helps to express the artist's ideas.

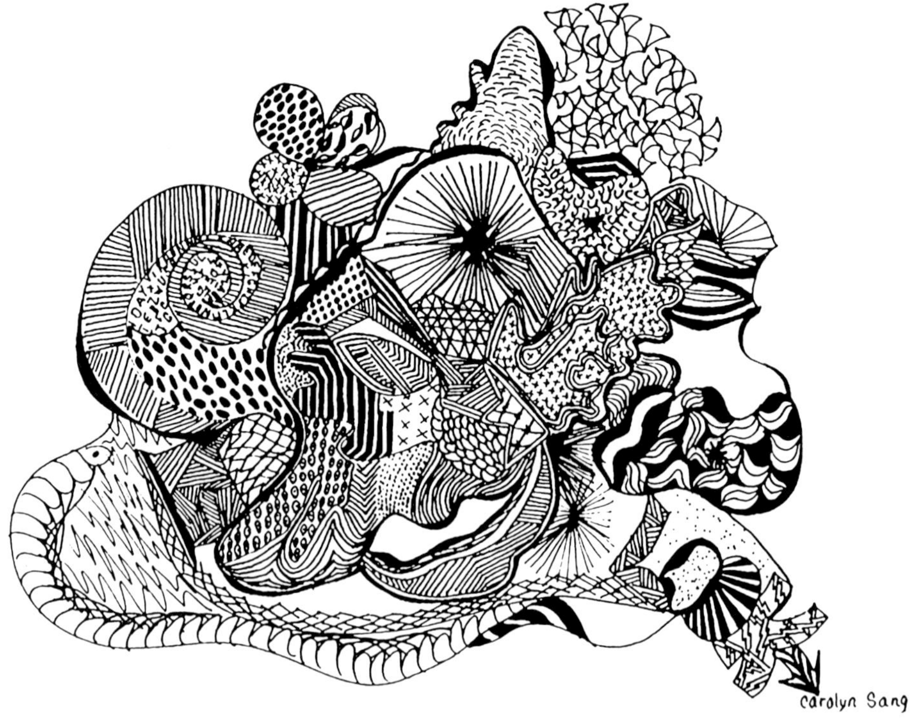

8-1 *Line*, Carolyn Sang
Line is used for its decorative quality in this felt pen drawing.

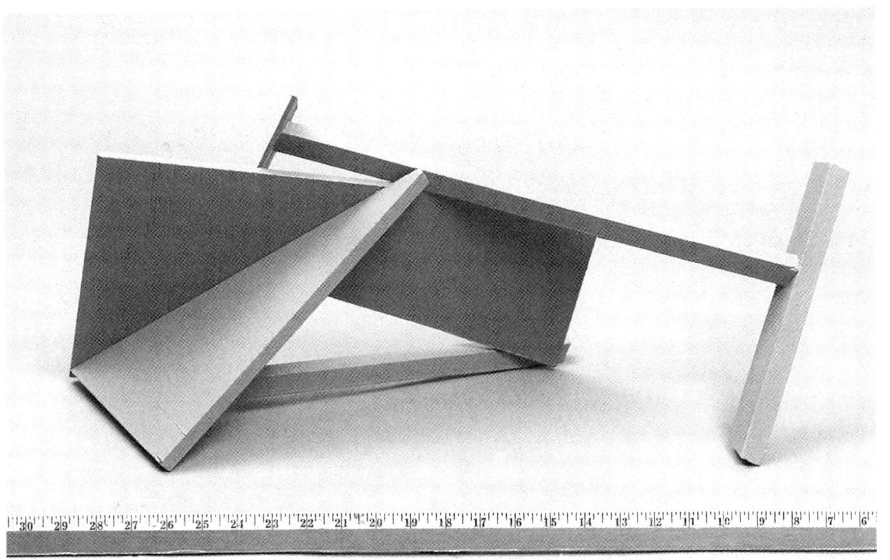

8-2 ***Shoaler Stretch*, Catherine Burgess**
The effective use of line is frequently seen in sculpture. Here Alberta sculptor, Catherine Burgess, has created a sculpture in which each line affects the way you see the others. The sculpture appears in the picture to be much larger than it really is. (Works with this effect are referred to as monumental.)

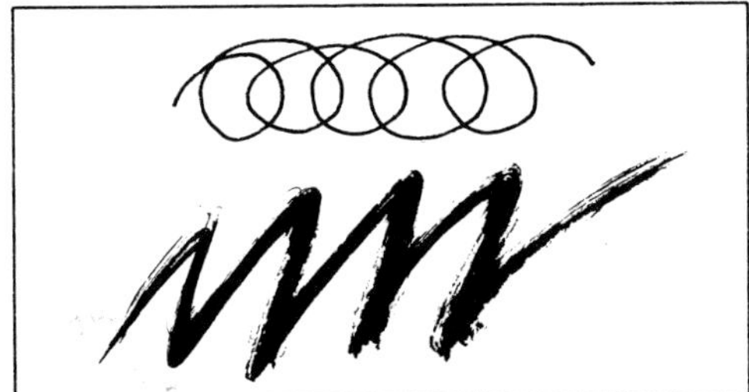

A line can say different things. A quiet, thin line represents a person walking, while a thick, diagonal line represents a person running.

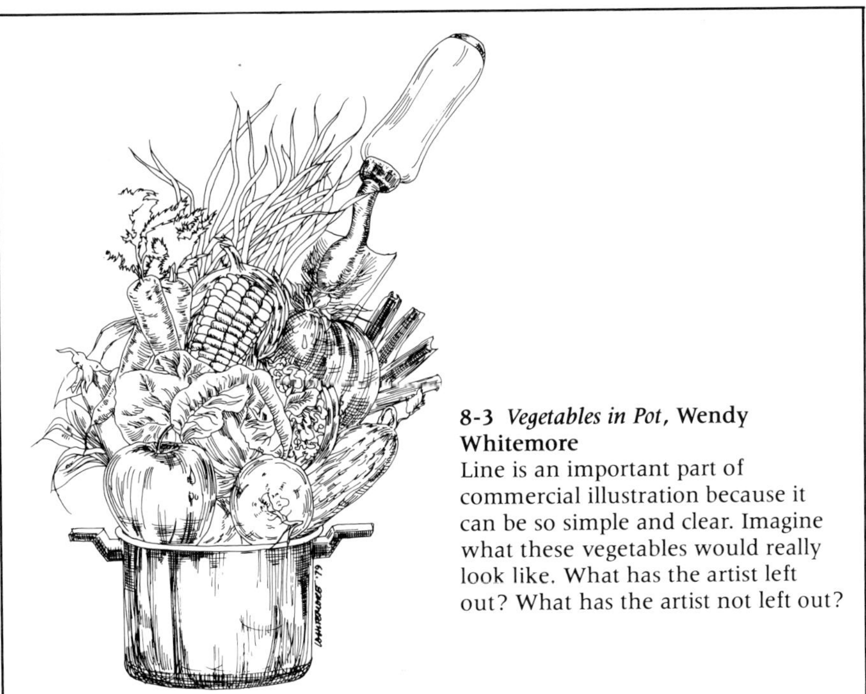

8-3 ***Vegetables in Pot*, Wendy Whitemore**
Line is an important part of commercial illustration because it can be so simple and clear. Imagine what these vegetables would really look like. What has the artist left out? What has the artist not left out?

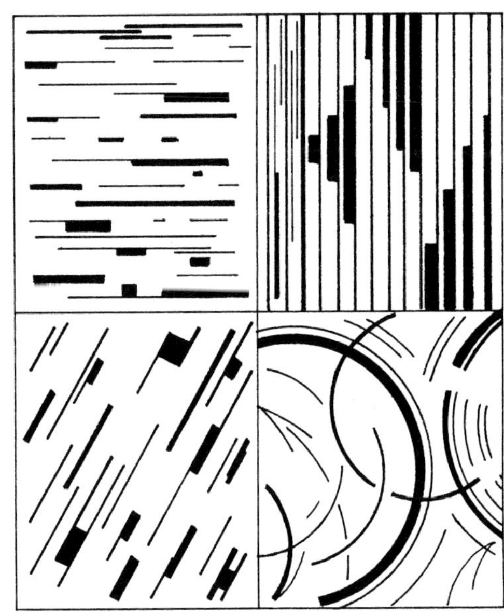

Simple line patterns can be varied in many ways. What words can you think of to describe the various lines shown here?

Look Again

- Look at 8-1, 8-2, and 8-3. For each piece of art, chose at least three words that describe the lines you see.
- Try to describe the kind of line you might use to show a feeling such as excitement or confusion.
- Name things you see now that seem to have an edge that appears as a line. Name those things that do *not* seem to have a line as their edge.
- Imagine your signature is a line. How can you show it expressing moods such as anger, fear, or happiness?

9. Shape and Volume

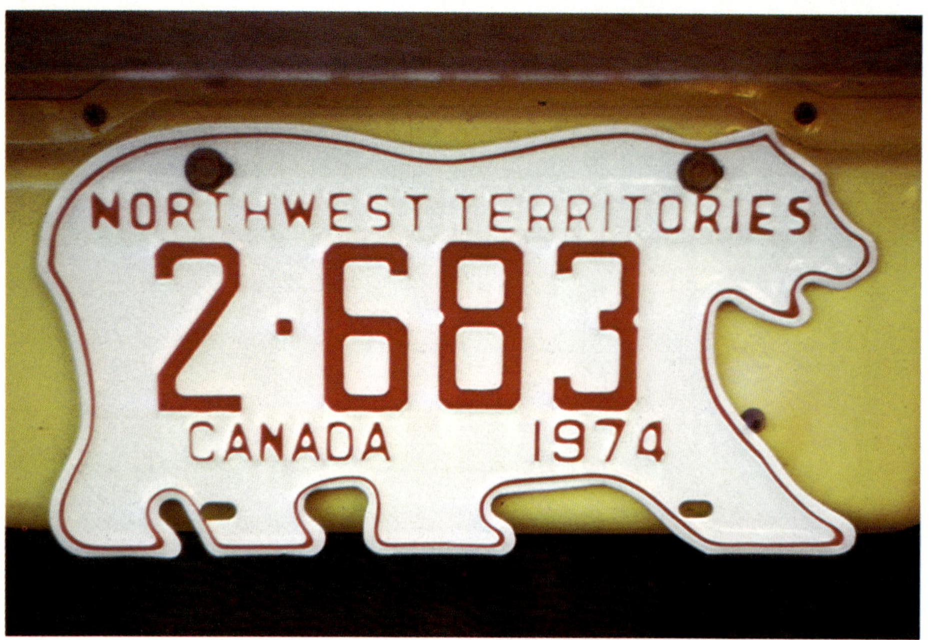

9-1 N.W.T. license plate
Shapes may be grouped into families or classifications that share common qualities. One such classification is based on shapes found in nature. Here the shape of a polar bear is used as the license plate for the Northwest Territories.

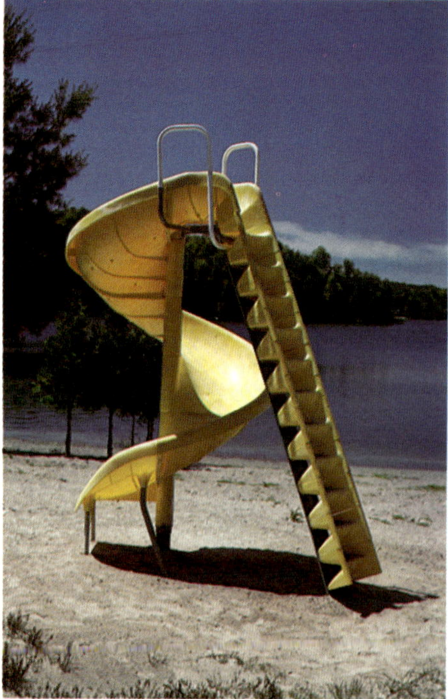

9-2 Dura Glide Slide, Kuypers, Adamson and Norton Research Planning and Design
In designing products, it is necessary to create a functional shape that is also visually pleasing to the eye. This unique design for a slide has been a Canadian entry in international design competitions.

When a line begins and ends at the same point, it makes a *shape*. A shape has two dimensions: length and width. The circle, triangle, square and rectangle are familiar shapes. The extra dimension of depth creates form. There are five basic forms that have depth. These forms are the cube, pyramid, cylinder, cone, and sphere. *Volume* is another term for each of these kinds of forms.

It is possible to depict a three-dimensional shape on a flat surface. The effect is often achieved with light and dark shading of values. Overlapped shapes usually give a sense of depth.

Shapes may vary from simple to complex. Shapes and volumes may be combined to form more complex arrangements. Some may closely represent an actual object. Others may be hard to recognize for what they are. If the shape or volume is distorted, the artist may be expressing dissatisfaction with the real world. A realistic form may be used to show the artist's appreciation of its beauty.

In art, shapes are the fundamental building tool for the artist. Size, position and colour are a few ways an artist makes shapes seem important in a work of art. Look for the kinds of shapes an artist uses to help you understand the visual message.

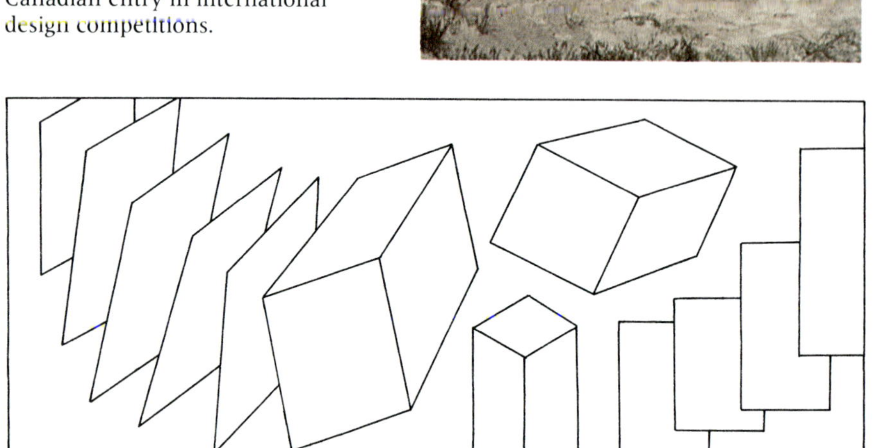

Shapes are planes having only two dimensions – height and width. Volumes have three dimensions – height, width and depth.

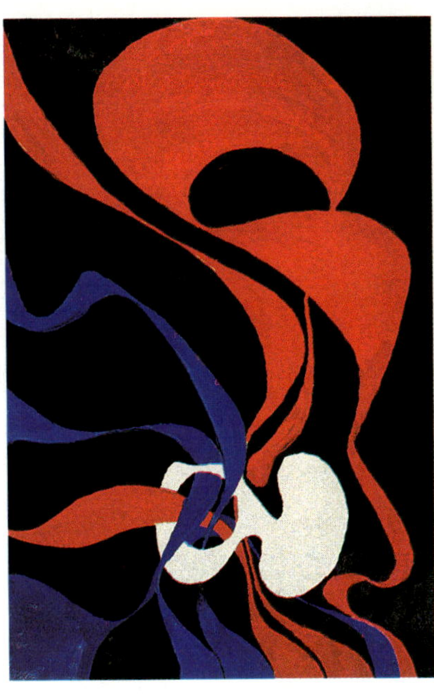

9-3 *Untitled*, **Darren Kindrachuk**
The irregular shapes in this student work are hard to classify. They do not clearly represent any known shape. (Artists call such shapes non-objective.)

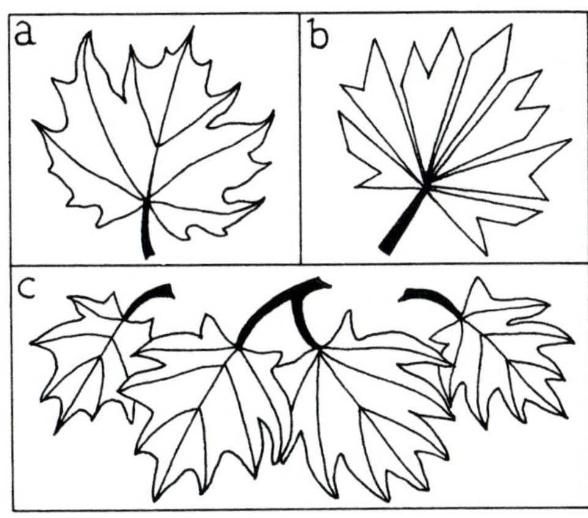

Shapes may be simple or complex. They may be representational like the first drawing in Fig. a or distorted as in Fig. b. Shapes may also overlap.

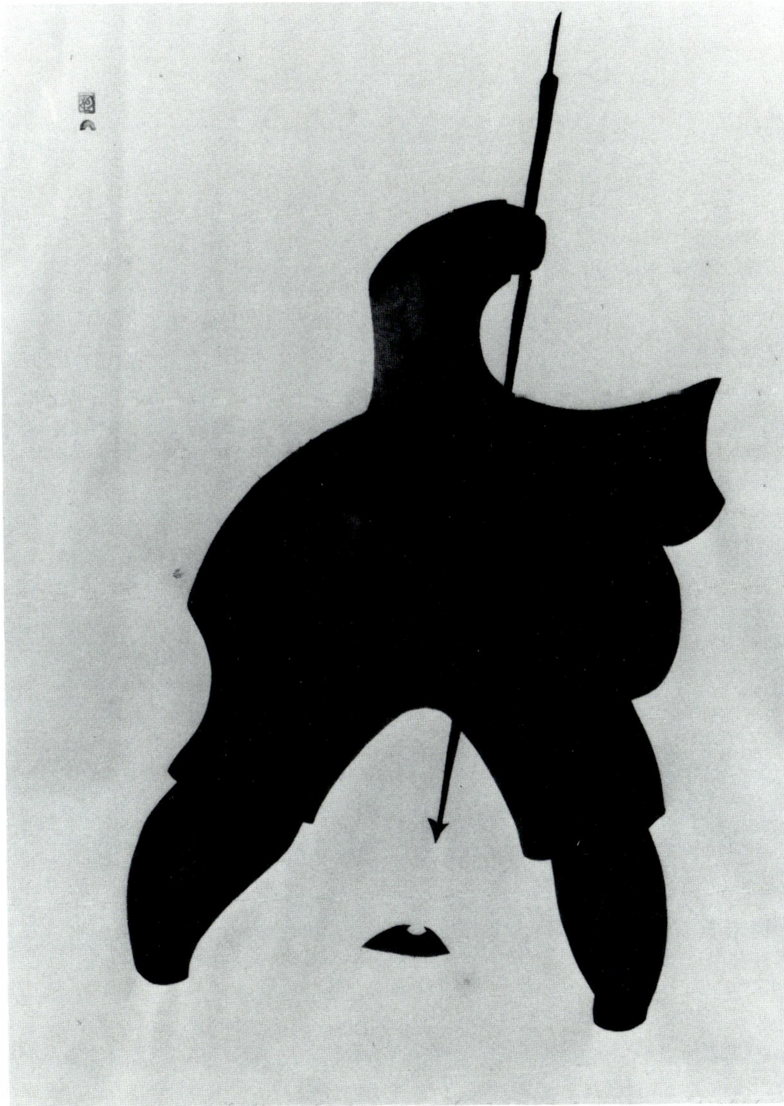

9-4 ***Man Hunting at Seal Hole*, Niviaksiak**
In this stencil print, the negative or background space of white suggests the cold of the ice and the air. Although there are few details, it is easy to recognize the shape of the hunter.

Look Again

- The basic shapes are the circle, triangle, square and rectangle. Where can you see any of these shapes in the art on these pages?
- Simple shapes can be put together to form an effective design by themselves. What shapes are used in the sculpture 8-2? In the quilt 10-2? In the sculpture 13-1? In the computer graphic 24-2?
- Describe the shapes you can see in the art room.
- What kinds of shapes might be dominant in city scenes? In rural areas?
- Look again at the polar bear in 9-1. You can imagine why it is used to represent the N.W.T. If you could design a license plate for your car, what shape would you choose? Why?

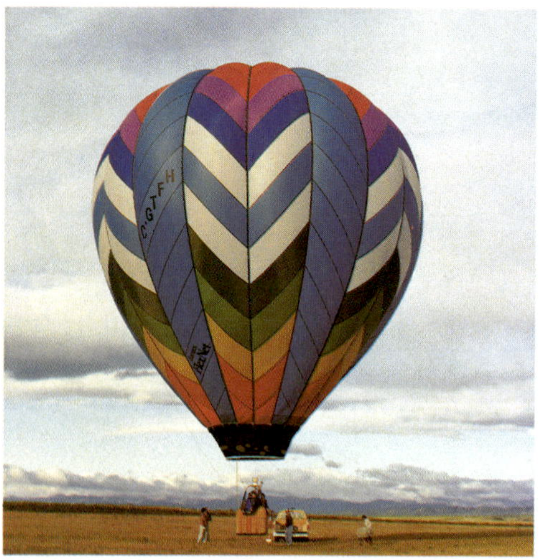

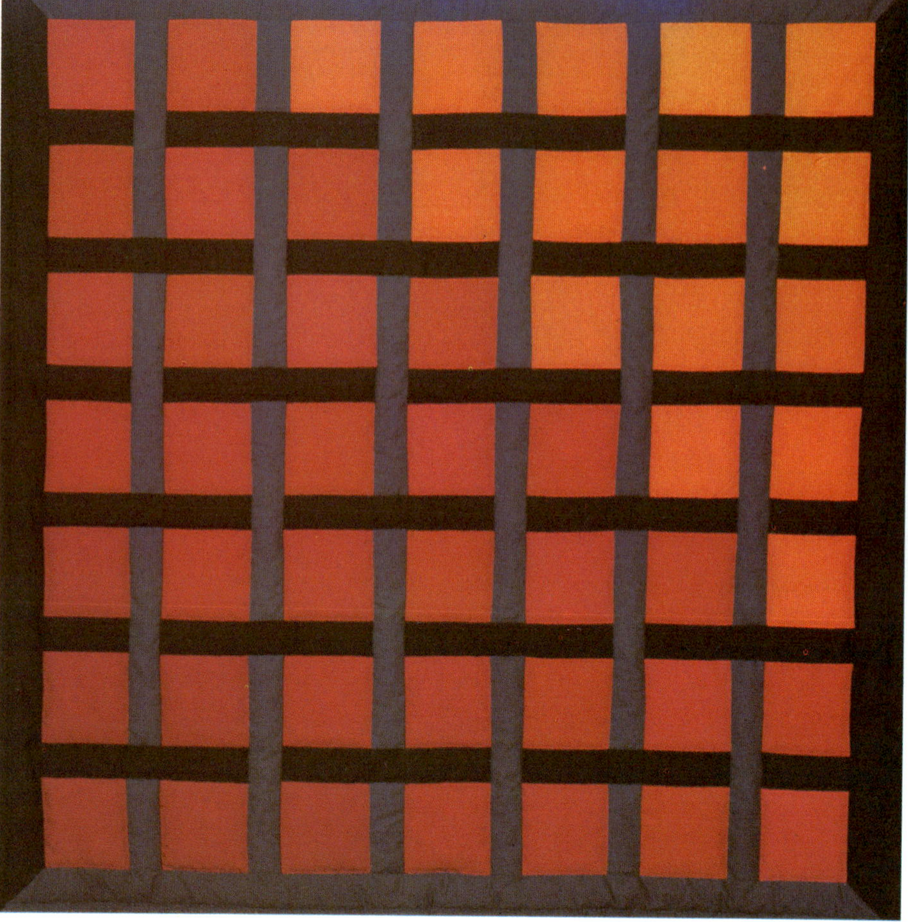

10-1 Balloon
Although many colours from the colour wheel are used on this balloon, the visual effect is pleasing. The colours have been organized into related groups of warm and cool colours.

10-2 ***Orange Becoming Red, Series #2,*** **Judith Dingle**
Red, red-orange and orange are examples of analogous colours. These colours are used in a subtle pattern of changing hues in this quilt by Judith Dingle.

10. Colour and Value

Colour is a large part of all you see. It is the element that is most expressive in art and one of the most complex. There are three important things to consider when describing colour. The most obvious is *hue*. Hue is the name of a colour, such as red, green and orange. The three *primary colours* are red, yellow and blue. The *secondary colours* are made by mixing two primary colours together. Red and yellow make orange. Red and blue make violet, and blue and yellow make green. Mixing a primary and secondary colour together makes a third set of colours called the *tertiary* or *intermediate colours*. Yellow-green, blue-green and blue-violet are some of the intermediate colours. The primary, secondary and intermediate colours can be organized into an arrangement called the *colour wheel*.

The colour wheel can help you see more relationships. For example, colours that are next to one another on the colour wheel are called *analogous colours*. Opposite colours on the colour wheel are called *complementary colours*. Complementary colours make strong contrasts in compositions. Red and green, blue and orange, and yellow and violet are examples of complementary colours.

Intensity helps to describe variations in the same colour or hue. For example, the sun is bright yellow while mustard is dull yellow. There are several ways to change the intensity of a colour. Mixing it with its complement is one way. Mixing with green will change the intensity of red.

Another physical property is *value*. It refers to darkness and lightness. A colour that is darker than the basic hue is called a *shade*. A colour that is lighter than the basic hue is called a *tint*. The *neutrals*, black and white, are used to change the value of a hue.

Knowing about colour helps you toward an understanding of the artist's message. Colours can generally be divided into two groups: *warm colours* and *cool colours*. Each colour group has been associated with things in the physical world. For example, reds, oranges and yellows are warm colours because they remind

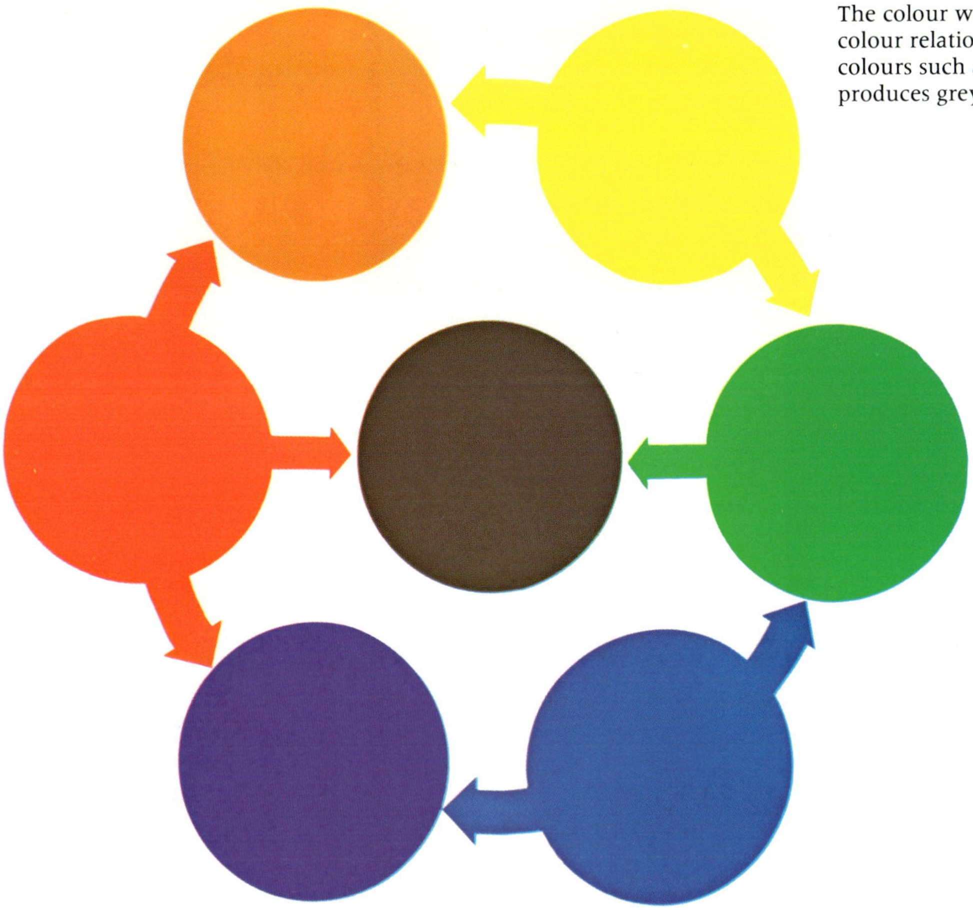

The colour wheel helps you see colour relationships. Mixing opposite colours such as red and green produces grey.

people of fire or the sun. Blues and greens and purples are cool colours that remind people of water, the sky or shade. This warm or cool effect can be changed by the colours used nearby. A warm colour will seem even warmer if placed near a cool colour.

Colour may be used realistically in art to represent a natural appearance. Colour may also be used to create a mood and to symbolize ideas. Bright colours may be used to express happy things such as birthdays. Darker colours may be used for serious themes and ideas such as death or war. When you look at art, think about whether or not colour is used realistically. Think, too, about the things that the colours remind you of. Try to relate your feelings to the artist's message.

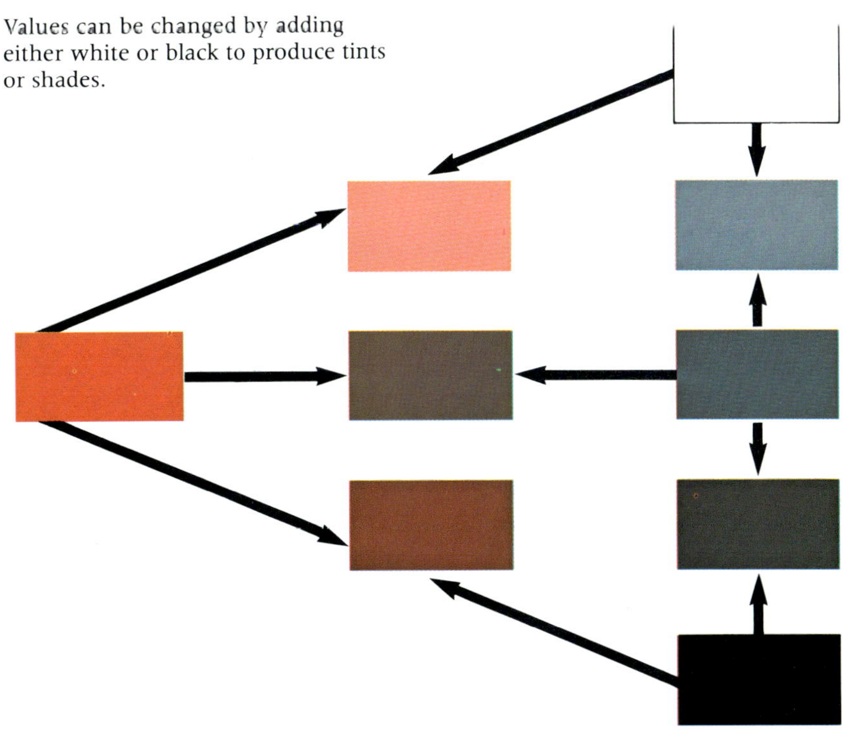
Values can be changed by adding either white or black to produce tints or shades.

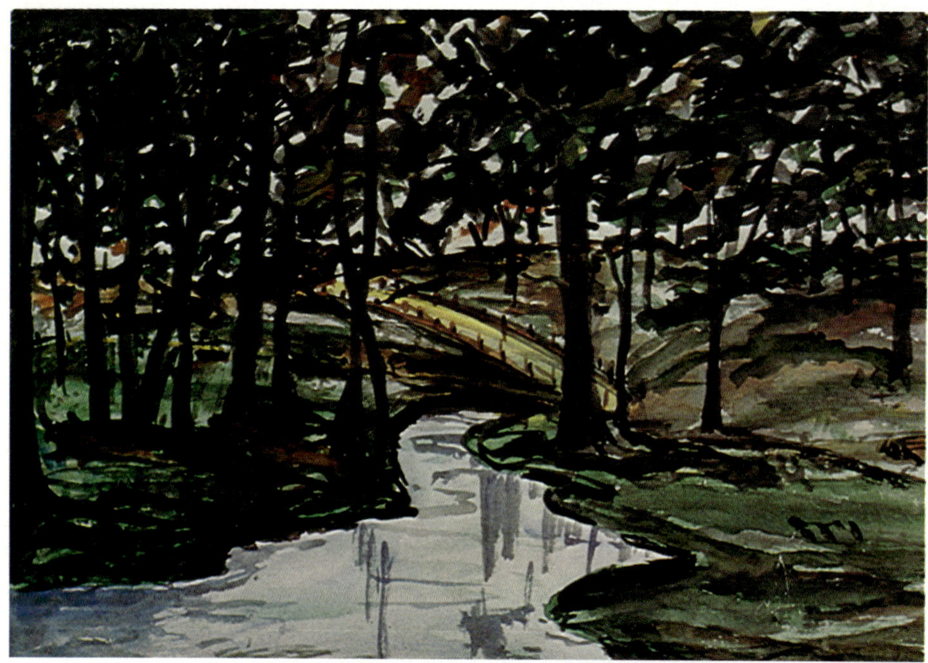

10-3 *Untitled*, **Barbara Phillip**
Value as well as colour is used to express dramatic moods. Notice the contrast in light and dark in this forest scene.

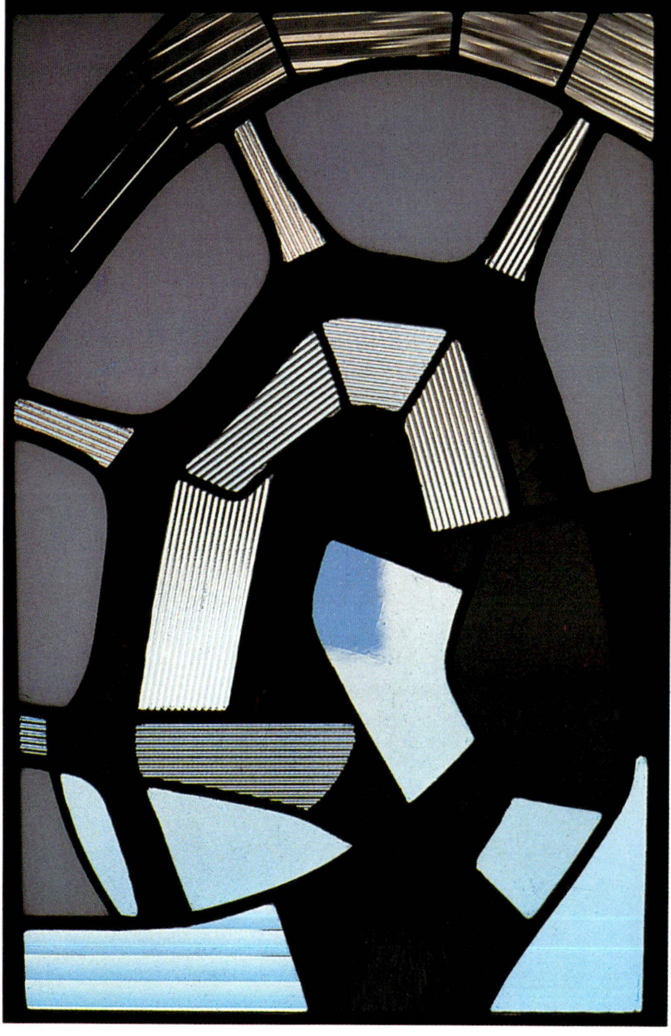

Look Again

- Do you think the balloon looks cheerful? Would it still look cheerful if it were just yellow and orange? Just pink? All black?
- What words would you use to describe it if it were any of these colours?

- Look at the colours that Barbara Phillip has used for the grass in 10-3. Do these colours look realistic? Why or why not?
- Why do you think she didn't just use green?

- Make a list of the colours you see in 10-4.
- In a second column, write down the *first* thing that you associate with each colour. Compare your list with someone else's.

- What is your favourite colour? Try to find it on the colour wheel.
- What five things does your favourite colour remind you of?

10-4 *Cambridge No. 2, 1977*, **Robert Jekyll**
Natural light helps to bring out the beauty of the colour relationships in this stained glass by Robert Jekyll.

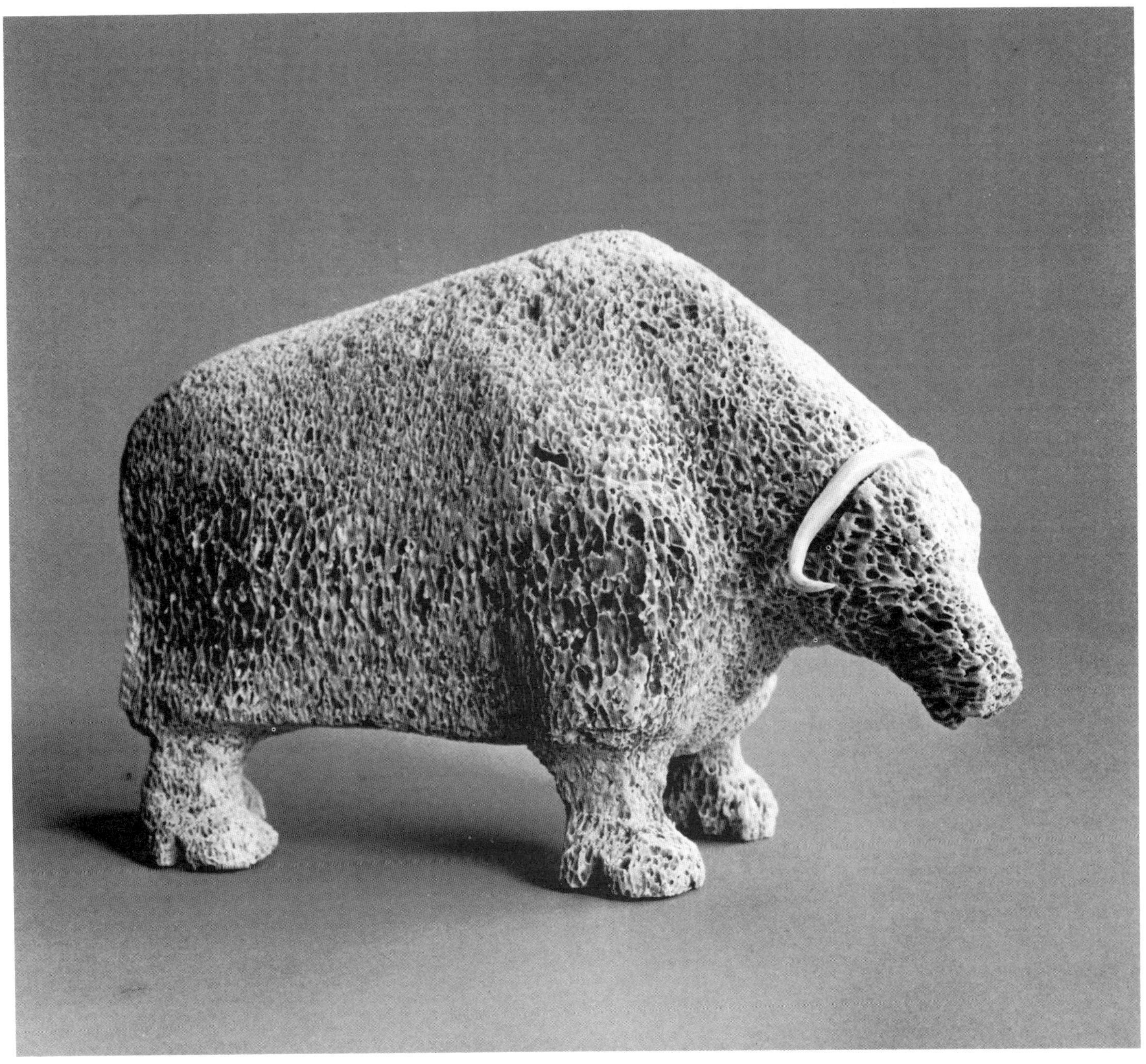

11-1 *Muskox*, Samon
The actual texture adds to the appearance of this whalebone sculpture. Whalebone, stone and ivory are some of the natural materials used by the Inuit carvers.

11. Texture

Texture refers to the feel or look of a surface. Each object or shape has a texture. You can discover texture by touching a surface, or by seeing light reflected from a surface. Your sense of sight and your sense of touch help you to understand texture. Two general categories of texture are rough and smooth.

Texture can be used by the artist to depict objects as they are in nature. For example, paint may be built up to produce a sense of the bark of a tree. This use of texture helps to identify objects, as well as to increase awareness of their true beauty. The artist also may deliberately alter the texture to suit the message. Adding a sense of texture is one way to create visual interest in a composition and to direct the viewer's gaze.

Each material that an artist works with has its own texture. For example, the artist who works with clay or wood is closely involved with the actual texture of the material. Be aware of how the artist has used or changed the texture of the materials when you look at art.

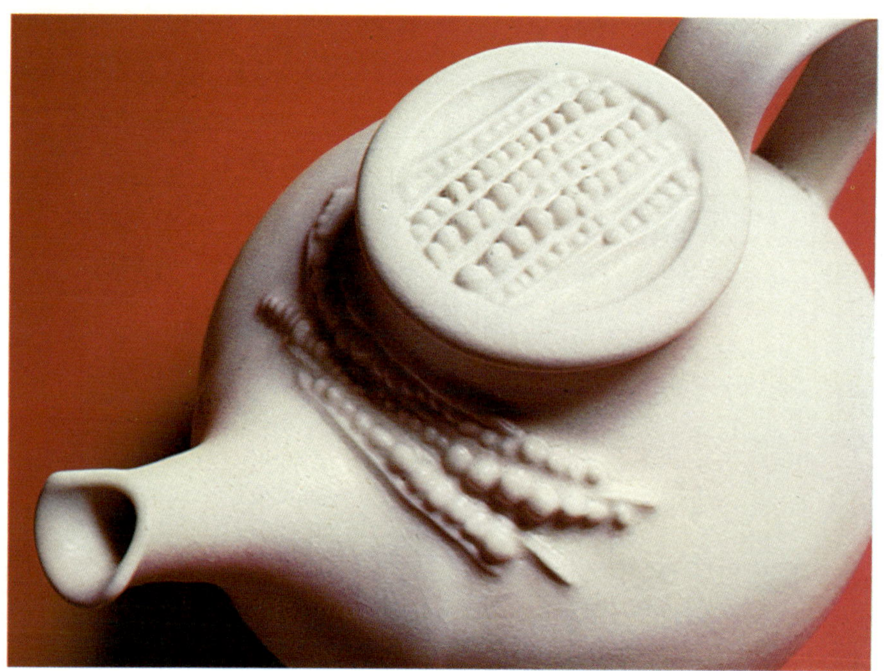

11-2 Porcelain teapot, Cynthia Root Texture is one of the most important concerns in ceramics. It is often the unique "handwriting" of the individual artist. This distinctive teapot is the work of Ontario potter Cynthia Root. Notice the use of a smooth, glazed surface. The decoration on the lid is based on shapes from nature.

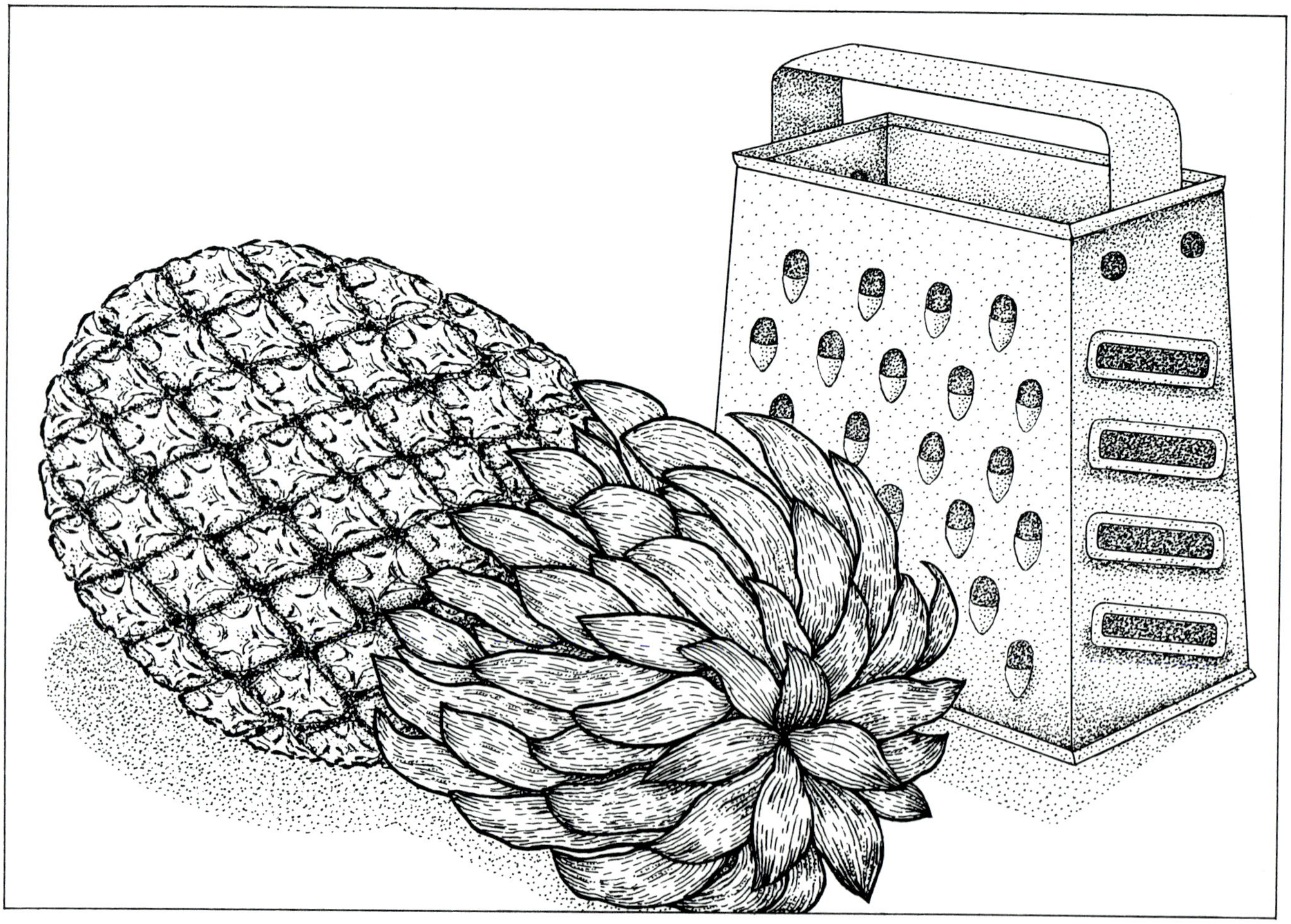

Texture may be actual, as it appears in nature, or it may be created or invented. This type of texture is often called artificial. It adds visual interest.

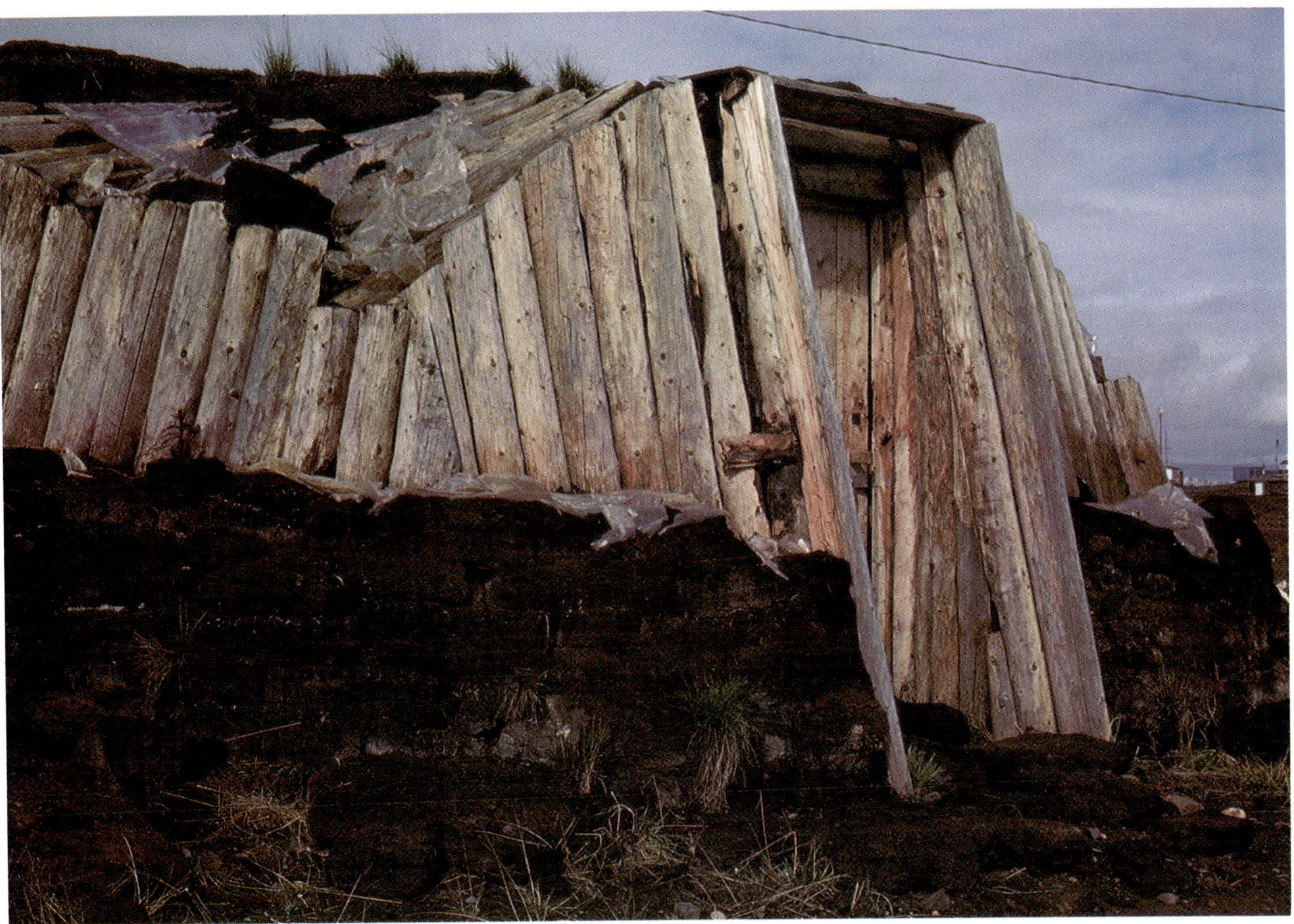

11-3 Sod house, Tuktoyaktuk, N.W.T.
The person who designed this house has chosen natural materials that blend in with the surrounding landscape. Here you see architecture being influenced by environment.

Look Again

- Imagine you could actually touch the Muskox sculpture (11-1). Describe how it would feel.

- What sort of cup would you buy to go with the teapot (11-2)? Describe its appearance.
- What texture would your chosen cup have?

- Look at the hat in 27-3. Describe the texures of the fabrics that are represented.
- The hat is made of porcelain! It is hard and rigid! No one could wear it. Why do you think the artisan chose the "wrong" materials for the hat?

- The sod house (11-3) matches its environment. Think about the materials used for buildings in your area. Say which ones have textures that match the environment, and which ones have textures that contrast with the environment.

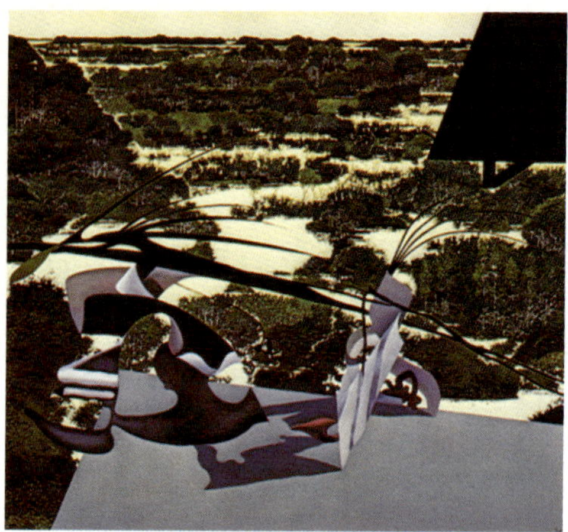

12-1 *Floodwood*, **Ivan Eyre**
Space influences all who live on the prairies. Artist Ivan Eyre was born in Saskatchewan and is now living in Manitoba. The large foreground object seems to emphasize the distance and expanse of the background in *Floodwood*.

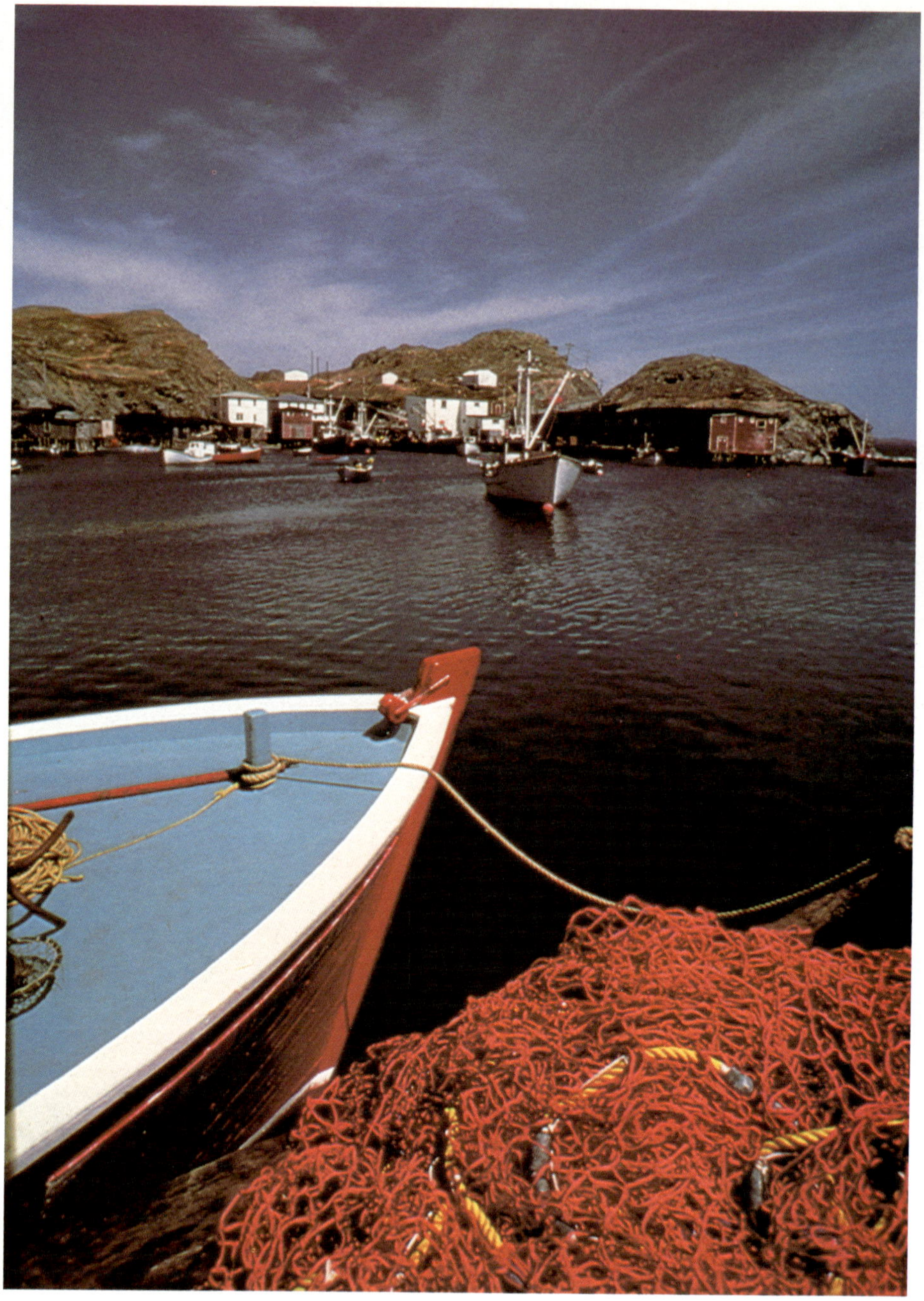

12-2 Port D'Grave, Newfoundland
Objects close to the lower edge of the picture appear nearest to you. Objects closer to the top of the picture appear to be more distant. Also, notice how the sky appears less blue at the horizon. This loss of colour intensity as a result of distance is called atmospheric perspective.

12. Space

Space refers to the distance between two points. People measure space in terms of length, width and depth. Three-dimensional art has its own depth. In two-dimensional art, depth is an illusion.

The surface of two-dimensional art is called the *picture plane*. The clever use of line, value and colour may give the illusion of space. When you look at art pictures that have the illusion of space, you feel that you could simply step into them. In much contemporary work, artists choose deliberately to avoid the illusion of space. Their work appears quite flat.

The illusion of space is added through a variety of techniques. *Linear perspective* produces the illusion of space on a flat surface. The artist who draws a road so that it appears wide at the front of the picture and vanishes as a point at the horizon is using linear perspective. Another technique involves the size and position of shapes. Imagine, for example, that you are drawing a country scene. You will likely draw the trees and flowers that are close to you next to the lower edge of your paper, and the hills in the distance near the upper edge. At the same time, you will draw the trees and flowers nearby larger than the hills. Also, they may be drawn so that they hide parts of the hills. It is generally true that large shapes

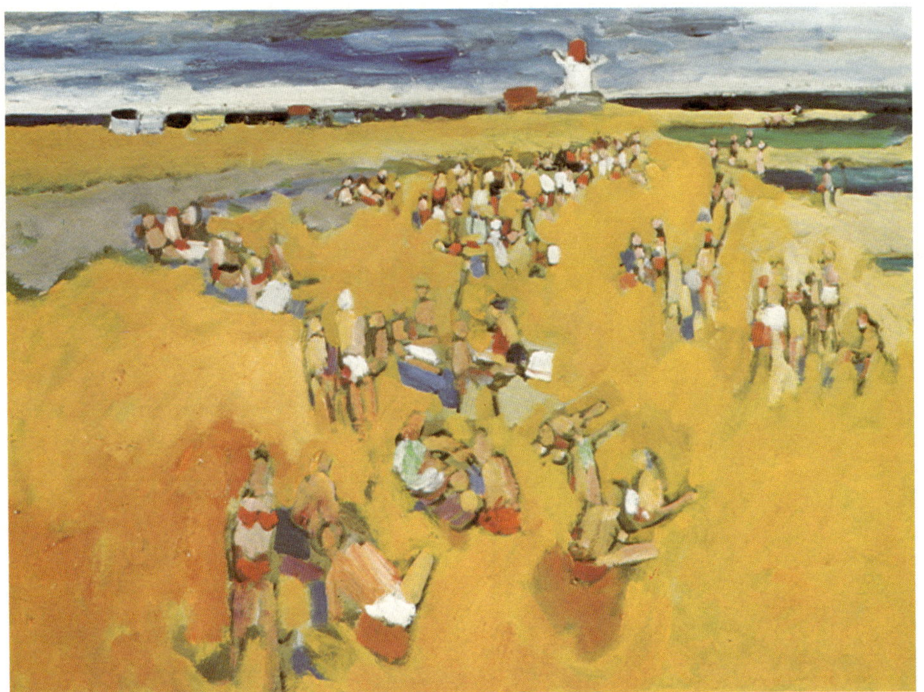

12-3 ***Shediac Beach (N.B.),*** **Molly Bobak**
How has Molly Bobak created a feeling of space in the painting *Shediac Beach*?

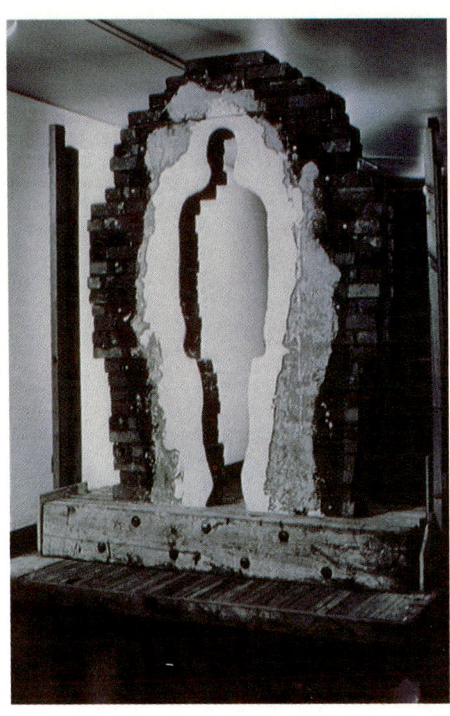

12-4 ***February 1975,*** **Colette Whiten**
Here the image of a person is created with space! The shapes of spaces are important in sculpture. Such shapes are referred to as amorphous.

placed near the lower edge of a picture appear closer to the viewer. Small shapes placed near the upper edge of the paper, and shapes that are partly hidden by others, appear to be farther away.

The use of detail can add the illusion of space to a composition. Detail added to a natural or decorative shape will make it appear close to you. By contrast, less detail or blurred edges on a shape will make it appear distant.

Look Again

- Look at 12-1, and 12-3. Take a ruler (make sure it is clean!) and measure, in centimetres, the distance from the front of the picture to the horizon.
- How far away from the objects in the front of the picture does the horizon appear to be?
- Name the techniques each artist has used to achieve this affect.

- The picture in 12-2 is a photo of the real world. But the photo is quite flat! How do you know that the actual scene isn't flat?

- The caption to 12-4 says that it is a sculpture. Can you be sure that is true? Might it not be a painting?
- How can you check whether or not 12-4 is a sculpture?

- Look at the painting 33-1. Does the space look realistic? Why or why not?

- What do you think a composition would be like without the element of space used? Can you find an example in the pictures in this book?

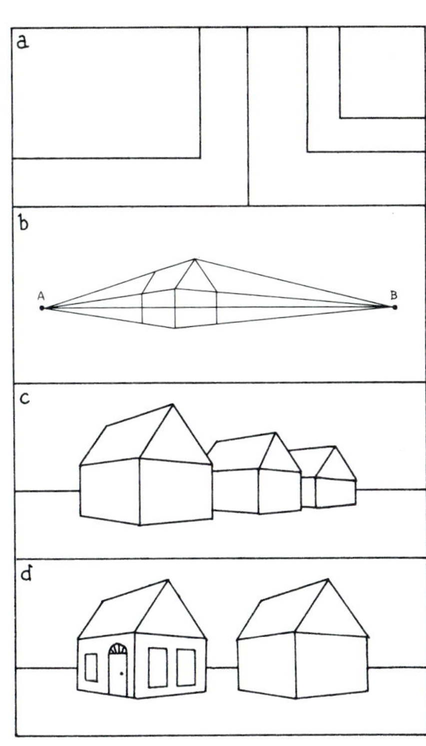

There is no illusion of depth in Fig. a, but the illusion of depth can be achieved by linear perspective, by overlapping shapes or by adding detail, as in the other figures.

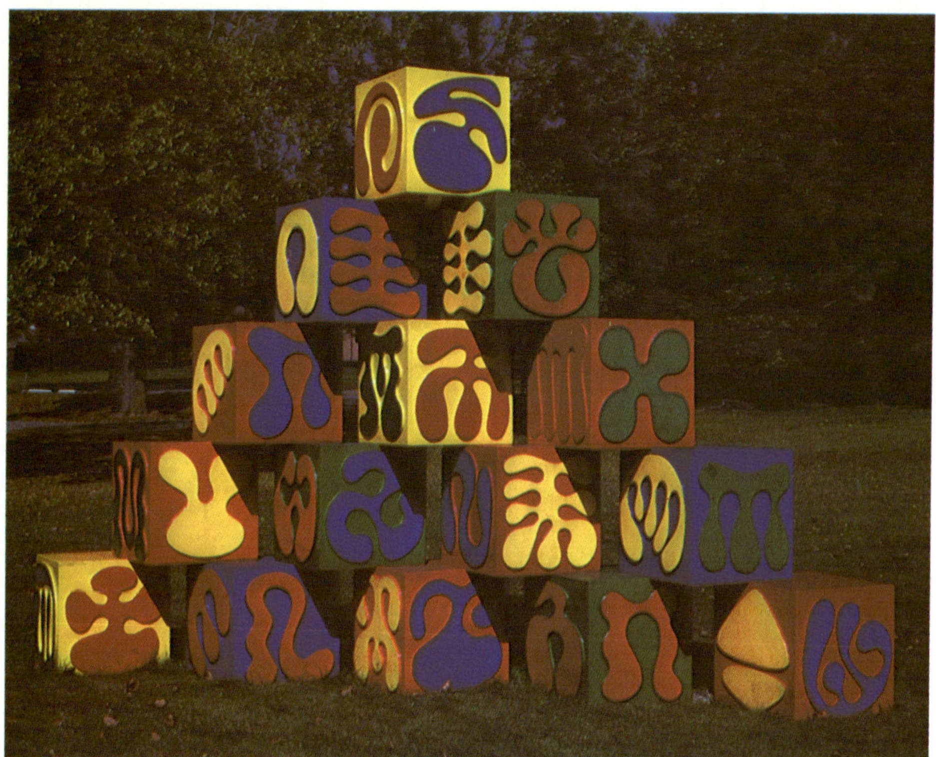

13-1 *Changes: Sculpture through Transition*, **Ted Turvey**
Ted Turvey used symbols based on primitive cultures to decorate these bright, colourful building blocks. They are arranged to form an outdoor sculpture. The blocks can be moved, to create many different effects.

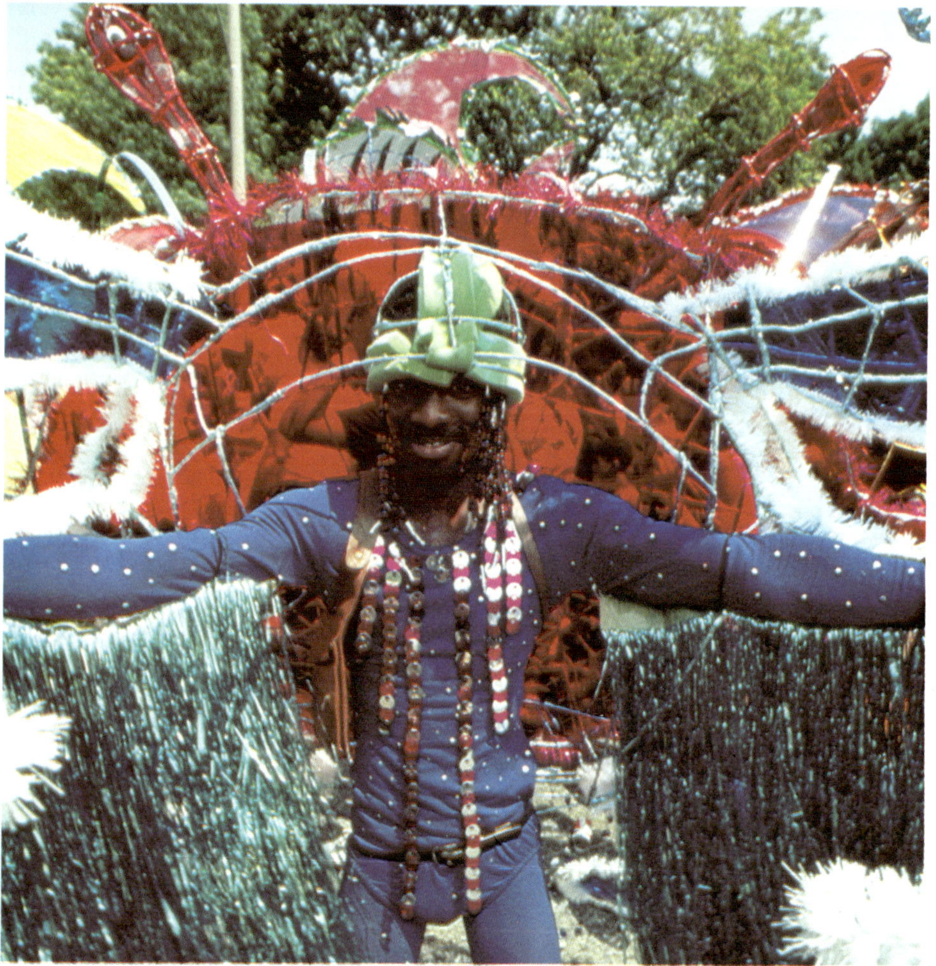

13-2 Caribana, Toronto
This costume is being worn at Toronto's Caribana festival.

13. Principles Help Visual Organization

In Chapters 7–12 you looked closely at some of the physical and expressive qualities of the elements of design. The artist organizes line, shape, colour and value, texture and space to create art forms such as paintings, sculptures and posters. The strategy used in arranging and organizing the elements is based on the *principles of design*. For instance, a painter uses the principle of dominance when placing a primary colour in the centre of a picture. Balance, dominance, movement, repetition, variety and unity are the principles of design used in organizing compositions.

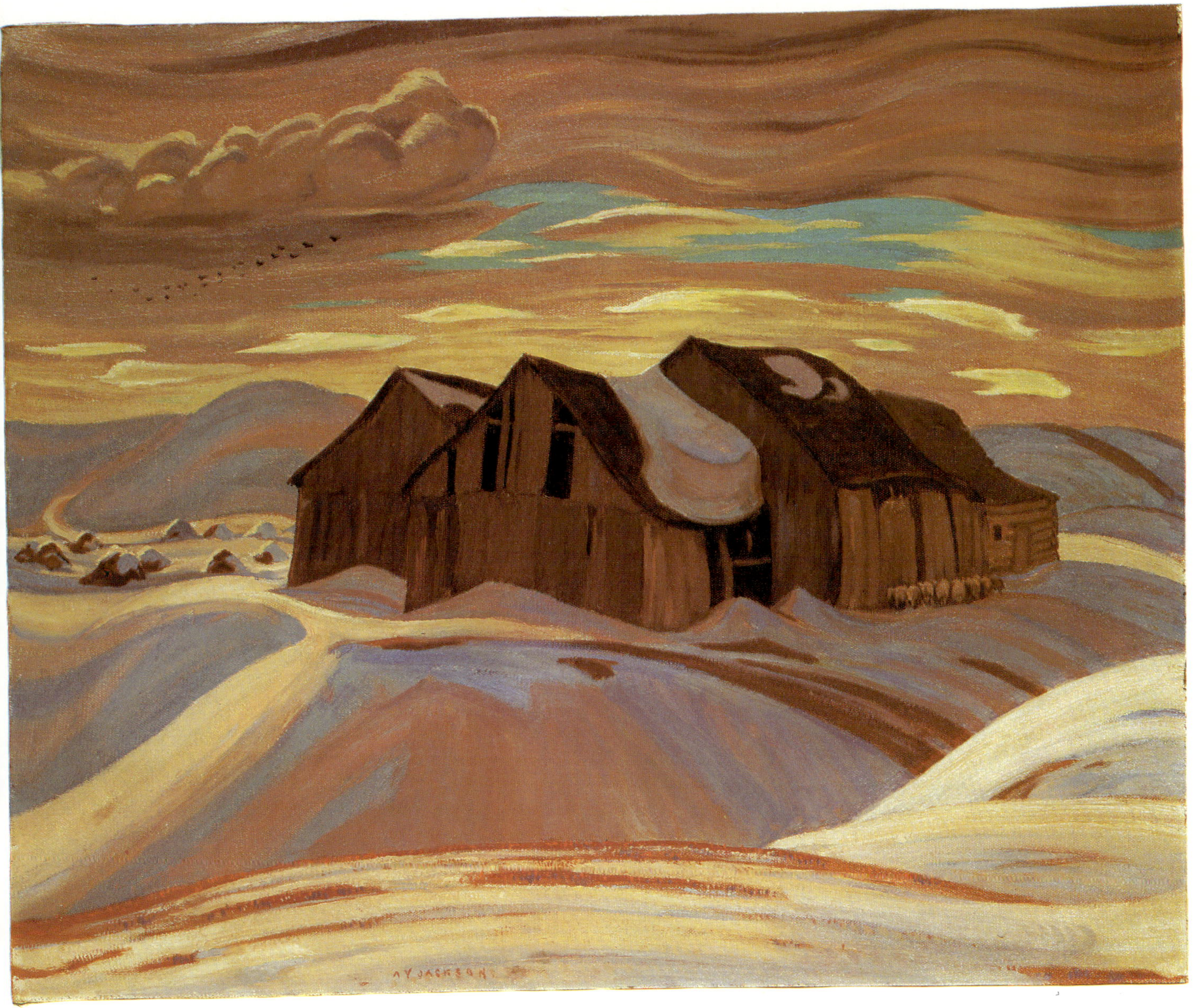

13-3 ***Barns*****, A.Y. Jackson**
A.Y. Jackson, an original member of Canada's famous Group of Seven, is well known for his use of rhythm and pattern. Notice how the same gently curving lines are repeated in the sky, buildings and the snow in *Barns*. Jackson was fascinated with barns and painted these near La Malbaie, Québec in 1926.

Look Again

- The regular triangular arrangement of 13-1 gives a feeling of stability. How would you re-arrange the cubes to suggest chaos? Loneliness?
- Look for each of the elements – line, shape, colour, value, texture and space – in the exciting Caribana costume. Describe how each has been used.
- Imagine a scene similar to 13-3 but in a different season or time of day. How would the colours change? Would the barns stay the same?

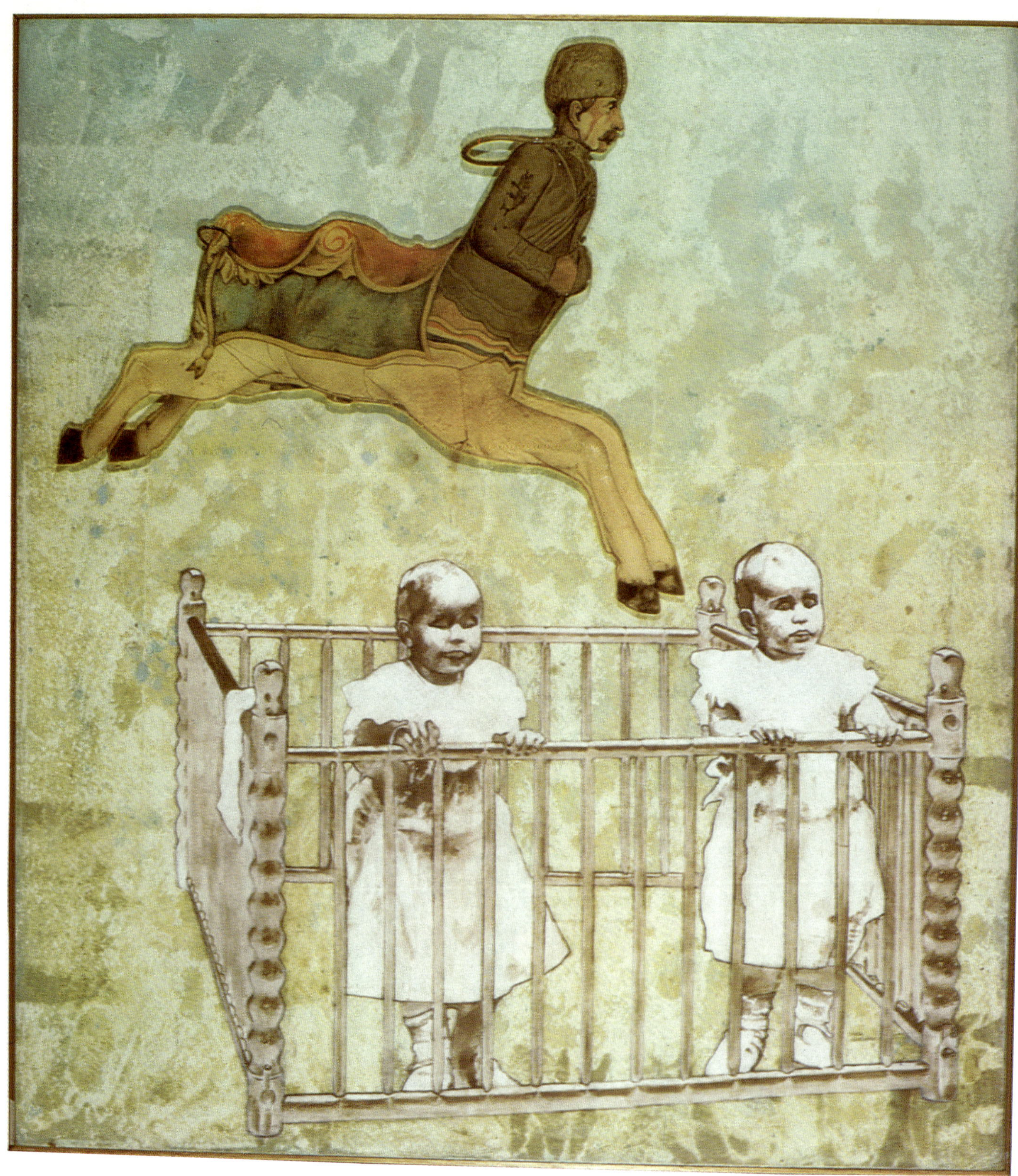

14-1 *How Many Days Has My Baby to Play?*, **Alexandra Haeseker**
Here Alexandra Haeseker has used asymmetrical balance. She has considered carefully the placement, size and colour of the objects in her picture. Notice how the single coloured shape balances the two paler shapes below.

14. Balance

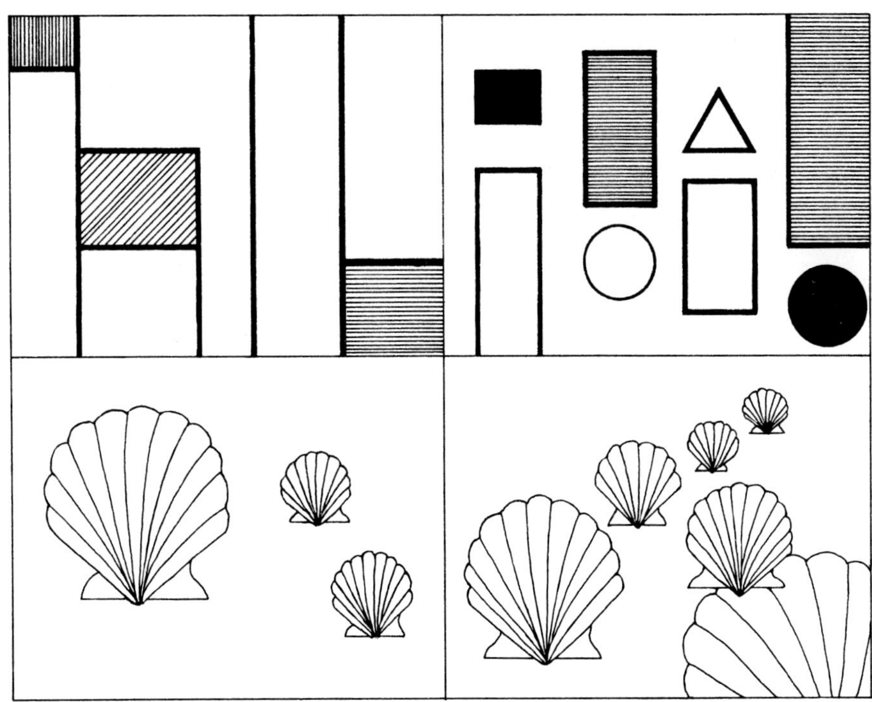

Informal balance adds interest.

If objects are to balance on a pair of old-fashioned scales, they must have the same weight. In art, parts of a particular work will seem balanced only if they have the same visual weight. In a work of art the position and size of each part must be balanced. For example, one large object on one side may balance several smaller ones on the other.

There are three main classifications of *balance*. They are symmetrical or formal balance, asymmetrical or informal balance, and radial balance.

If a work of art has *symmetrical balance*, the parts are visually equal. For example, a drawing of the side view of a bicycle that has both wheels the same size has symmetrical balance. This type of balance creates a feeling of structure and stateliness.

If a work of art has *asymmetrical balance*, the parts are visually unequal. For example, two small shapes can appear to balance one large shape. This type of balance creates a sense of activity and interest. Nowadays, many artists like to explore the use of asymmetrical or informal balance.

If a work of art has *radial balance*, it revolves around a real or imaginary central point. For example, a hubcap, an orange half and a sewer cover have radial balance.

When organizing the elements within a work of art, the artist always thinks about balance. Balance is important to achieving unity in a composition. The type of balance to use depends on the ideas and feelings the artist wants to communicate.

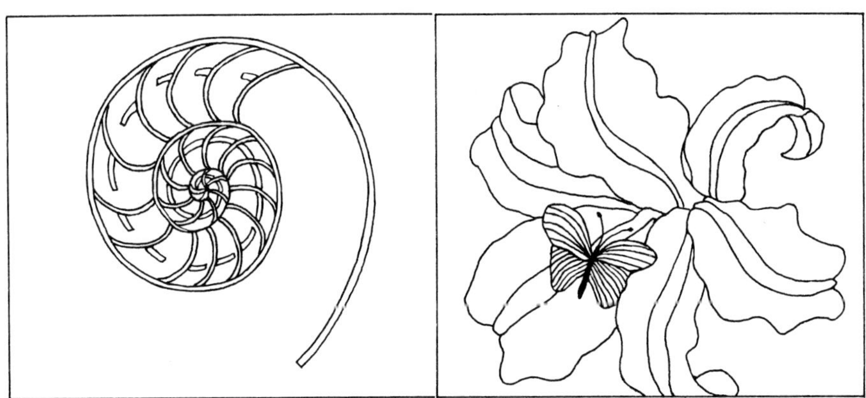

Radial balance creates a feeling of symmetry around a central point.

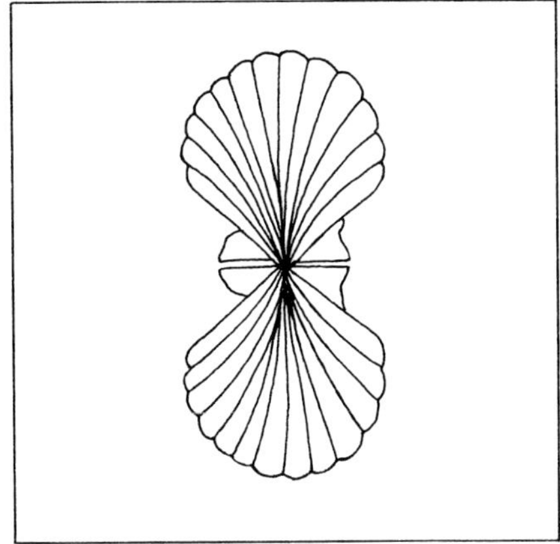

Symmetrical balance is achieved by placing two shapes of the same size together.

Look Again

- Imagine the picture **(14-1)** if the upper, coloured shape was pale like the others. Would it still look balanced?
- Imagine the picture without the lower, pale shapes. Would it still look balanced?

- Describe an arrangement of Ted Turvey's blocks (13-1) that would look unbalanced.

- Look at the church interior in 17-2. What kind of balance do you see in the church? Name all the things that contribute to the balance.

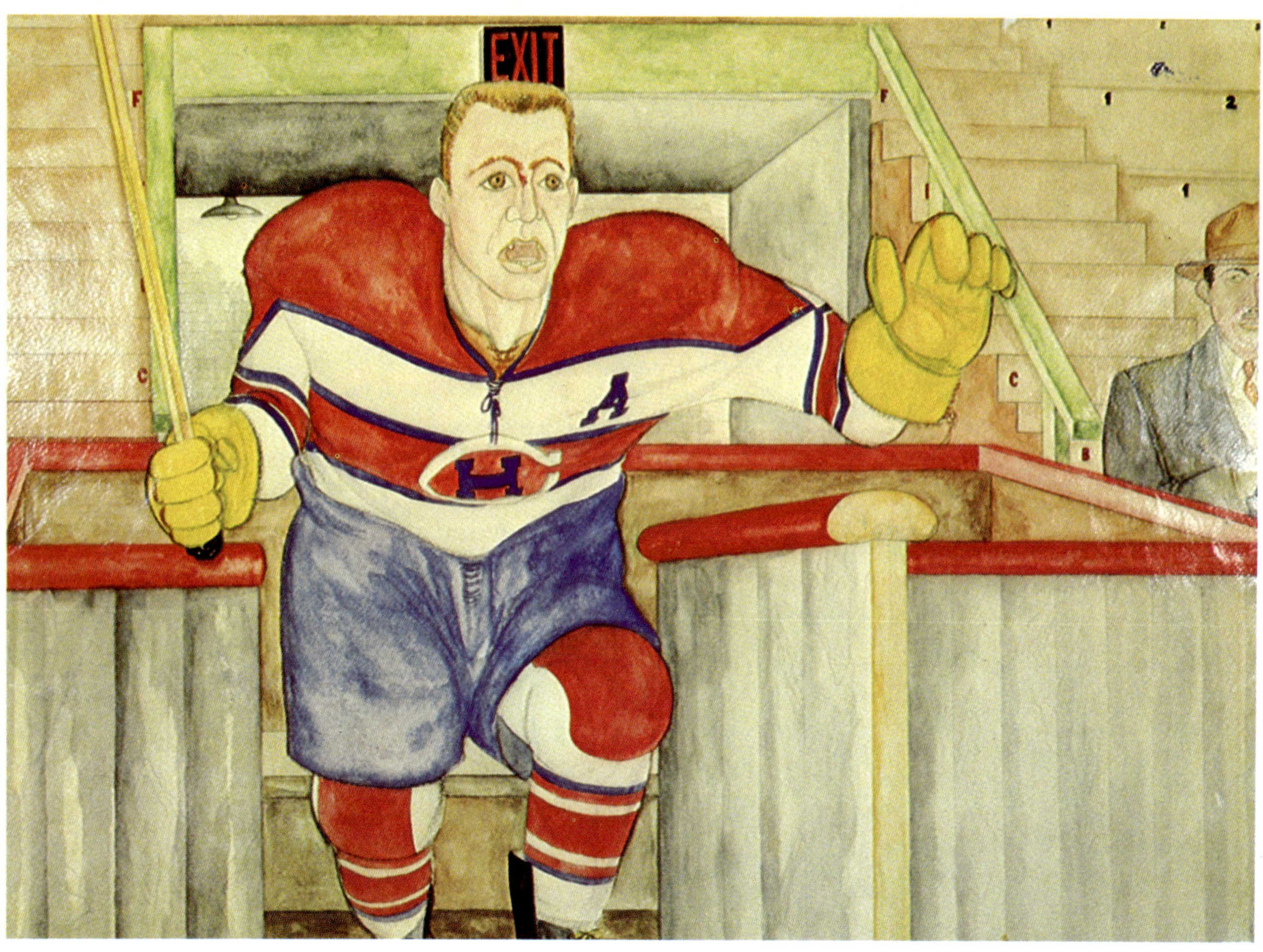

15-1 *Untitled*, Frank Routledge
There can be no doubt about the dominant feature of this picture! What techniques has the artist used to make the hockey player dominant?

15. Dominance

When something is dominant it is important. It stands out from everything else. In nature, a tall tree may dominate an area of low bushes. In art, a picture may have one or more areas of special emphasis that dominate other areas. There are many ways to create important areas or *dominance* in works of art. For example, the artist may emphasize an area by making it large, or by giving it a strong colour. It may be completed in greater detail than other areas. It may stand out from its background because of a sharp contrast between light and dark. Its shape may be distorted in some way that catches the eye. It may be placed in an important position, such as the centre of the picture.

The way the artist has organized the lines, shapes, colours, textures and space in a composition tells you about its visual message. For example, lines may have been arranged so that they lead your eye to a dominant area. Look for a centre of interest or dominant part as you view a work of art. Then you will discover what the artist thinks is important. This will help you understand the message within the composition.

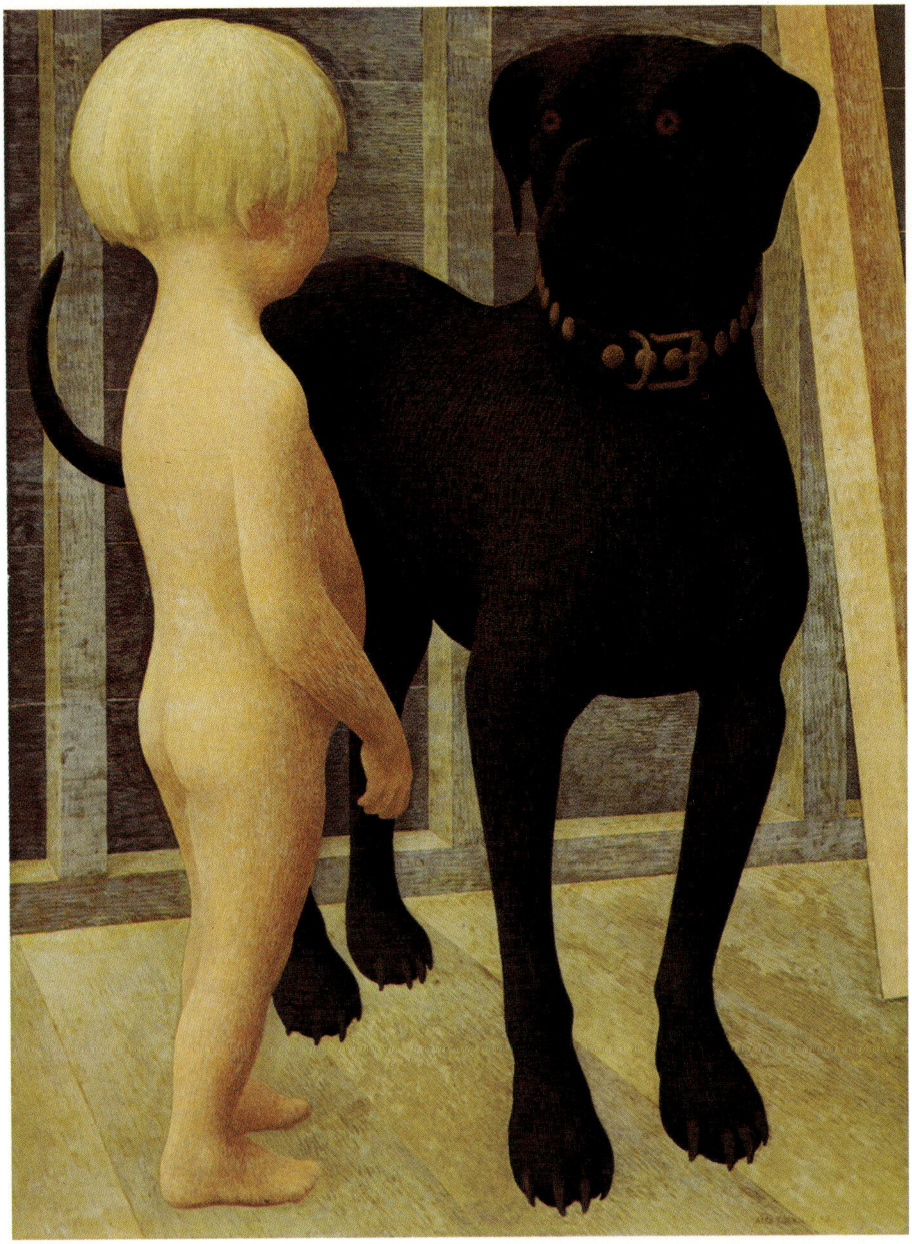

Look Again

- Look at 15-1. Do you think Frank Routledge likes hockey? Why or why not?
- Do you think the person in 15-1 plays a good game of hockey? What words would you use to describe him?
- Do you think it is appropriate to make such a person the dominant feature of a picture?

- Look at 29-2. Discuss which person you think dominates this picture.

- Put your hand over the child in 15-2. How does this seem to change the image of the black dog? Now cover the dog. What effect does this have on the image of the child?
- Imagine that the dog is larger. How would the feeling change?

- Photographs advertising products appear on billboards, posters and in magazines and newspapers. Where do you think the Azzaro perfume advertisement would appear?
- Look for examples in magazines where photographs are used to focus your attention.

15-2 ***Child and Dog*****, Alex Colville**
Two elements of design are used to create a dominant centre of interest in this painting by Alex Colville. The location of shapes in the centre of the picture and the use of contrast in dark and light emphasize the relationship between the child and the dog. Alex Colville was born in Toronto and now lives in Wolfville, Nova Scotia.

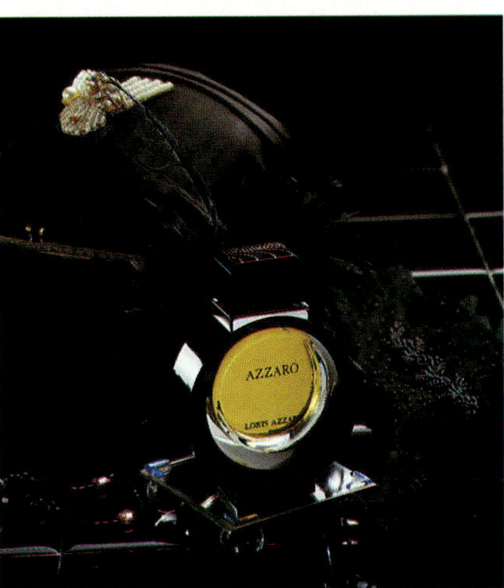

15-3 Azzaro perfume, Taffi Rosen
Photographer Taffi Rosen has carefully composed an advertisement for Azzaro perfume. Your eye is drawn to the perfume bottle as the brightest spot in an otherwise darkened image. The perfume is also the only part of the composition that is in colour.

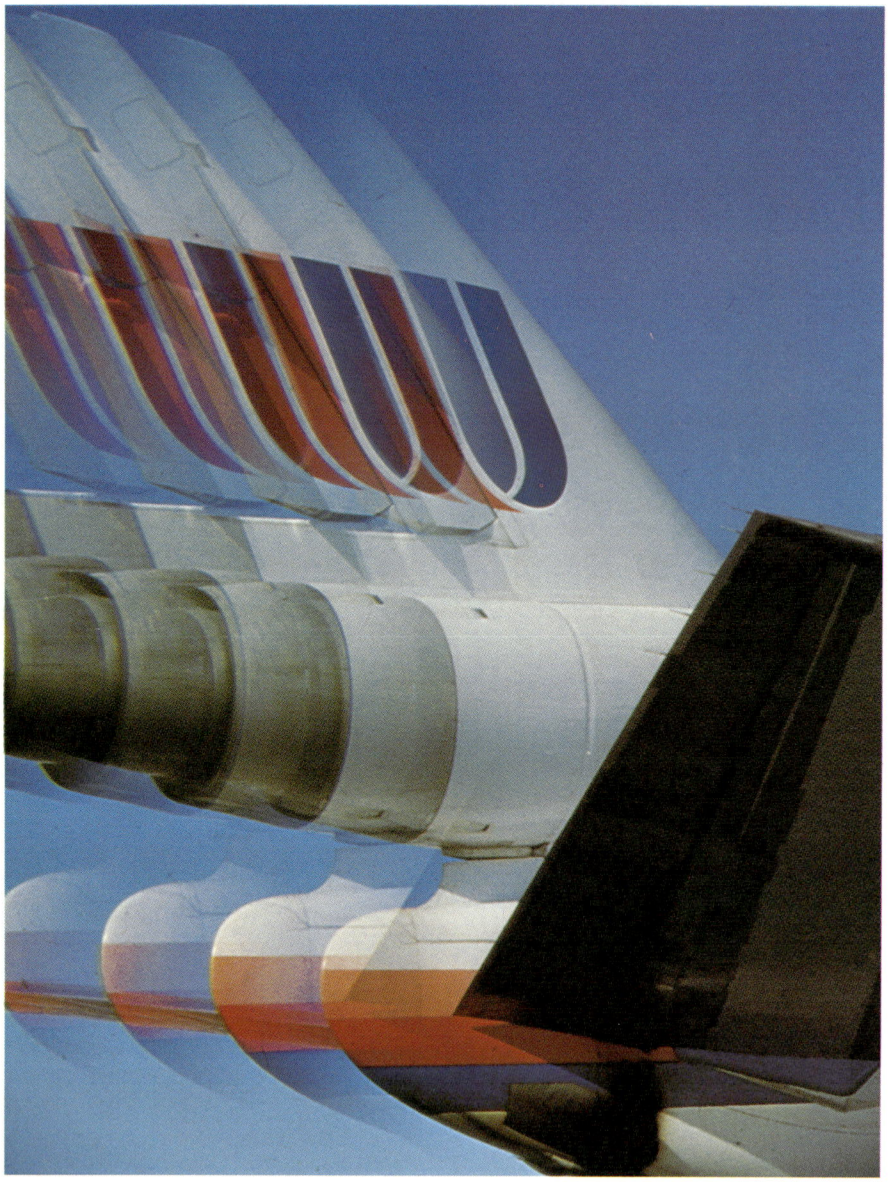

16. Movement and Repetition

Movement is meant to show activity in a picture. A picture may show physical activity such as skating or running. This is called *physical movement* in composition.

Compositional movement is different from physical movement. This type of movement is created by *repetition*. Repeated lines or shapes lead the eye from place to place in a rhythmic way. Other methods of creating compositional movement may be to repeat colours or patterns of texture or light. The artist plans the type of movement that is needed to direct the viewer's gaze in a particular way.

16-1 Pacific Western tail fin, Toronto International Airport
The sense of movement may be created by repeating shapes. By overlapping the image, the photographer has made the plane appear to move from left to right.

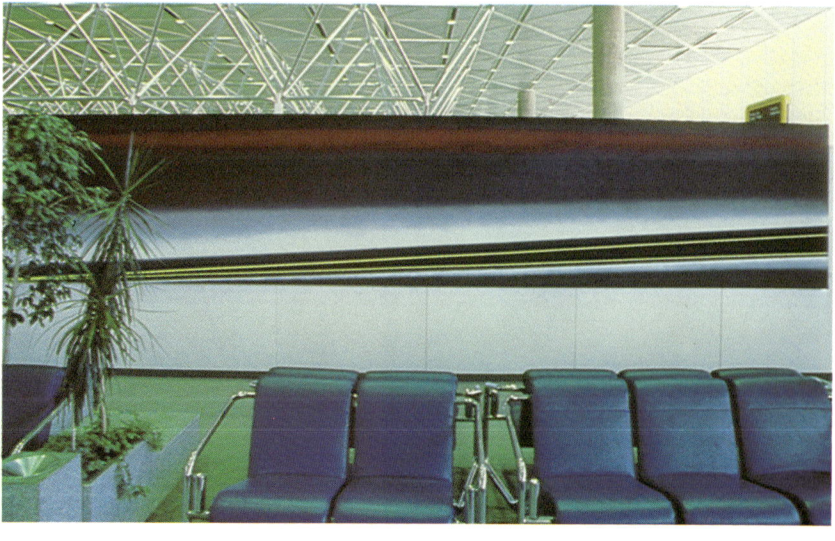

16-2 *Kodawanda*, Rita Letendre
A feeling of jet-like speed is produced by the converging, repeated lines of Rita Letendre's *Kodawanda*. Gradual changes in value also help to increase the sense of movement. A fitting setting for this picture is at Montreal's Mirabel Airport.

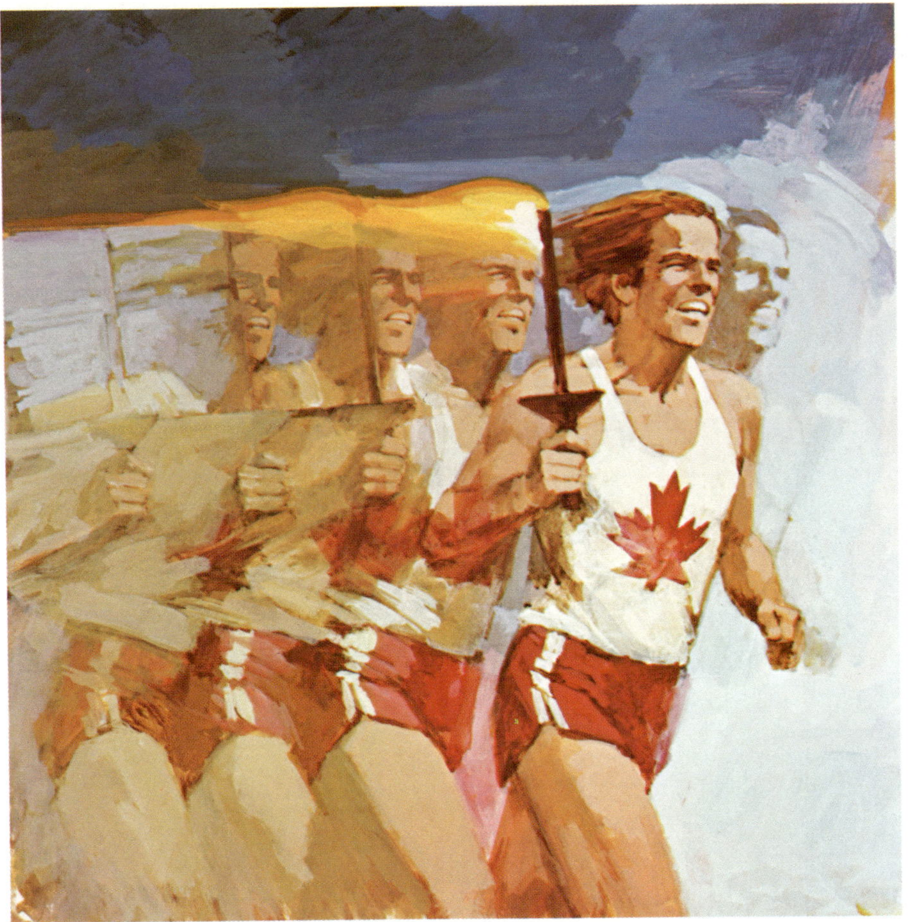

16-3 *Olympic Torch Runner*, **Fred Oakley**
The artist uses repeated shapes that recall the rhythm and physical action of running in this highly expressive Olympic poster.

Look Again

- When looking at a work of art, notice how the artist uses movement. Describe which kinds of movement are used in the works of art on this page.
- Is the movement in *Kodawanda* (16-2) from left to right or from right to left? Give reasons for your answer.
- Imagine 16-3 without the "shadow" figures. Is the single figure still running, or is he just walking into a strong wind?
- Look at the quilt in 10-2. Notice the repetition of shapes. Does this repetition give a feeling of movement? Why or why not?
- Look at the glass window in 10-4. Does your eye follow a path when you look at this picture? If it does, describe the direction.

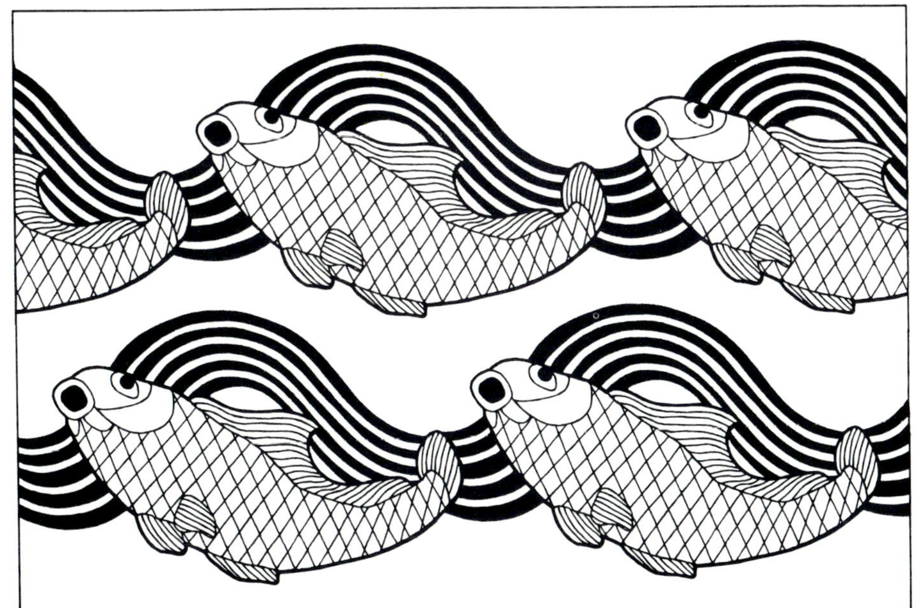

Works of art often have repeated motifs or themes. These repeated shapes create movement and rhythm.

17. Variety

Variety adds interest to a work of art. The artist uses it in a controlled way to hold the viewer's attention. One of the ways to achieve variety is through *contrast*. For example, contrasting values are dark against light. Contrasting colours are warm and cool; contrasting shapes may be large and small. Contrasting textures may be rough and smooth. These kinds of contrasts help the artist to achieve areas of interest.

Another way to create variety is through *elaboration*. By adding detail, the artist increases the variety of patterns.

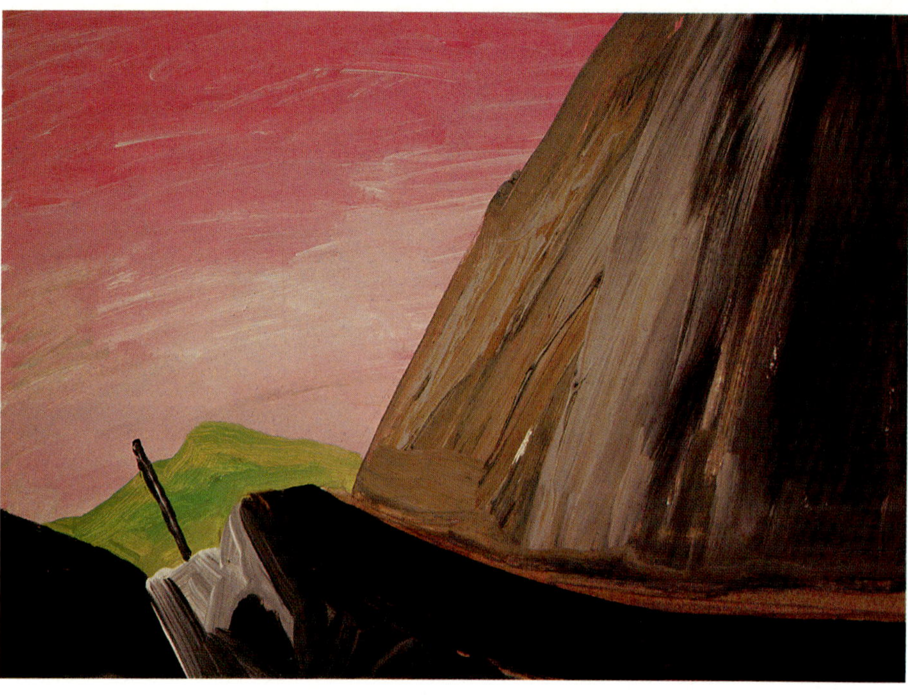

17-1 ***Highway*, Wanda Koop**
The simplicity of the landscape represented in Wanda Koop's *Highway* is balanced by interesting brush stroke variations.

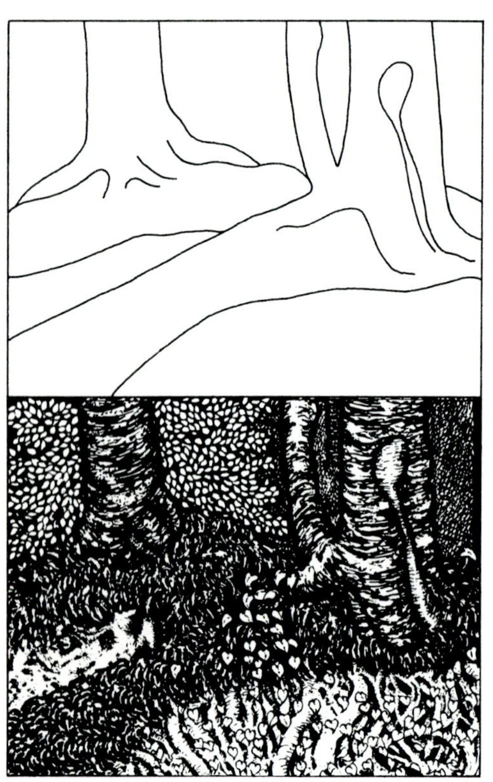

An artist begins to work with an idea. The shapes are then re-worked to make the idea more interesting. The final result is often very elaborate.

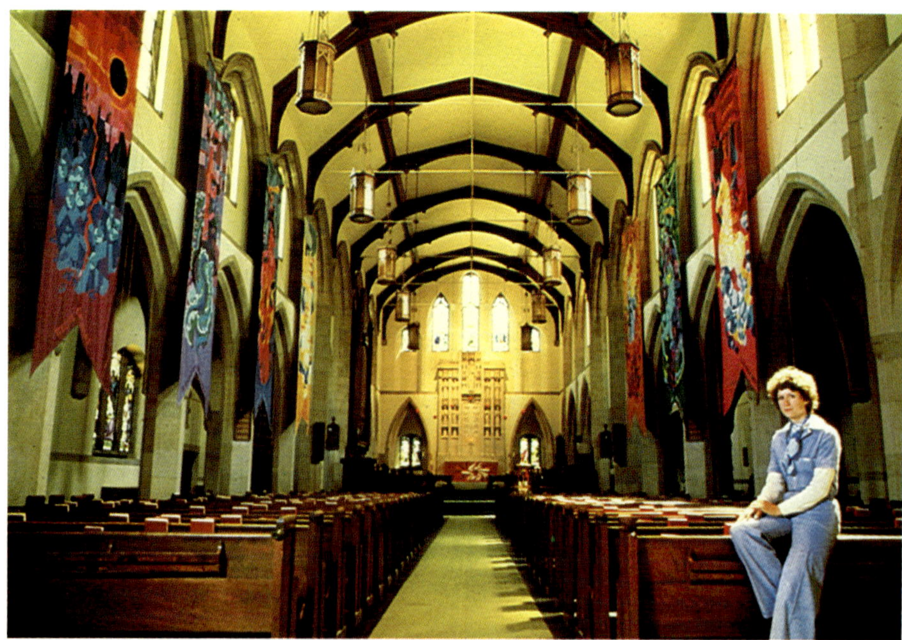

17-2 Banners in church, Marion Spanjerdt

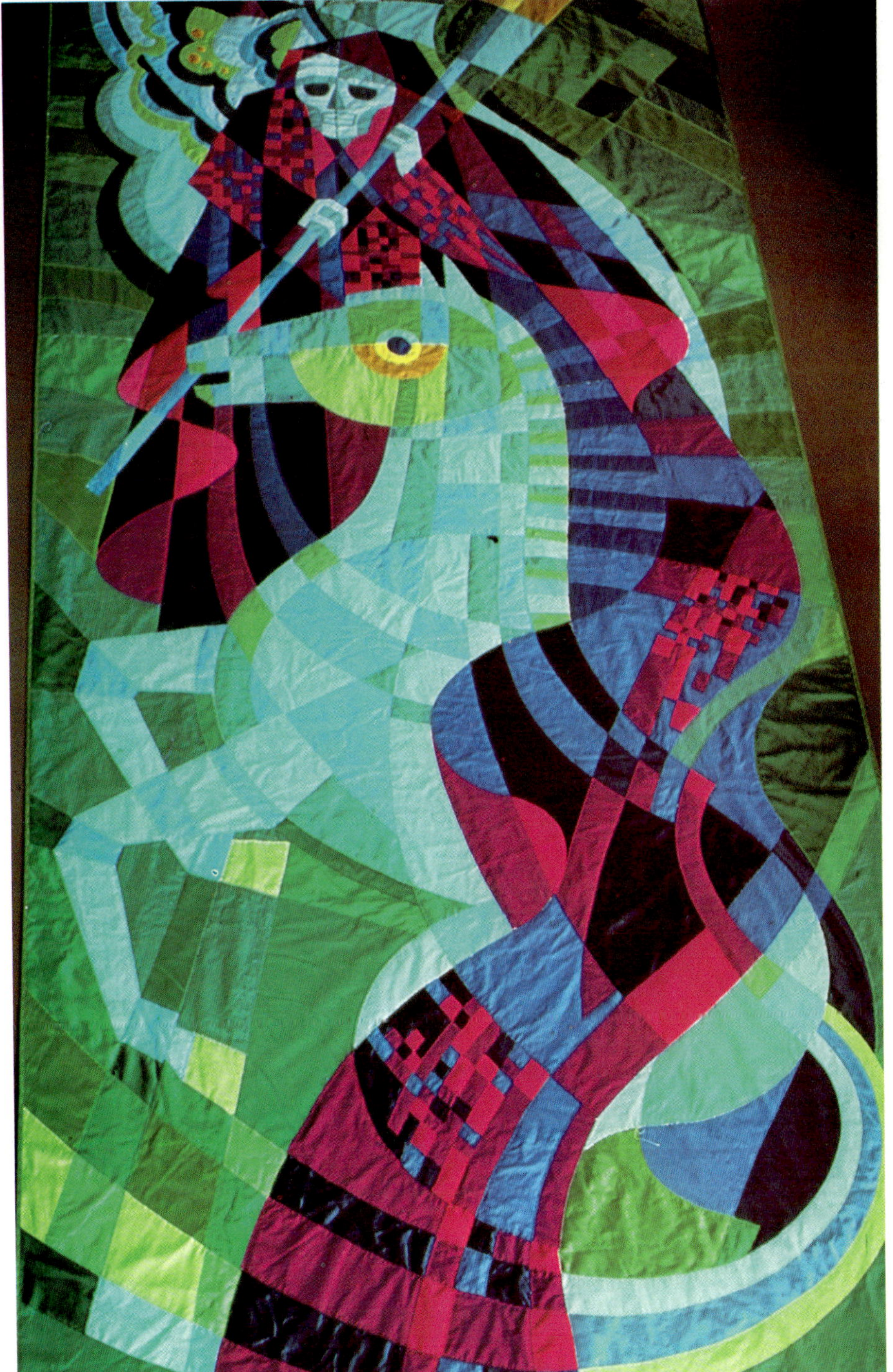

17-3 ***Devil and Horse*****, Marion Spanjerdt**
Symmetrical balance is evident in the interior design of the church, but the banners add variety. Here is a close-up of one banner called *Devil and Horse*. Although variations appear in both figures, the artisan has shown concern for visual harmony and unity.

Look Again

- How is colour used for variety in 17-1 and 17-3?
- Look at the interior in 17-2. Does the room look restful? Give reasons for your answer.

18. Unity

Throughout this section, you have seen how individual principles of design can be used by the artist. These principles are primarily guides to organizing the elements in order to produce visual *unity*.

Artists achieve unity by their careful choice of the visual elements. They may use similar lines, shapes, colours and textures. For example, using neighbouring colours on the colour wheel, such as blue-green and yellow-green, can increase unity.

Unity without variety could be boring. However, the balance between unity and variety is not always equal. In some instances, a lack of apparent unity is quite deliberate. Topics such as war and violence may be depicted in what may seem to be a disorganized way. Look for the artist's strong feelings about the subject as the visual message in this type of art.

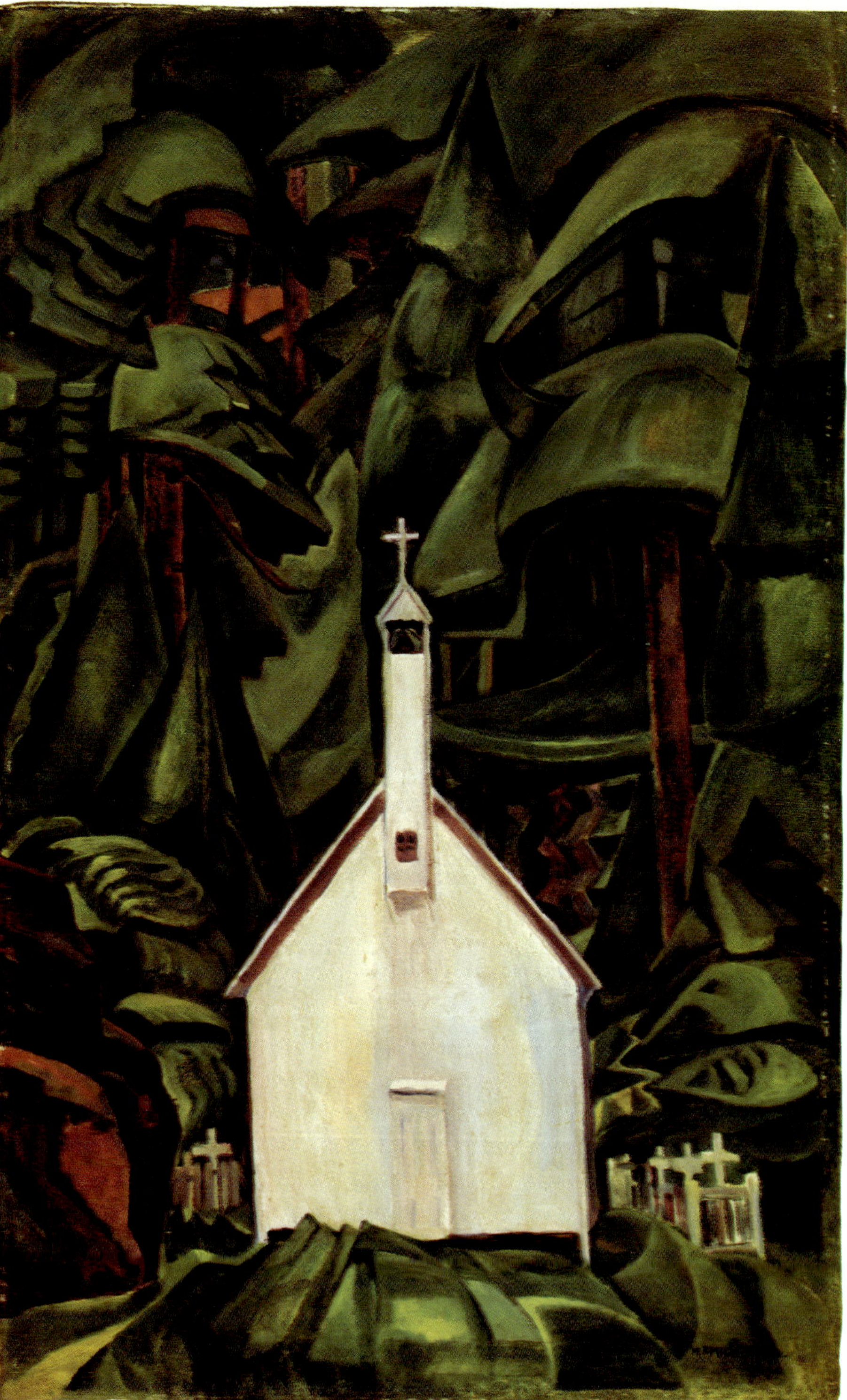

18-1 *Indian Church*, Emily Carr
Although the church stands out against the forest, Emily Carr created a sense of visual harmony in the painting. Emily Carr painted *Indian Church* in 1930 as part of her continuing themes about the Indians of British Columbia, as well as her own religious feeling.

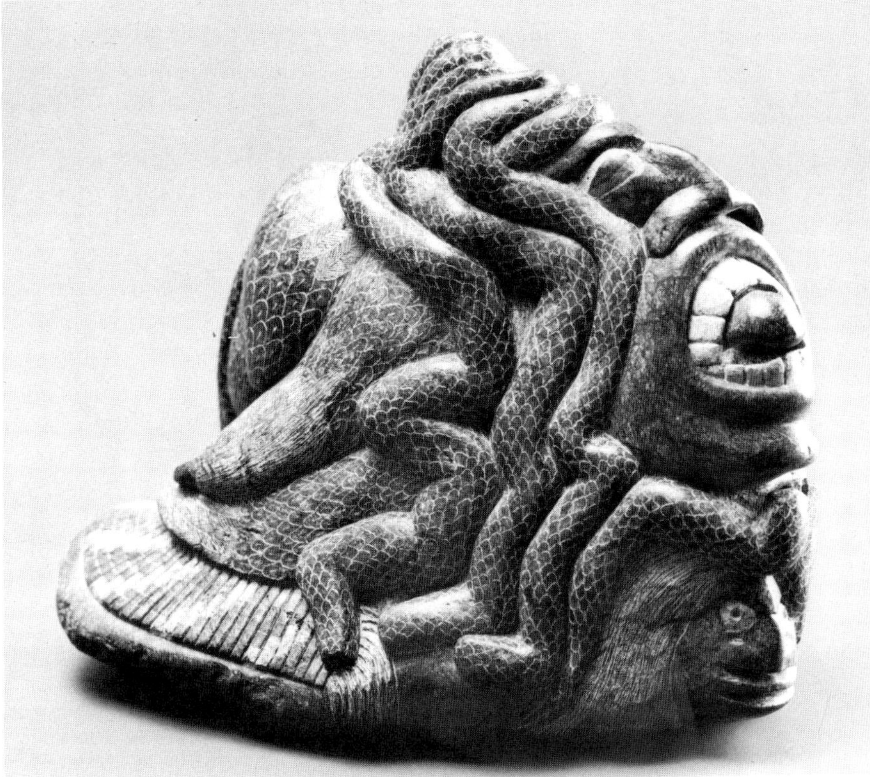

18-2 *Ta do da ho*, **Duffy Wilson**
Artists who work in three-dimensional materials are concerned with visual unity. Notice how Duffy Wilson has repeated lines in this stone carving.

Look Again

- Similarities help create harmony. What elements are repeated in each of these two works to create unity and harmony?
- Variety makes art seem lively and interesting. How does line help to create movement and variation in each of these works of art?

- Look at the photo of Inuvik, N.W.T. in 26-2. What things are all the same in this residential area?
- What things are different?
- If you lived in this area, would you want your home to match the others, or would you want it to look different? Choose which house you would buy. Describe what you would do to it to achieve your aim.
- How do you think your choice would affect the appearance of the street?

- Many people say they find a walk in the country restful. How does harmony appear in nature? For example, what colours and shapes are repeated?
- What adds variety in nature?

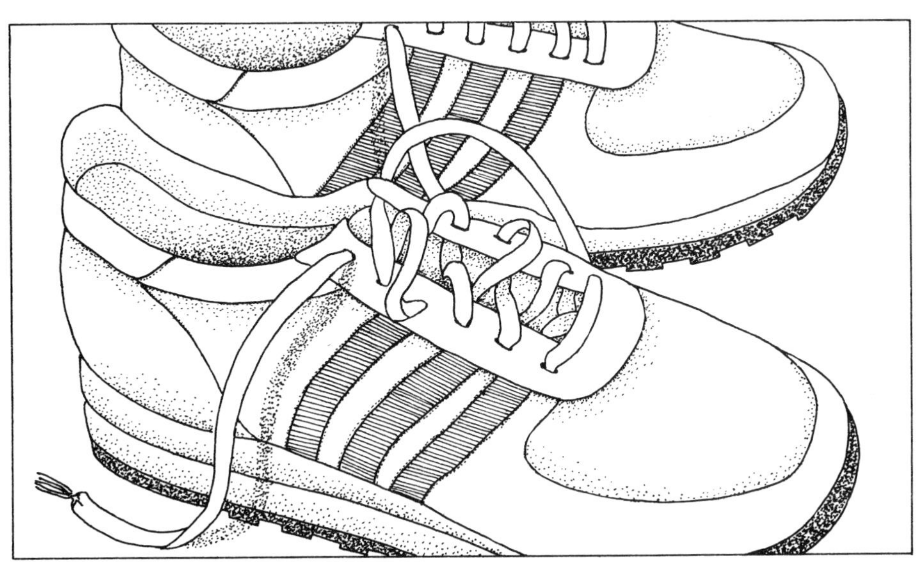

An artist strives to create a unified visual message.

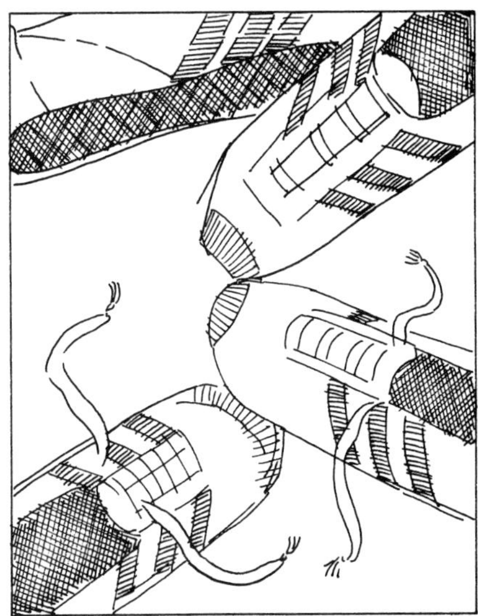

Without using the principles, an artist may have difficulty organizing the elements of a picture. Disorganization and a lack of harmony may be the result.

19. A Closer Look at Forms of Art

Art as a language needs materials that the artist can use to express ideas. This book has already shown you some different forms of art. Now it is time to take a closer look. What materials were used in each art form? Looking closely at how an artist uses materials will help you understand the artist's message.

20. Drawing

Drawing refers to making lines on a surface such as paper. Some drawings are plans for other works of art. Others are art in their own right. Drawings may be very detailed or consist of simple lines. Many kinds of drawing materials and tools are available today. It is impossible to describe them all, but here are a few that are seen quite often.

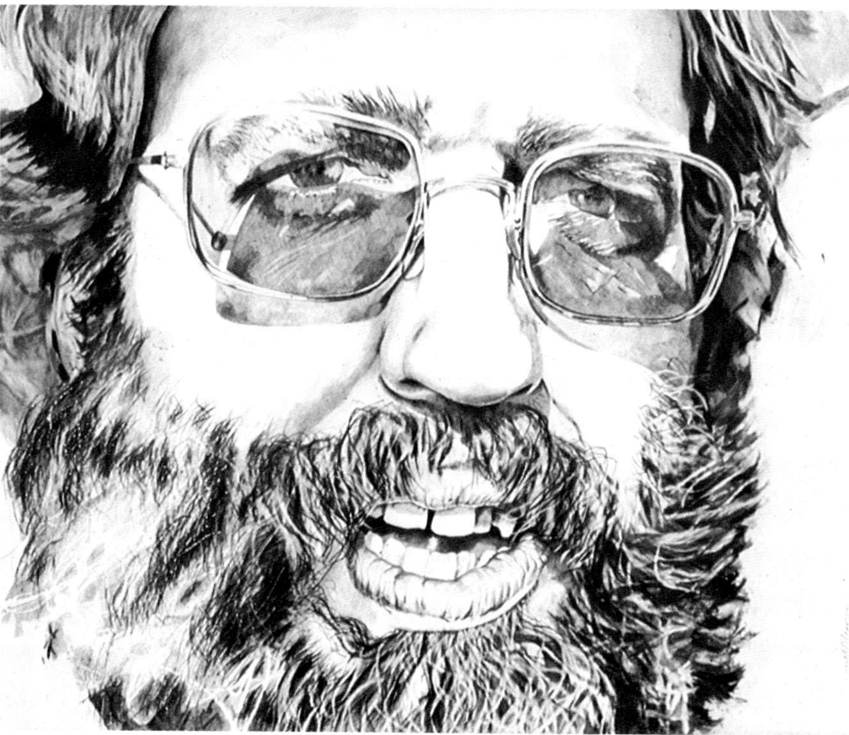

20-1 *Big Dick*, Gary Olson
Gary Olson, a contemporary artist from Alberta, uses balance between the negative and background space and the positive shapes made of closely grouped lines.

Pencils are commonly used in drawing. These pencils vary from soft to hard and from thick to thin. The softest pencil is 6B. The hardest is 9H. Each one makes a distinctive type of line or shaded area depending on its size or quality. An eraser can be used to correct mistakes. Charcoal and graphite are two materials for pencils.

India ink is a traditional drawing material. It is permanent which means a drawing will last for a long time. Ink is opaque and covers other marks such as pencil outlines. It is applied with a pen that may be fitted with pen nibs of different thicknesses. Ink also may be used with a brush, which may be used to apply an ink wash. The ink may be diluted with water to give the right colour strength. Using a brush with the wash technique is similar to painting.

Conté crayon is another traditional drawing material. It comes as a dry stick. It, too, is permanent and is available in a variety of neutral colours such as brown, black and white. Conté crayon can be used to outline objects by using an edge of the stick to make a thin line. A wider line can be produced by drawing with the full stick. Some areas may be shaded with crayon.

Charcoal also comes as sticks or in the form of pencils. Unlike conté crayon, it blends easily because it is soft. Areas on a drawing may be shaded from light to dark. A kneaded eraser will remove charcoal lines. Charcoal is a favourite sketching material because of the interesting line quality it can make. It can be used to make a thin or thick line by changing the angle or pressure within the same stroke.

When colour is desired in drawing, materials such as felt pens, coloured markers, wax crayons, chalks and pastels can be used. Felt pens and coloured markers are relatively new drawing tools. Their ink is permanent and comes in a wide range of colours. They produce crisp, bold colour. Chalk, on the other hand, is used when colours are to be blended. Pastels are similar in colour range to chalk. They, too, can be blended to produce a variety of colours. Coloured wax crayons have a distinctive texture. Coloured pencils also leave a texture. They may be used dry to draw lines, or

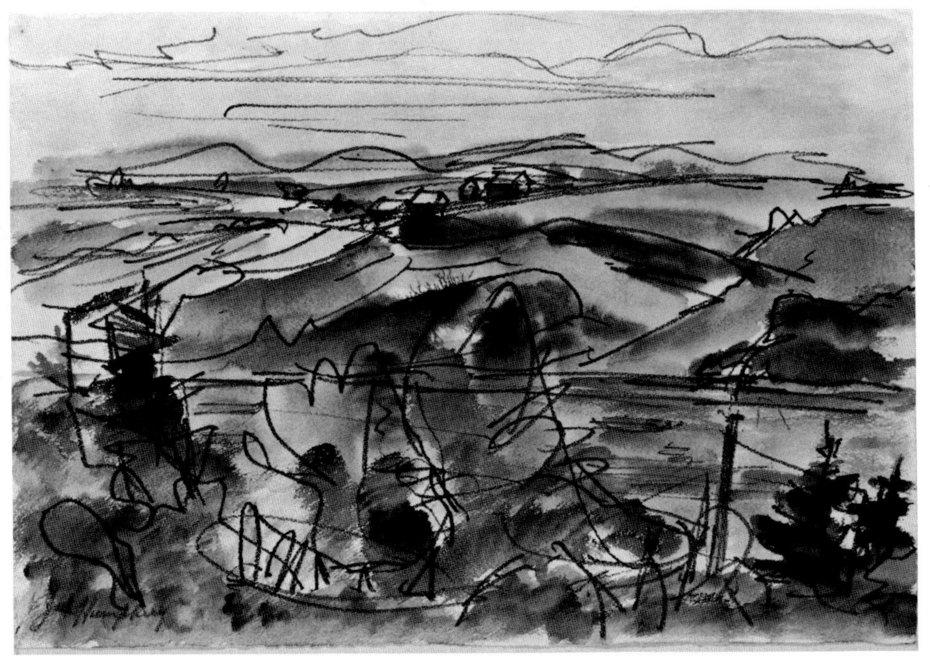

20-2 *From Perry Point*, **Jack Humphrey**
Expressive use of line is combined with watercolour in this drawing by New Brunswick artist Jack Humphrey.

wet to draw in an area of colour.

Many of these drawing materials may be used together to produce mixed media compositions. For instance, crayons may be used with inks, or pencil with charcoal. Artists today have a variety of drawing materials to choose from to express their ideas.

Paper is the most common base for drawing. There are many types of paper. Some are glossy, some are dull; some are smooth, others are rough. Some are coloured. Different types of paper are suitable for different media. An important part of drawing is choosing a base that is right for the medium.

20-3 *Cat Series – The Permanent*, **Ted Larson**
Cartoon illustrations such as Ted Larson's *Cat Series* add an entertaining quality to advertising.

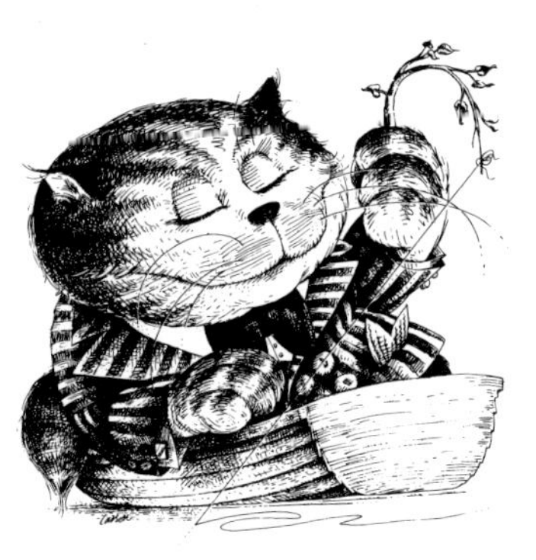

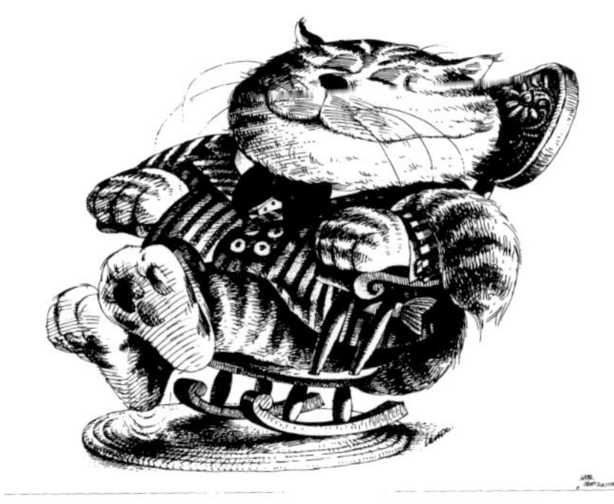

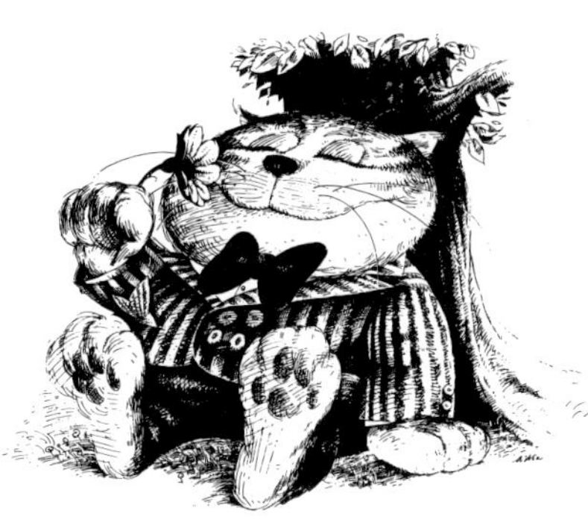

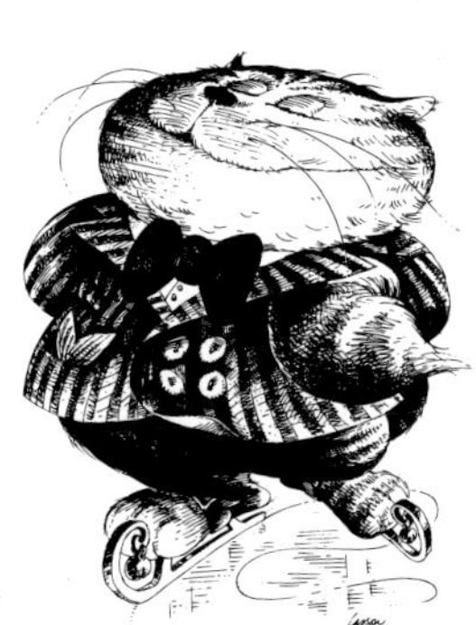

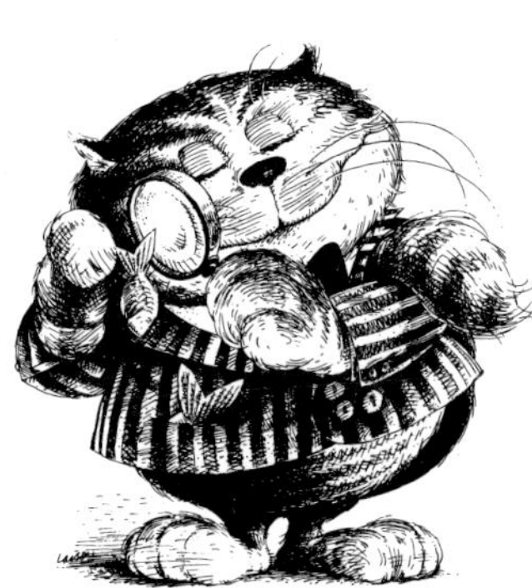

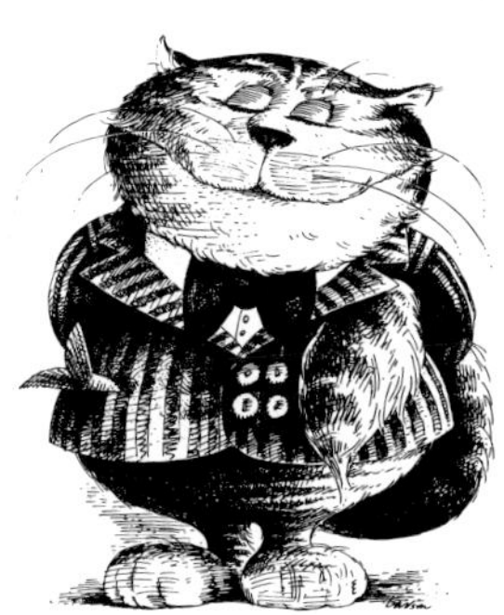

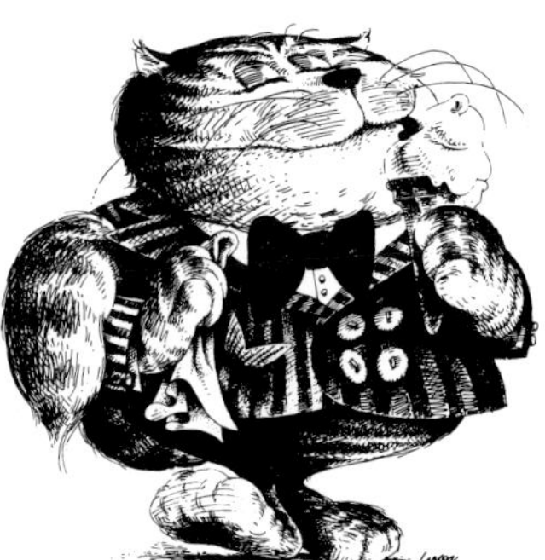

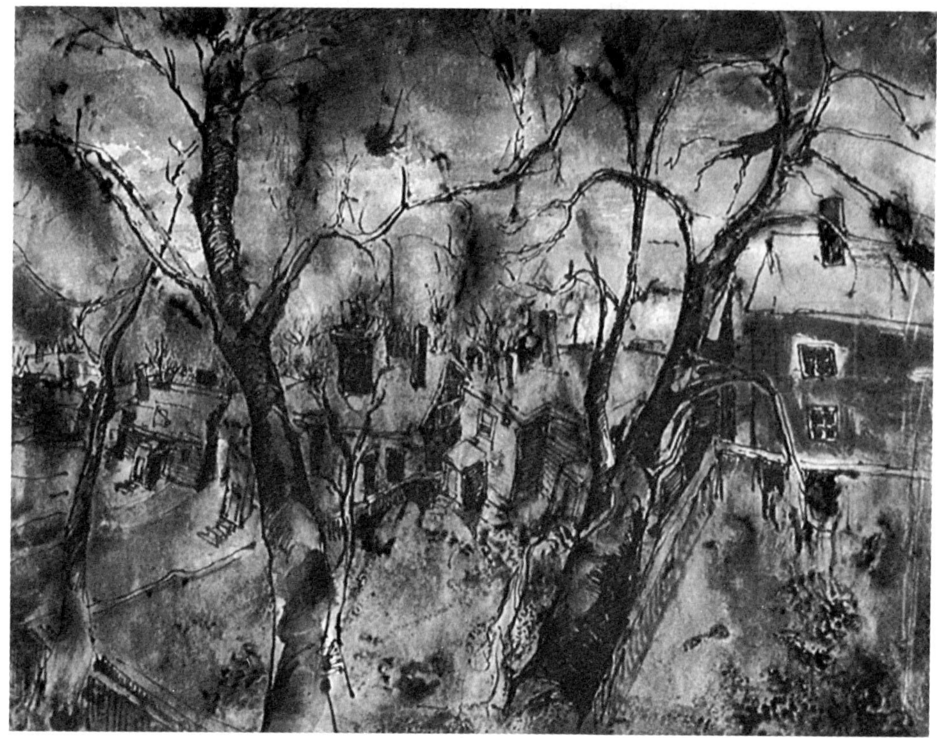

20-4 ***Gloomy Day in Halifax,*** **Carol Fraser**
Drawings may be very detailed or may be very free. Here Nova Scotia artist Carol Fraser has drawn with ink on wet paper to express a gloomy day.

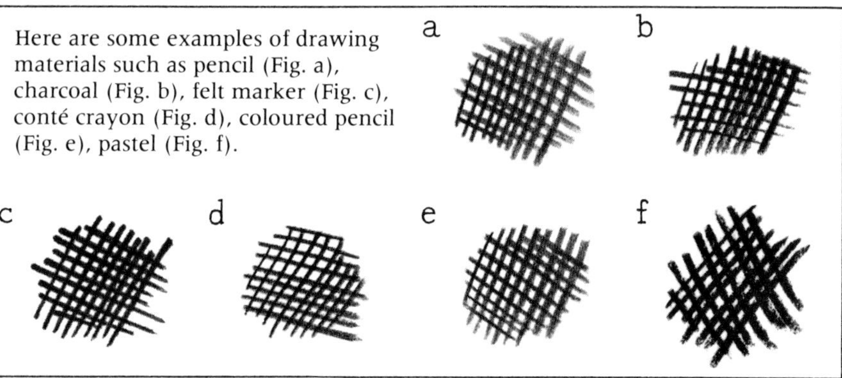

Here are some examples of drawing materials such as pencil (Fig. a), charcoal (Fig. b), felt marker (Fig. c), conté crayon (Fig. d), coloured pencil (Fig. e), pastel (Fig. f).

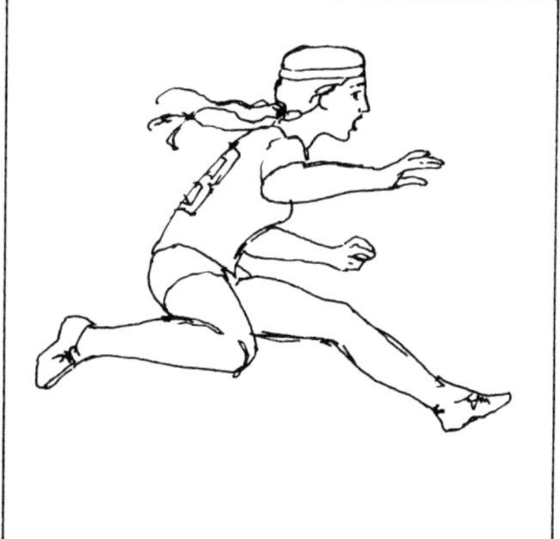

A contour drawing is done by following the exterior outline of a person or object. Often it is done by looking only at the figure and not at the line on the paper.

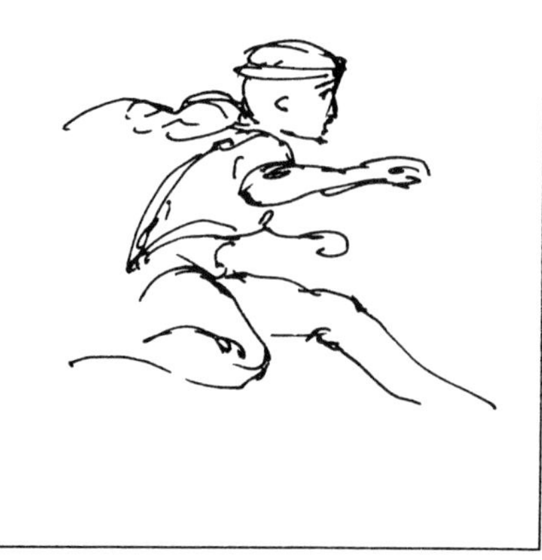

A gesture drawing gives the feeling of the action; *not* the actual appearance.

Look Again

- Look at Big Dick (20-1). Try to describe him. For example, how old is he? What does he do for a job? Is he fierce or friendly?
- Would you like to meet this person?
- What has the artist done to suggest these ideas to you?

- Which of the drawn lines in 20-2 outline the real edges of things in the scene? Which do not?
- How would you describe the lines that do not show real edges? What things do they show, if not edges?

- The cat cartoons (20-3) consist of black lines drawn on flat, white paper. The artist uses them in a number of ways. Can you tell the following:
- How he indicates texture? What textures?
- How he indicates shape?
- How he indicates volume? For example, how can you tell if the cat is fat or thin?
- How he suggests colour?

- Look closely at 20-4. How has the artist used line and colour to achieve the feeling of a gloomy day?
- What lines and colours would you choose for a hot summer day? A windy day?

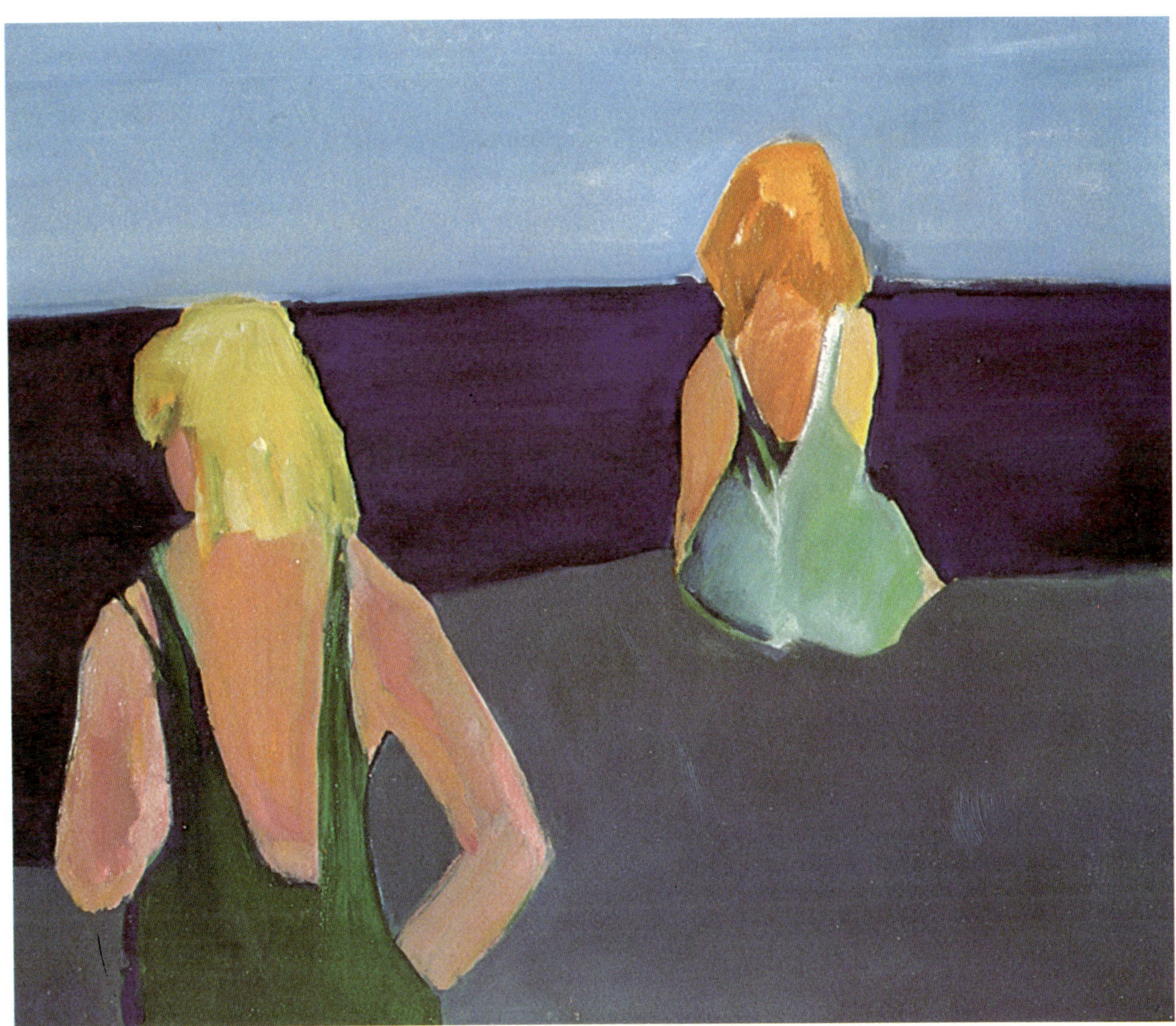

21-1 *Girls*, Nita Forrest
The flat application of coloured oil paints and the obvious brush work in Nita Forrest's *Girls* tell you immediately that this picture is a painting. The term "painterly" is used to describe works that have this effect.

21. Painting

A paint is made by mixing powdered colours or pigments with a liquid. *Painting* itself means that colours are applied to a surface to create a picture or design. Traditional paints include tempera, oils and watercolours. Modern paints include acrylics.

You are probably familiar with *tempera* paint. Tempera can be bought in liquid form or as powdered pigments to which water is added. The paint needs to be stirred before it is used until it is smooth and creamy. The colours are usually bright and bold as they are applied but dry to a less bright finish. Colours may be mixed in flat trays. Black or white may be added to make shades or tints. Tempera paint may be used on bases such as paper, masonite or cardboard. It can be brushed on with stiff, bristle brushes or floated on with soft hair brushes. It dries relatively quickly and is opaque. This means it covers the surface and does not allow the underlying layers to show.

Watercolours come in the form of small cakes or in tubes. Water is used to wet the cakes of colour, or used to thin the paint from the tubes. Watercolour is described as being clear or transparent, because underlying layers of colours show through top layers. These paintings are usually created on textured paper. Many special effects are possible with watercolours. Some artists draw ink lines into wet areas of colour so that the ink spreads out in feather-like patterns. Crayons or other wax-like materials can be used with watercolours to make still other variations. In working with watercolours, it is necessary to keep the colours pure and fresh-looking. Brushes and wash water need to be kept clean. Although watercolours are mixed in a similar way to tempera paints, traditionally no white is used. A colour is lightened only with water. The artist obtains white areas by leaving sections of the background paper showing. There are several kinds of brushes to use, but most artists prefer soft hair brushes, such as camel or sable.

Acrylic paint is also water-based. The colours are made from synthetic materials rather than from natural pigments. They can be thinned with water to be transparent. Thick acrylic paint is opaque. It dries quickly to a permanent waterproof layer. The paint may be brushed on with stiff bristle brushes. Alternatively, it may be applied with a palette knife in bold strokes. A thick application of acrylic paint creates heavy textures that form rough, raised surfaces when dry. Acrylics are used on paper, wood, canvas or masonite. There is a greater variety of colours available in acrylic paint than in tempera paint. White and black are used to make tints and shades. Acrylic paint dries to a bright finish.

Oil paint, like acrylics, is permanent. Unlike the other paints, it is oil-based. This means it is thinned with turpentine and mixed with linseed oil and varnish. It dries very slowly. The artist can change and re-work areas with a brush or palette knife before it dries. Oil paintings are usually done on canvas stretched on a wooden frame. Masonite, wood, canvas board or other heavy paper may be used as a base. The surface may be covered with several coats of gesso, or white latex paint, to produce a white background on which to work. Oils may be applied in thin, smooth layers, or in short, textured dabs of colour. There is a wide range of colours, as well as black and white.

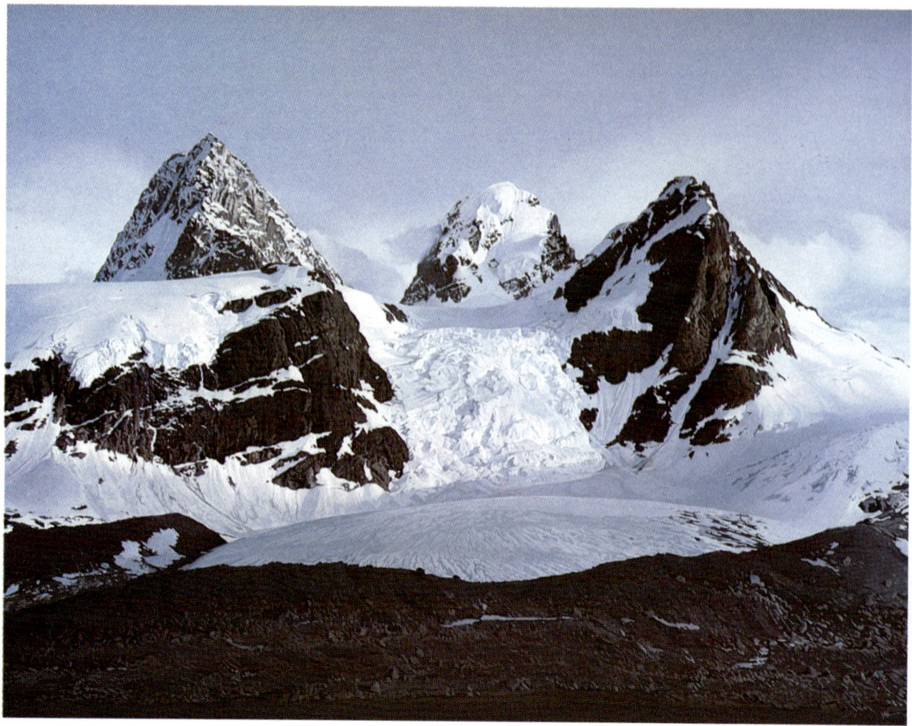

21-2 *Mt. Jacobsen #2*, **James Spencer**
Acrylic paint is a popular medium for large paintings. Here James Spencer has achieved photographic detail in his large acrylic painting of Mt. Jacobsen.

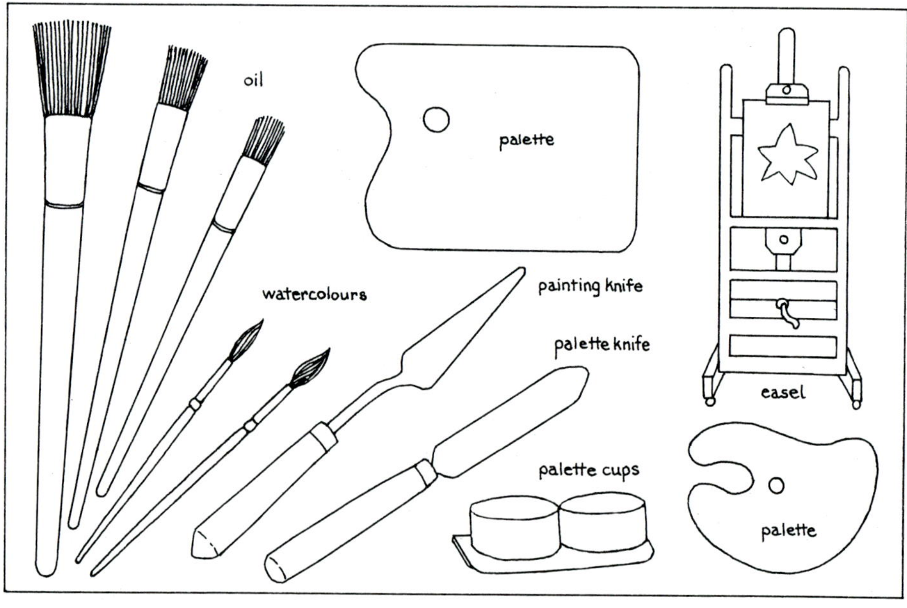

Some specialized equipment is used in painting, such as flexibile steel blades with handles, or palette knives. Easels, brushes and palettes are also part of the painter's equipment.

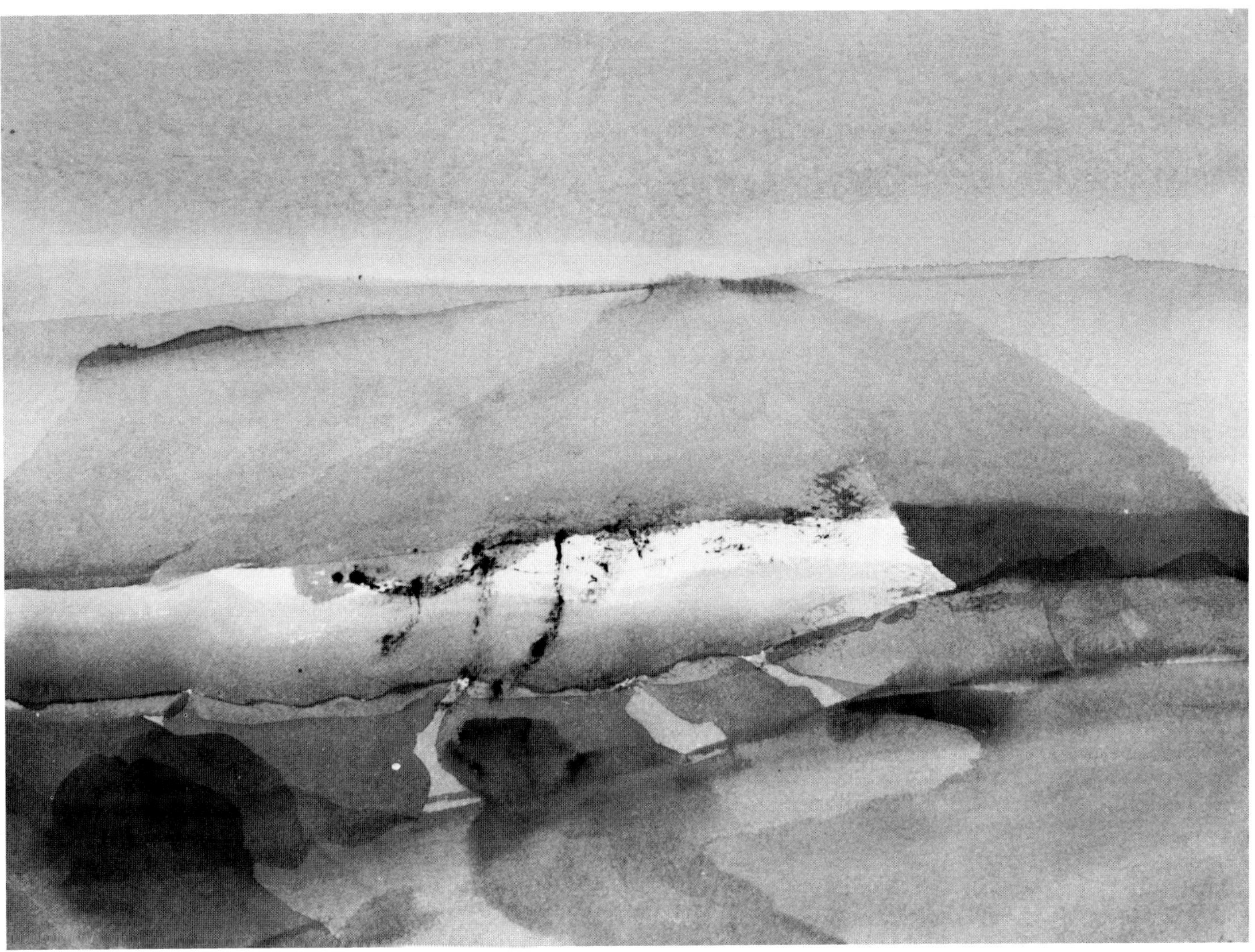

21-3 ***Badlands, Red Deer Valley, Alberta*, Toni Onley**
The transparent quality of watercolours creates a feeling of delicacy.

Look Again

- Why do you think it is important that an artist understands colour relationships before beginning a painting?

- What kinds of decisions do you think an artist needs to make about the choice of painting materials?

- It would be possible to photograph a scene similar to the one in *Girls*? In what ways would such a photograph differ from the painting? Think about colour, detail and shape.
- What special mood does the painting have that a similar photograph might not have?

- *Mt. Jacobsen #2* (21-2) is almost as large as some walls. What special impact would this have on the viewer?
- What other subjects could be presented effectively on such a large scale?
- If you were going to paint a detailed scene, what would you choose as the subject?

- Toni Onley's use of shape is very important in *Badlands* (21-3). Identify the shapes.
- What effects would be lost if the artist had used cut-out paper instead of watercolour paint to make a similar picture?

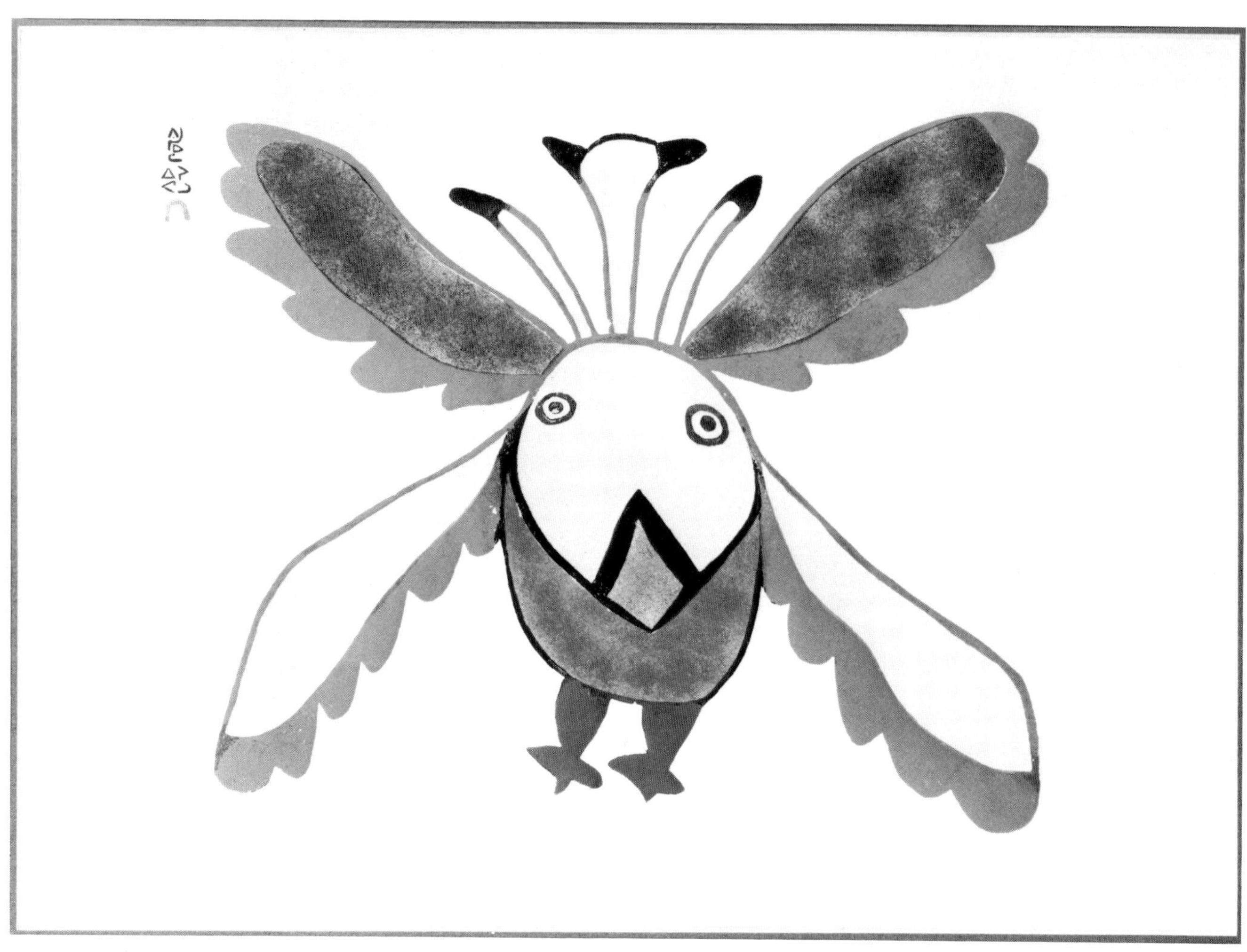

22-1 ***Gay Bird*, Pitseolak**
Printmaking techniques such as lithography were introduced to the Inuit in 1959. Since that time their prints have become widely known. Each fall a new edition of Cape Dorset prints is awaited with much excitement and enthusiasm by collectors and art galleries throughout Canada. The themes include animals and legends, as in the print called *Gay Bird*.

22. Printmaking

Printmaking involves repeating a design from a specially prepared surface. Although there are many ways to make a print, here are a few basic processes.

One is *relief printmaking*. The printing block is made from a soft material such as linoleum, soft wood, cardboard or styrofoam. Part of the surface is carved away, leaving behind the shape that is to be printed. Ink is applied to this raised surface and pressed on to a paper or cloth background. The area carved away will not print, leaving a plain background. More than one block may be used to apply different areas of colour on each print. Relief prints have characteristically sharp edges, although some blocks have a natural texture (such as blocks made of soft pine). By creating dramatic contrasts in dark and light, the printmaker can express strong emotional feelings.

Stenciling is another way to create a print. There are several methods of stenciling. One of the simplest is to use a paper stencil and a hard, bristle brush called a stipple brush. The stencil is made by cutting a design or picture out of paper. The cutout stencil is then placed over another piece of paper. Paint is applied around the edges of the stencil in short brush strokes with the stipple brush. More than one stencil and colour can be used in a print. This method allows for experimentation with simple, bold shapes.

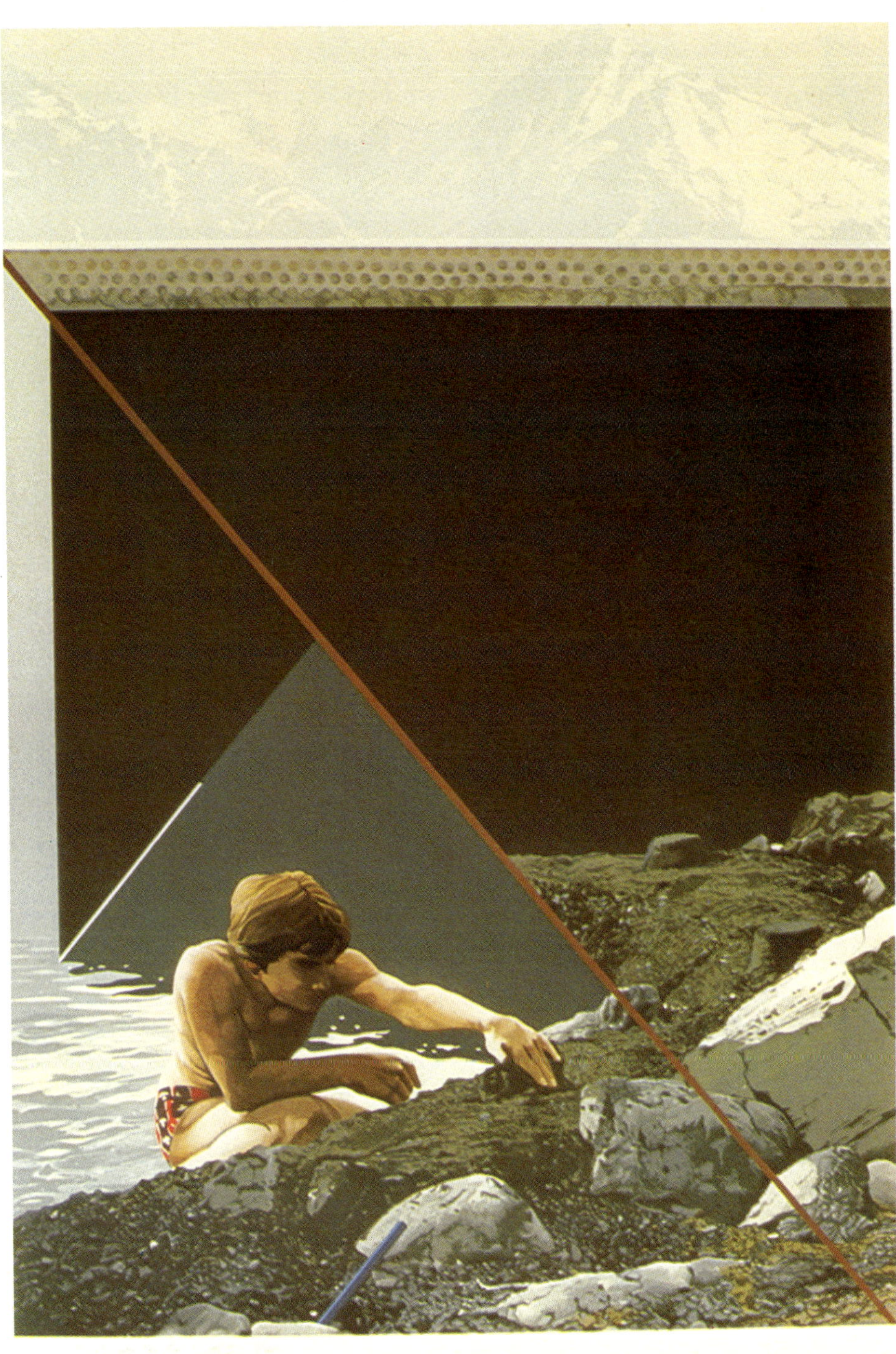

22-2 *Architecte (1982)*, **Lauréat Marois**
A series of prints is called an edition. Each print is usually numbered as it is "pulled" or taken. The numbering system used contains two numbers. One indicates the total number of prints; the other indicates the order of a particular print in the sequence. Often you will see the number and the artist's signature in the lower right-hand corner of each print. This screen print by Québec artist Lauréat Marois was produced in an edition of 40.

Serigraph or *silkscreen* printing is a form of stenciling. The basic idea is to stretch a silk screen over a frame, and then block out parts of it so that ink or paint will go through only the unblocked areas. The screen may be blocked with special film that is glued on, or with glue or shellac that is painted on to the silk. Then, paint or ink is drawn across the screen with a squeegee (a wooden scraper with a rubber edge) and the design is transferred to the printing surface, often paper. Different areas can then be blocked if more designs or colours are to be added.

Another process is *lithography*, which means making a print from a flat surface, such as a piece of limestone. There are several methods for making the design or picture. One method is to use a lithographic crayon or tusche to draw a picture on to the stone. Then water is used to wet the stone. Because grease and water do not mix, only the uncrayoned areas take in moisture. Next ink is applied. The ink sticks to the greasy areas where the crayon marks are and not the damp areas. The inked stone then can be used to stamp a print on to paper by means of a press.

Intaglio, like lithography, requires a printing press. This process involves lines that are recessed or incised into a plate of copper or zinc. A special steel tool called a burin is used to cut the lines. The printing ink is spread into the incised lines as the plate and paper are rolled through the press. The paper is pressed onto the inked lines. Etching and aquatint are similar processes, but different methods are used to cut the lines. Intaglio is used by professional printmakers because prints with fine detail and clarity are possible with this method.

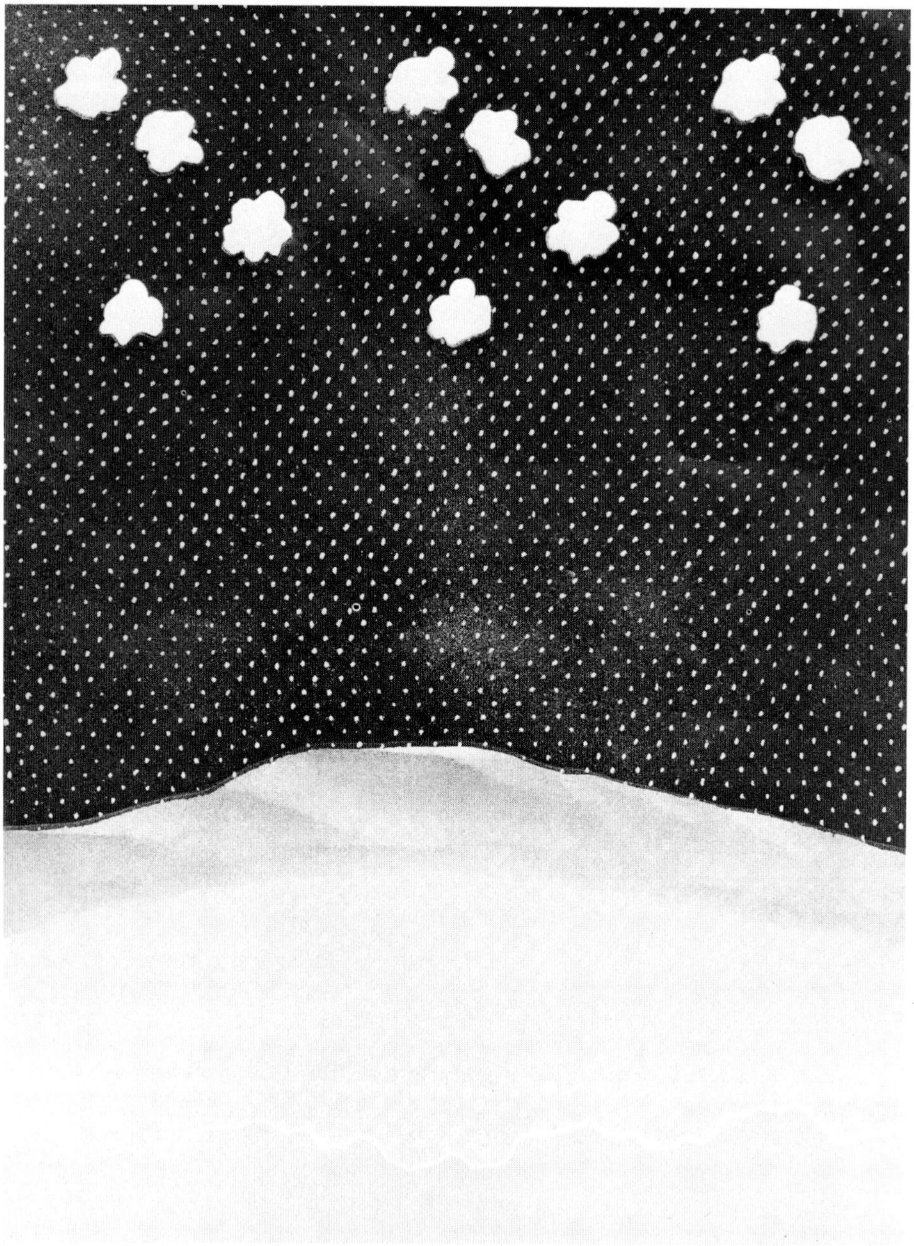

22-3 ***Summer Rain*****, John K. Esler**
Born in Manitoba, John K. Esler teaches at the University of Calgary in the Department of Art. He is interested in landscape as subject matter for his prints, but his style is often abstract. *Summer Rain* is an etching.

Look Again

- Compare *Gay Bird* (22-1) with the watercolour called *Badlands* (21-3). Try to imagine what *Gay Bird* would look like in the style of *Badlands*. What would happen to the edges of things?
- What would happen to the mood of *Gay Bird*?

- What textures do you see in *Architecte (1982)* (22-2)?

- Can a screen print have an actual texture – one that you could feel if you touched the surface? Why or why not?
- What techniques would the printmaker use to create textures in a print?

- How does John Esler use the principle of variation and repetition?

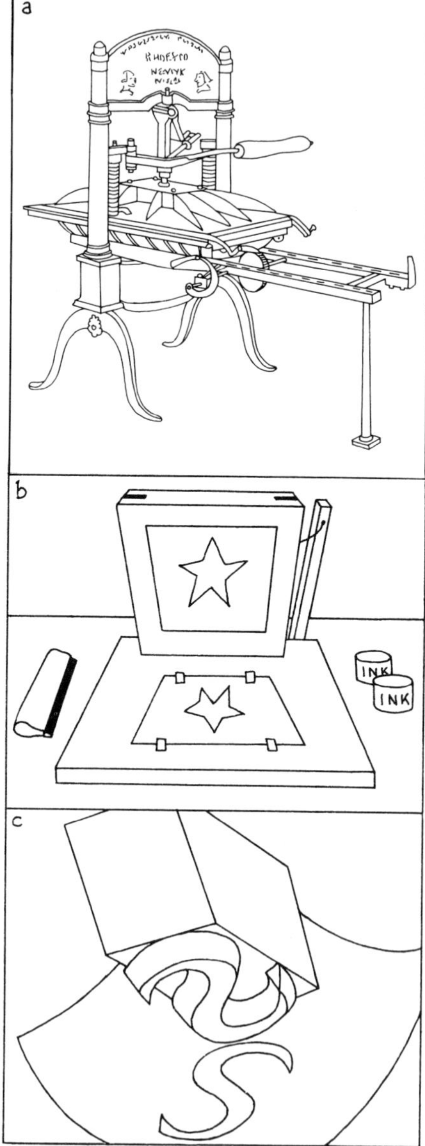

Here are some of the methods for making a print. Fig. a is a printing press used with a flat surface that is rolled through the press. Fig. b is a silkscreen. Fig. c is a stamp print.

23. Sculpture

Sculpture involves using three-dimensional space. Sculpture that can be seen from all sides is called *sculpture-in-the-round*. Statues are this type of sculpture. A sculpture that is raised or juts out from a flat background is called *relief sculpture*.

There are several basic methods used in sculpture. One is the subtractive or carved method. Another is the additive or construction method. A third method involves casting. These methods can be used with a variety of materials. Some materials may be flexible and soft, while others are firm and hard.

The choice of method often depends on the choice of material. For example, the carving or *subtractive method* can easily be done from a block of plaster of Paris formed in a cardboard box. A drawing is made of the image and then outlined on the plaster. Areas are carved away with a variety of tools such as chisels and rasps. With this technique, the artist does not have the opportunity to change ideas once the material has been carved away. Planning is important! Stone and wood are frequently used to make carved sculpture.

If the sculptural image is built up by adding material, then it is the *additive method* that is being used. Typical materials include clay, wax and plasticine. These flexible materials allow the sculptor to make changes from the original sketch as work develops. Additive sculpture is often used to complete a small model before work begins on a larger sculpture in another method. For example, before carving a life size figure, a sculptor may create a miniature figure first. In this way, artistic as well as technical problems can be solved before tackling the actual block of stone.

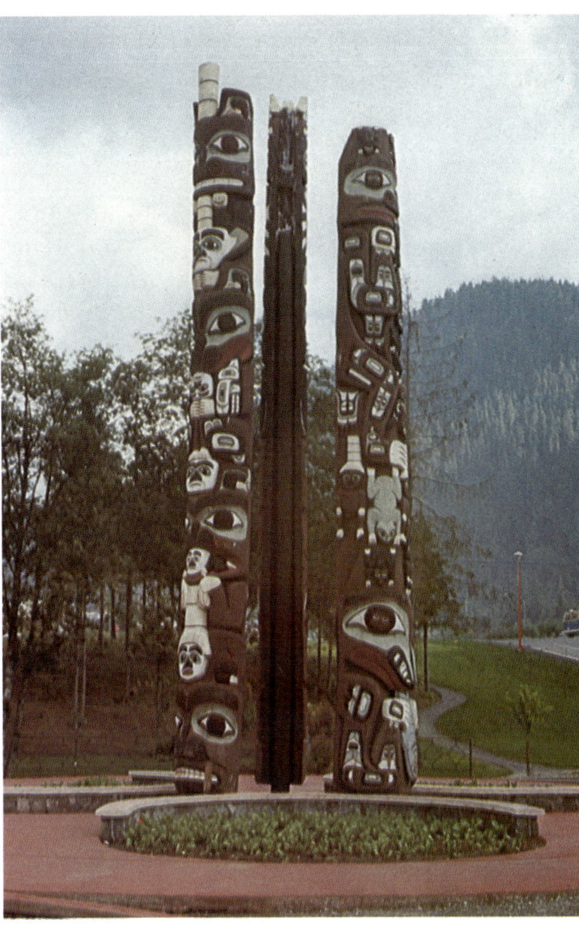

23-1 Totems, Prince Rupert, B.C.
Traditional materials such as wood have been carved by the Indians of the West Coast to depict their legends.

A variation of the additive method involves construction. When materials are joined rather than modelled or carved, the sculpture is called a construction. Gluing cardboard or wood pieces together would be one example of the *construction method*. Another would be the welding together of pieces of metal to create a three-dimensional sculpture.

Metal can also be used for the *casting method*. A sculptural image is first created in a flexible material such as clay or wax. It is then covered with plaster of Paris. After the plaster is dry, it is carefully removed from the clay or wax so that it can be allowed to cool and used as a mold. Liquid metal is poured into the mold, and sets in the shape of the original clay or wax. After this stage, the surface can be polished as a finishing touch. Variations of this technique allow sculptors to make the images hollow. The bronze sculptures seen in special places to commemorate Canadian historical figures, for example, are often made by the hollow casting method.

Many different materials are used for sculpture. Some materials, such as wood and marble, have been used for centuries. The surfaces of these kinds of sculpture may be left their natural colour and texture, or may be smoothed and polished. Wood may be painted. Sculptural materials such as plexiglass or fabric can involve a wide range of colours. Unusual materials for sculpture are often selected from the everyday world. For example, junk, plastics, neon lights, and found objects have been used to express ideas about people, places and things.

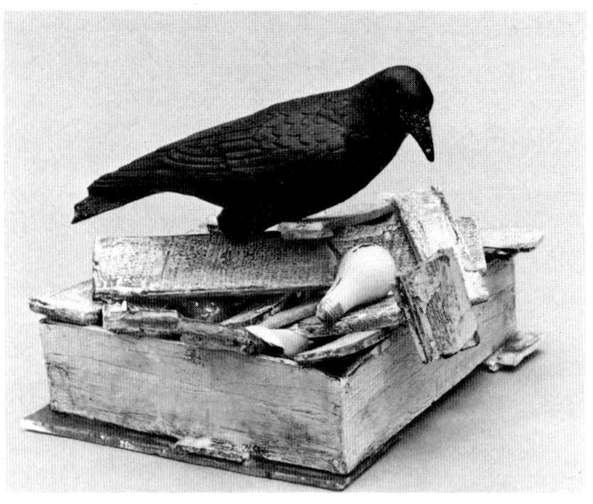

23-2 ***Bird and Green Cup*****, Annemarie Schmid Esler**
The additive method has been used by Annemarie Schmid Esler in her sculpture of earthenware clay titled *Bird and Green Cup*. Note how the artist has made the clay look like other materials, such as wood and glass.

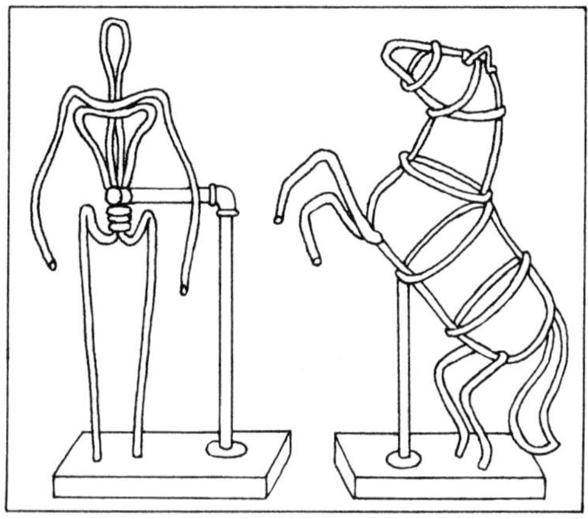

When soft modelling materials like clay or wax are used in a sculpture, a support frame, or armature, is needed. The armature must be made from material that is stiff and strong, such as wood, wire or metal rods.

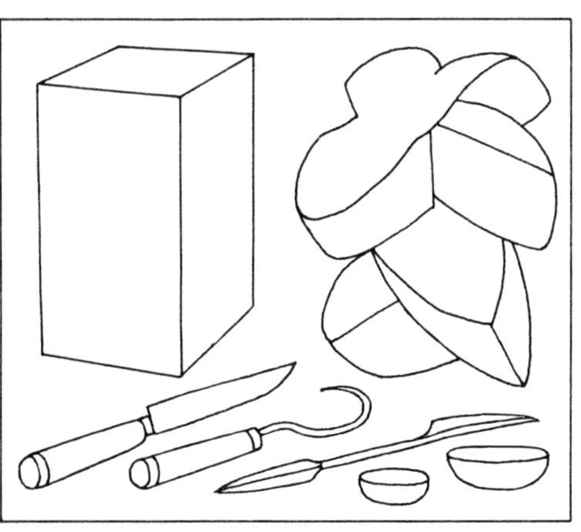

Materials such as stone, wood or plaster are often carved into three-dimensional pieces of sculpture. This is the subtractive method.

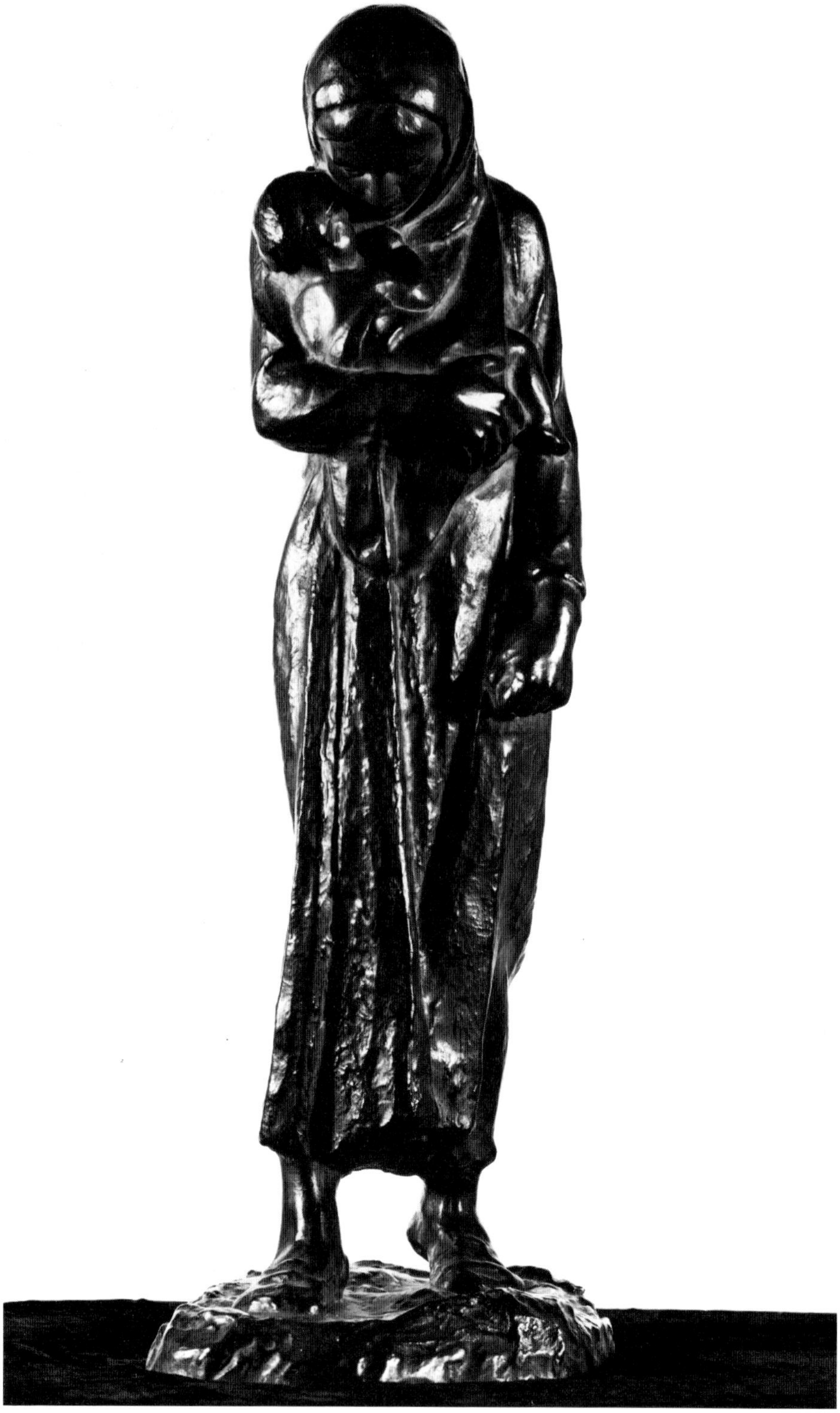

23-3 ***The Derelicts*****, Frances Loring**
Frances Loring added strong emotional feeling to the bronze sculpture called *The Derelicts*. She was one of the founding members of the Canadian Society of Sculptors.

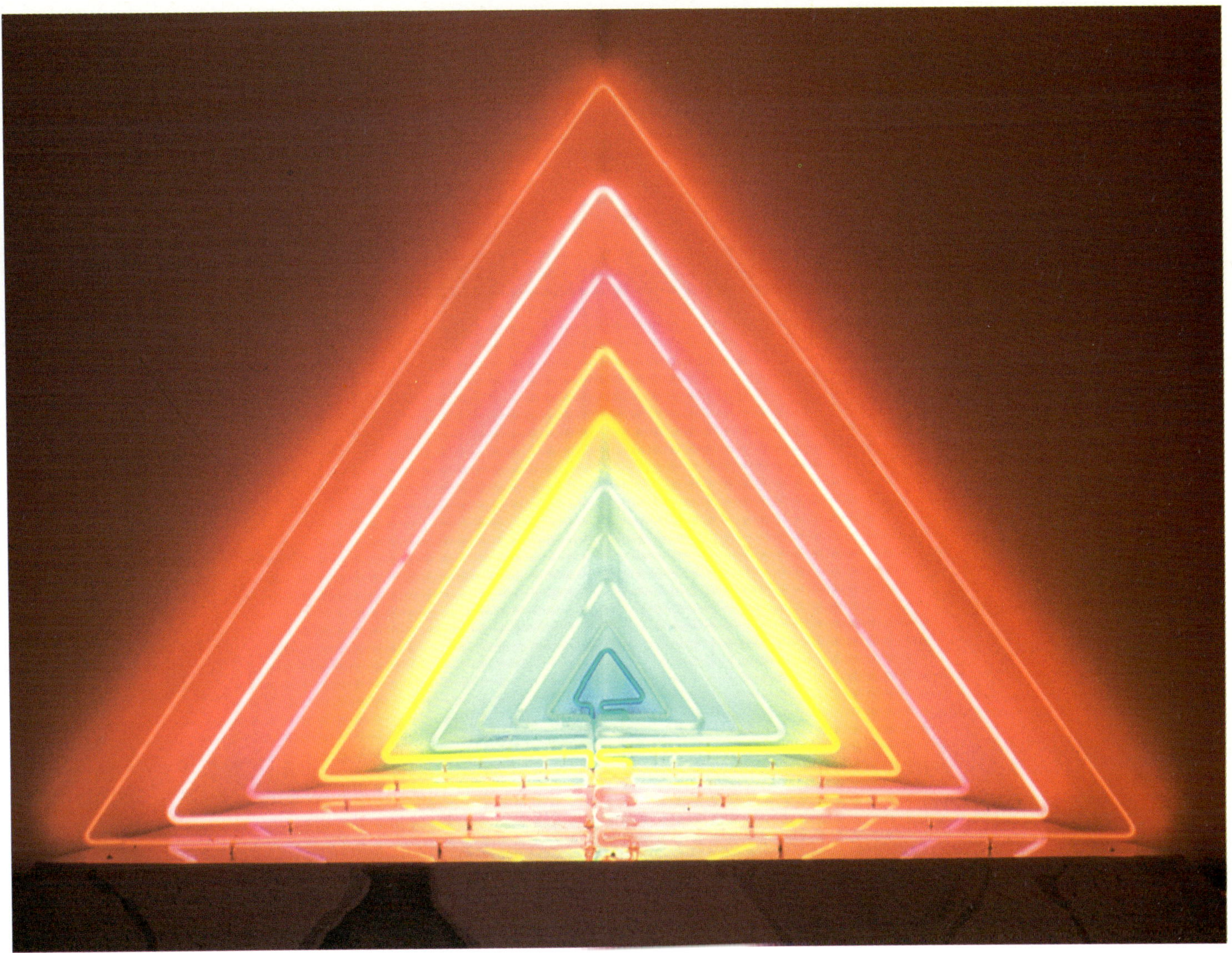

23-4 *Dive*, **Michael Hayden**
Line and colour are part of Michael Hayden's neon light sculpture titled *Dive*.

Look Again

- The totem poles in 23-1 are three-dimensional. Imagine the same faces on a flat picture. Could you use the picture in the same way? In the same place?
- Would the picture have the same impact as the sculpture? Why or why not?

- Imagine you are going to make a sculpture just like *Bird and Green Cup* (23-2). However, instead of modelling clay, you are going to find all the items and construct it. First, make a list of all the things you will need. Describe how you will assemble them.
- Your sculpture looks just like the artist's! But, which one would you prefer to display in your home? Why?

- What makes Frances Loring's *Derelicts* (23-3) look so derelict (outcast, poor, sad)?
- Could she have achieved the same visual effect if she had used wood? Gold? Maple sugar?
- Would you feel the same way about this sculpture if she had used these other materials?

- Name the three things you like most about *Dive* (23-4).
- Where would you display a sculpture like this one? Where would you not display it?

- Look at all the craft objects shown in Chapter 27. Which of them might be called sculptures? Give reasons for your answers.

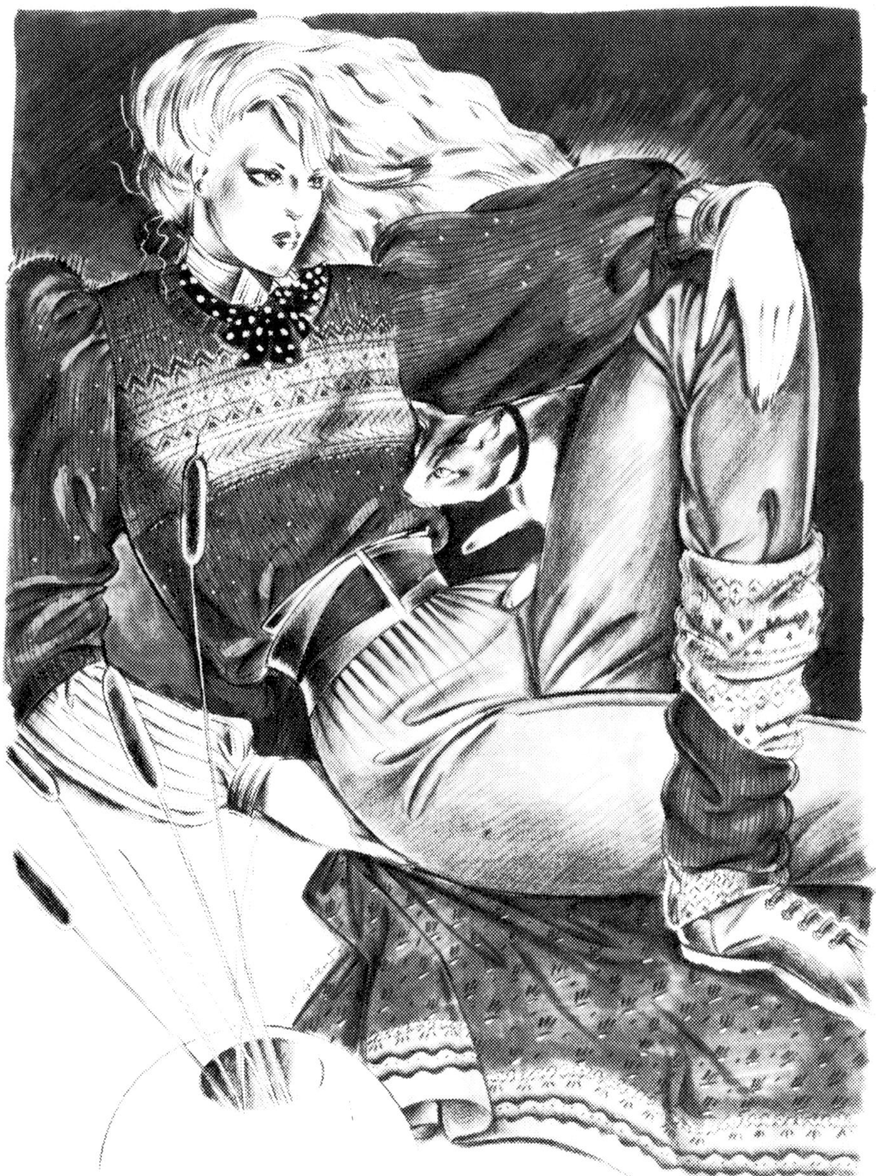

24-1 Fashion illustration, Sheila McGraw
Illustration plays an important role in communication.

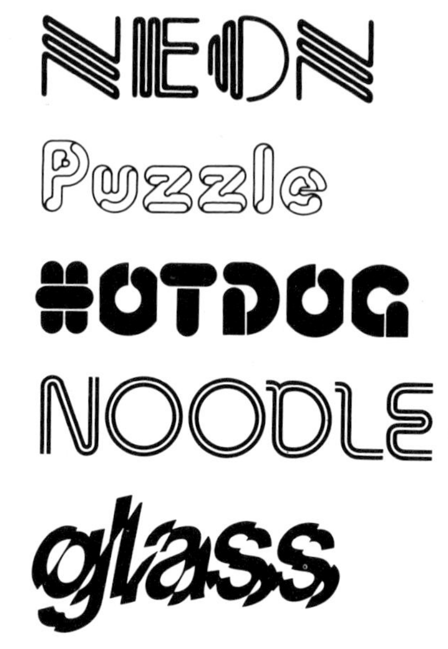

The style of lettering often helps to get the message across.

24. Graphic Art

Graphic art aims to communicate information. It uses visual symbols, such as lettering and illustrations, to do so. Graphic art may be used to sell a product or to promote a service or an idea. There are many forms of graphic art. One form is the advertisements that appear in newspapers, in magazines, on posters, or on outdoor signs and billboards. Window, store and counter displays, and the labels and packages of products are other examples of graphic art. The design and illustration of books involves graphic art.

Graphic art is prepared by graphic artists and designers. They decide how the art will look and then arrange the materials, usually on cardboard or paper. This arrangement of the artwork is called the *layout*. Once the elements have been laid out, they can be reproduced, or printed, into labels, advertisements, books and other products.

Preparing the layout involves a knowledge of a number of basic processes. For example, in advertising the graphic artist must have a knowledge of *typography* or *lettering*. Depending on the desired results, lettering can be done by hand, with a brush or a pen. Lettering done by pen may be stately and formal because of the rigid pen point used, while lettering done by brush may be broad and flowing. Lettering also may be mechanically transferred from commercially prepared

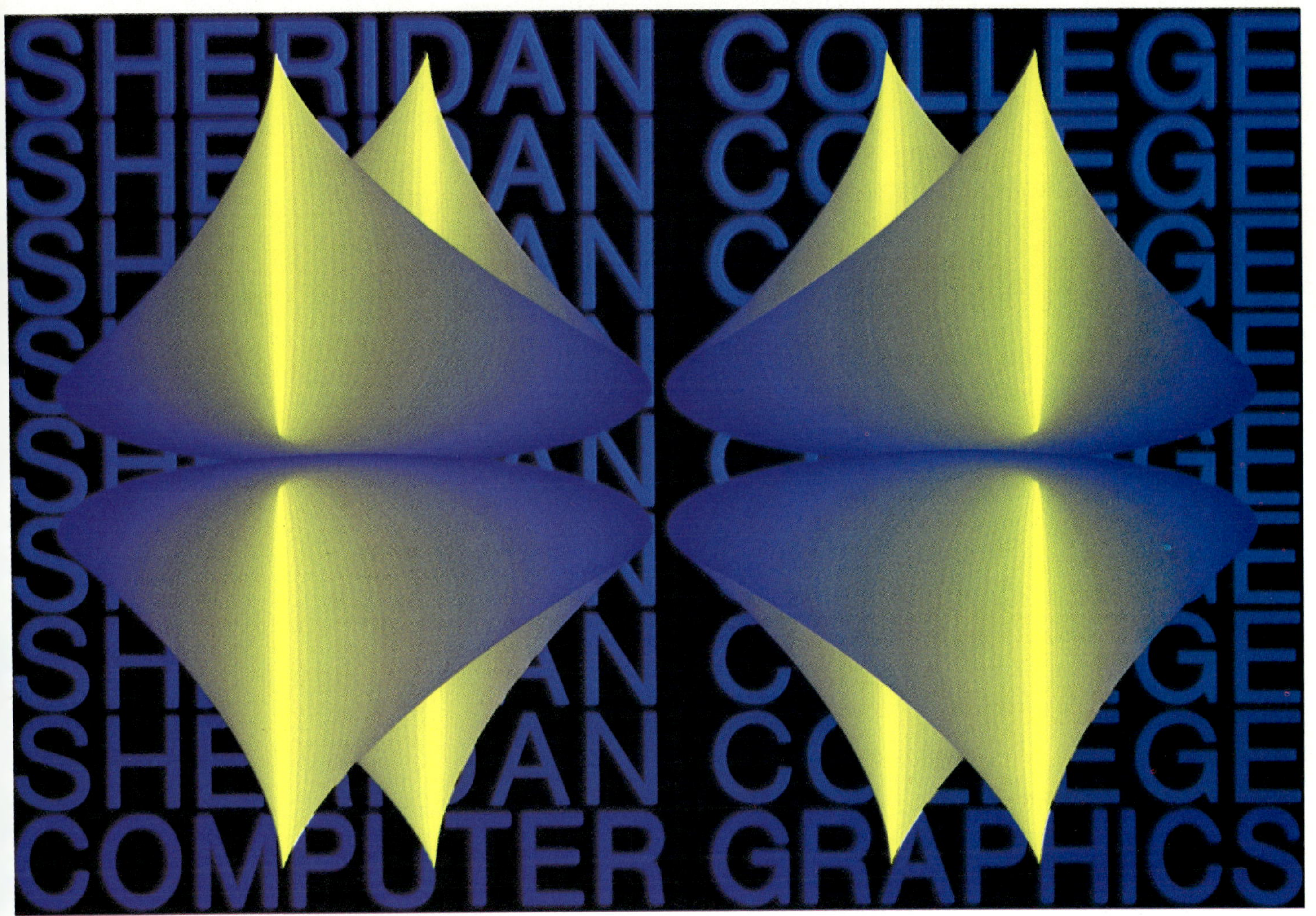

24-2 *Sheridan College*, **Paul Griffin**
Computer graphic art, like other forms of design, is based on the use of the elements organized according to the principles. Here the artist uses shape to create symmetrical balance. Describe how he does this.

plastic sheets of letters. Often lettering, or print, is prepared by a typesetter.

Another basic process is *illustration*. Illustrations may be technical drawings, pictures for children's stories, cartoons, photographs, landscape scenes or portraits. The artist must choose the illustration that will best help to communicate the information.

Once the type of lettering and illustration has been chosen, the artist must use the basic design principles of balance, dominance, space or colour to attract attention and to communicate the information. The function of the art is important. In a poster, for example, a strong design and few words may be right. Illustrations must be carefully chosen to make a book more interesting, or to make an advertisement eye-catching.

Nowadays, the computer is often a useful tool for the graphic designer. The artist may type information into the computer, or draw it in by using a graphics tablet. The artist can see the picture on the screen, and may change it many times until it is just right. Then the computer can print the picture. Computers can also be programmed to design their own pictures. Art or designs produced with the aid of a computer are called *computer graphics*.

You can see that graphic design is a wide and varied field. Every day, you see around you more examples of graphic art than of any other art form.

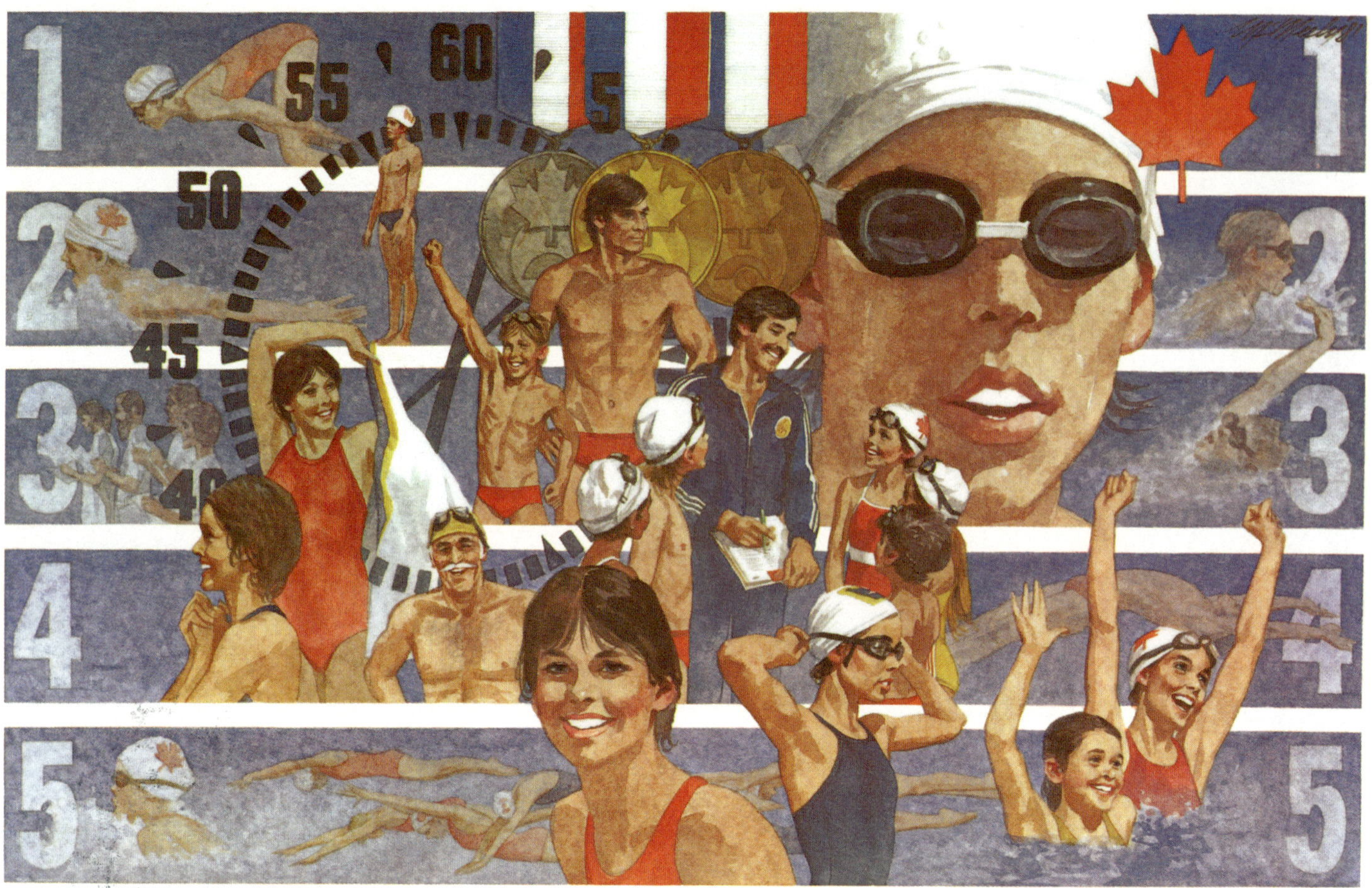

24-3 *Canadian Amateur Swimming Association*, **Tom McNeely**
Tom McNeely created this exciting illustration about swimming for the Canadian Amateur Swimming Association.

Look Again

- Fashion designers use different types of illustrations at different stages of the design process. First, the designer may quickly sketch the basic idea. Then, a more detailed sketch must be made so the pattern cutter can turn that idea into a wearable garment. Finally, an advertising illustration may be drawn to show buyers what the garment will look like when worn.
- Which type of illustration is 24-1?
- Try to draw the other two types of illustration for the trousers.

- What message is Paul Griffin trying to convey in the computer graphic? State the message in three sentences.
- What does he do to convey the message visually?

- Look at the poster 4-1. How does the illustration help repeat the message of the words – Dragon Fyre?

- When the manuscript of this book was given to a designer it consisted of the following: over 100 typed pages, some quick sketches prepared by the authors, and box full of envelopes containing slides of the Canadian art you see.
- What has happened to the typed pages? Who might have done this work?
- What has happened to the sketches? Who might have done this work?
- What has happened to the slides? Who might have done this work? Note: Look at the acknowledgements on page 5. All the people involved are listed there.

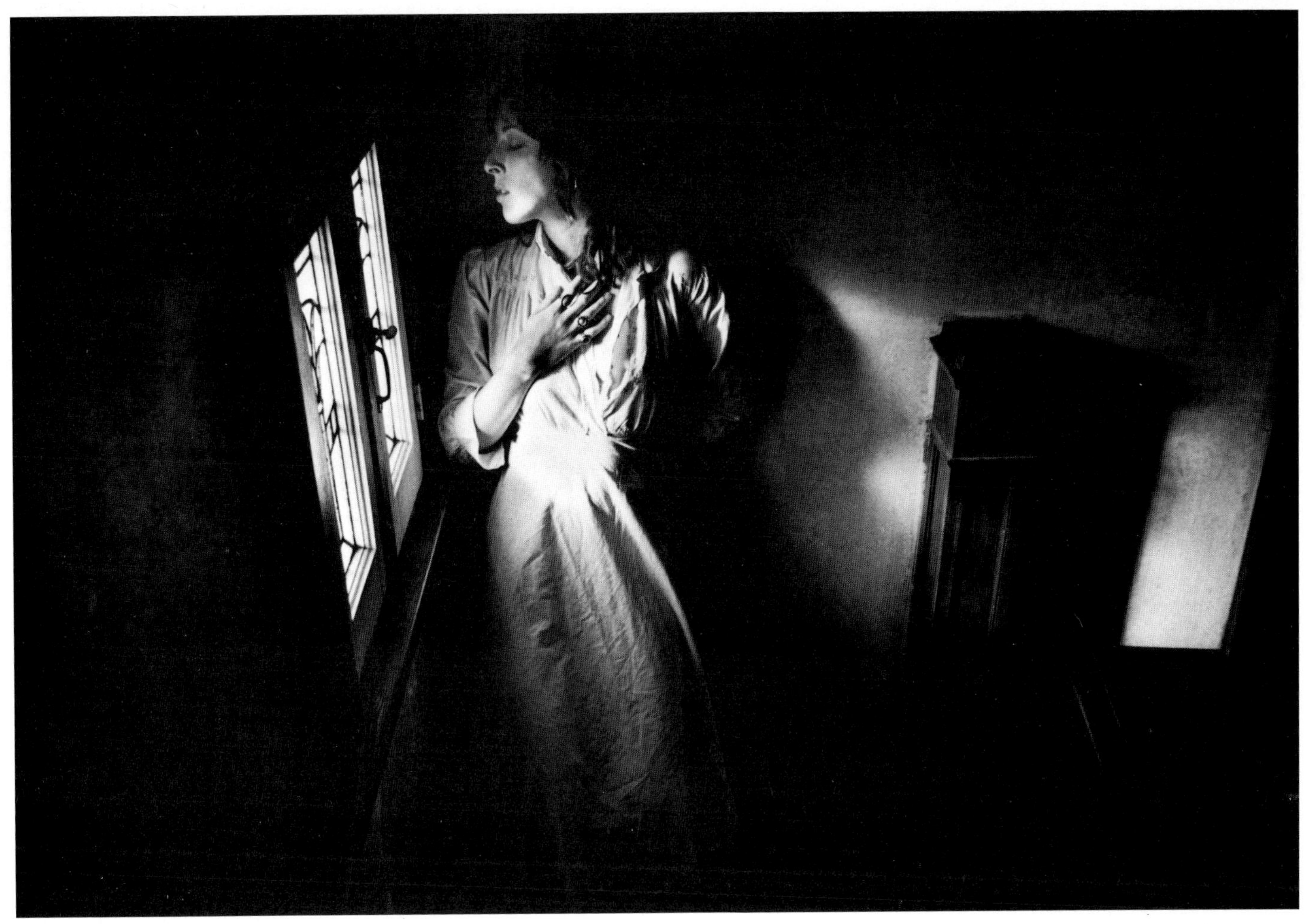

25-1 *Woman in a Stairwell*, **Barbara Astman**
Here the photographer has made use of a single natural light source to create dramatic light effects. The photographer, Barbara Astman, has taken a photograph of herself by using a method called a time exposure.

25. Photography

Photography is the process of producing images on film. It is a medium that relies greatly on a machine: the camera. You must understand how the camera works before you can take good pictures.

First of all, there are several types of cameras available. One popular type is the 35mm single-lens reflex camera. Different lenses can be attached. The choice of lens depends upon the subject to be photographed. Three basic types are normal, wide-angle and telephoto. A normal lens produces the same narrow image you would see if you held a paper tube to your eye. The wide-angle lens increases the width of the image you see. A telephoto lens brings distant objects closer to you. The photographer can adjust the focus of the camera, to give objects a clear, sharp outline. It is also possible to adjust the amount of light that passes onto the film, so that the picture will not be too pale or too dark.

There is also a choice of film. Some require less light than others to take a picture. Some films produce black and white pictures, other films produce colour pictures. The image recorded on the film is actually the opposite, or negative, of what is seen through the viewfinder of the camera. On the negative, light areas will be dark, and dark areas will be light. Then the film is processed by using chemicals to turn the image back into its natural, or positive, image. The final picture is called a photographic print.

The photographer as an artist selects and arranges images to make interesting pictures on film. To do this, the photographer must understand the elements and principles of design. Sometimes the photographer will compose a picture as carefully as any painter. These types of pictures include advertising displays and posed portraits. Elements and principles such as balance, colour and unity are used carefully. Some photography is concerned with a particular choice of subject. Perhaps the subject is scenes of everyday life. The photographer cannot adjust the real world to achieve a balanced picture. Instead, the photographer must move around to choose the best angle from which to shoot.

Other photography makes use of special techniques. One of them is the close-up. This means the subject appears larger than you would normally see it. For example, the texture of a stone, or a bee inside a flower, or the picture on a stamp may be the entire photo. Another special technique is stop action: the photo may be blurred to show fast movement. Two photographs may be taken on the same piece of film, to show people and objects in unlikely combinations. This type of photograph is called a double exposure.

The photographer artist always has a message to communicate to the viewer, just as the painter or the graphic artist has. For each artist, the ability to make the message clear depends on an artistic sense and on the proper and controlled use of the equipment or materials.

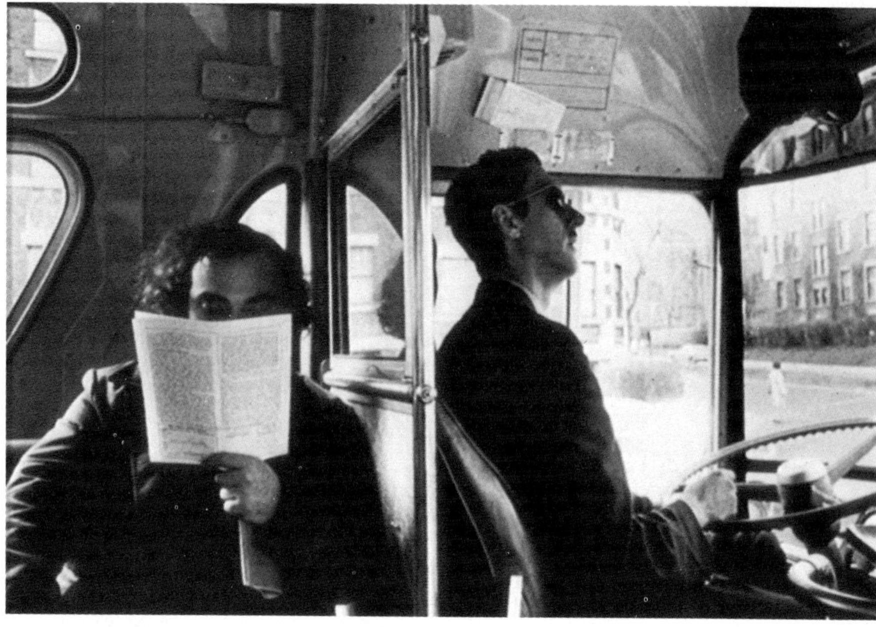

25-2 ***Bus, Sherbrooke St. W., Montreal,*** **Sam Tata**
The photographer helps us study the world around us.

The way an image is magnified depends on the lens used. Here are a close-up (Fig. a), a normal (Fig. b) and a wide angle (Fig. c) view.

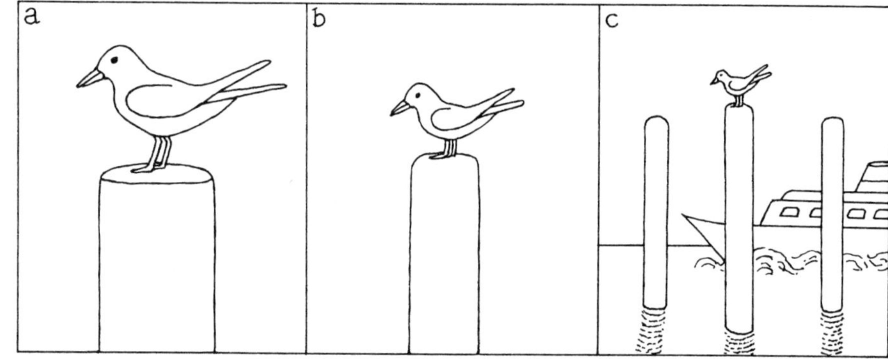

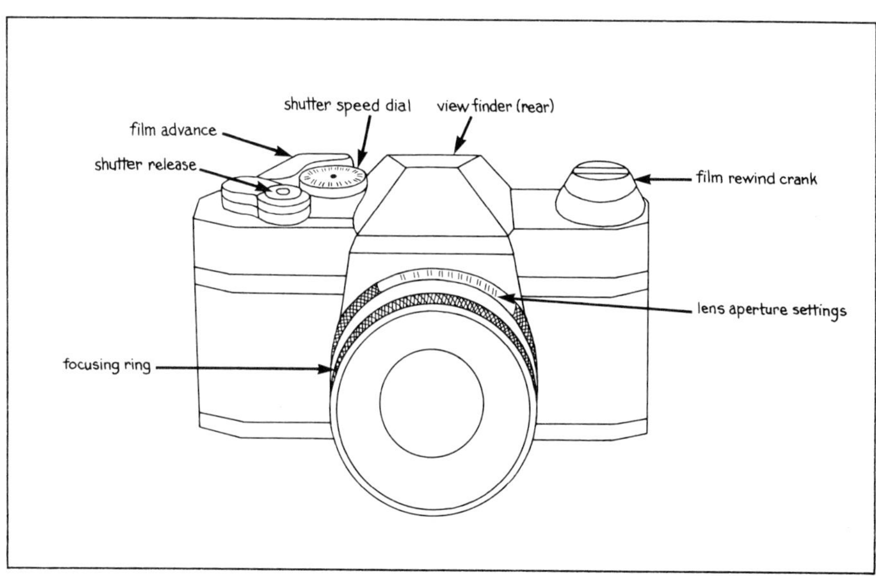

A 35 mm single-lens reflex camera is by far the most widely used type of camera for nature photography and in photography for newspapers, called photo journalism.

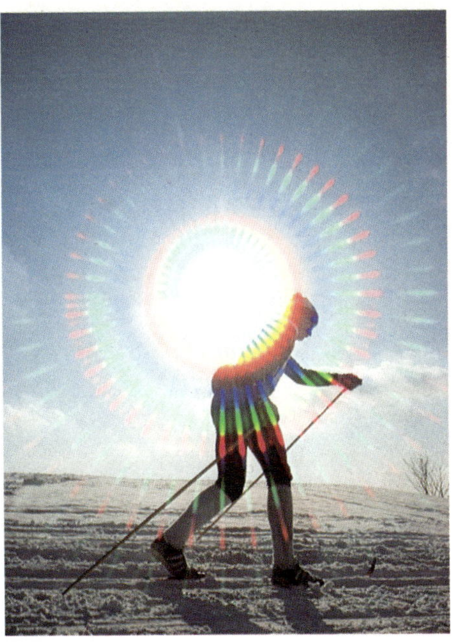

25-3 Skier, Ottawa region
Light is used by the photographer to create special visual effects.

Look Again

- Which elements of design seem to be most important in black and white photography (25-1)?
- Which elements are not important?

- Where did Sam Tata have to sit to take the photo in 25-2?
- What different view would he have obtained if he had taken it from the back seat?
- Compare the impact of the two different views.

- Imagine yourself to be out skiing. Suddenly a rainbow-coloured halo of light appears round you! Does the ski trip seem more pleasant? Warmer? Why or why not?

- Would photograph 25-3 be as good an advertisement for skiing if the special rainbow effect were missing?

- Look at Chapter 6. It shows a number of photos of the real world. For any one of those photos, complete this sentence: The photographer chose to take the picture from this angle because . . . . .

- Describe the ways in which Ellie Forrest's reworked photograph does not reflect the real world.
- For what reason do you think the photographer has created these special effects?

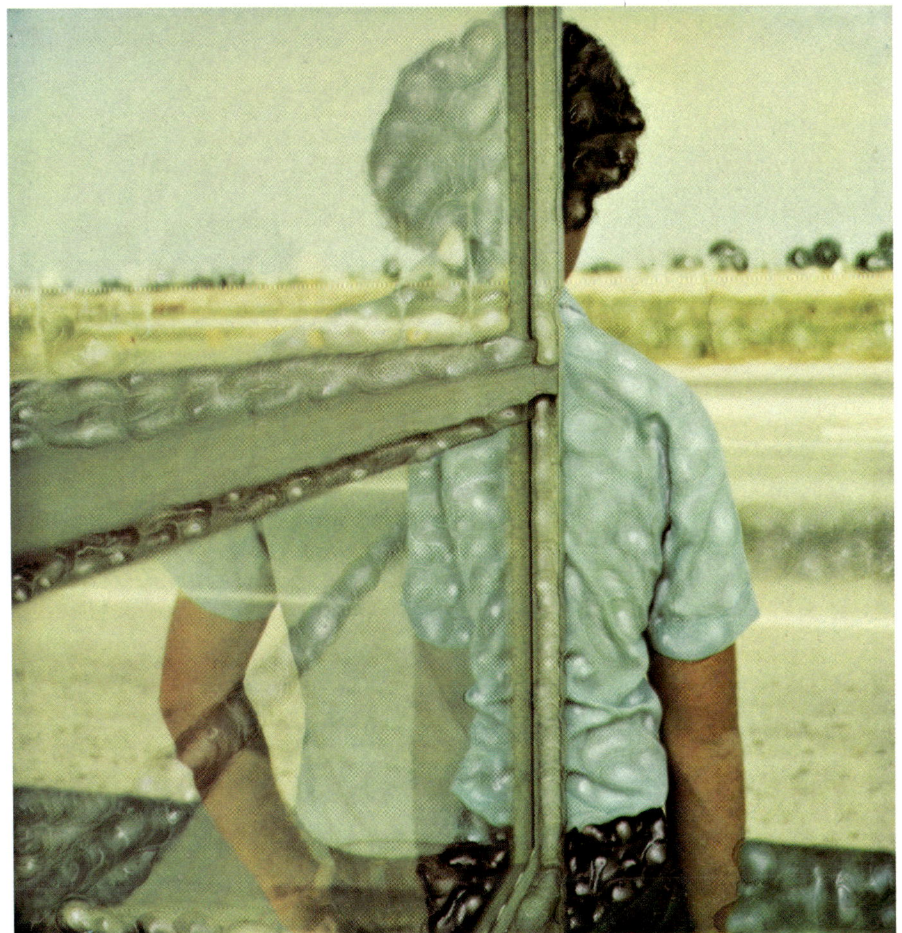

25-4 ***Boy Waiting for Bus*, Ellie Forrest**
Sometimes the photographer reworks the photograph to give very special effects.

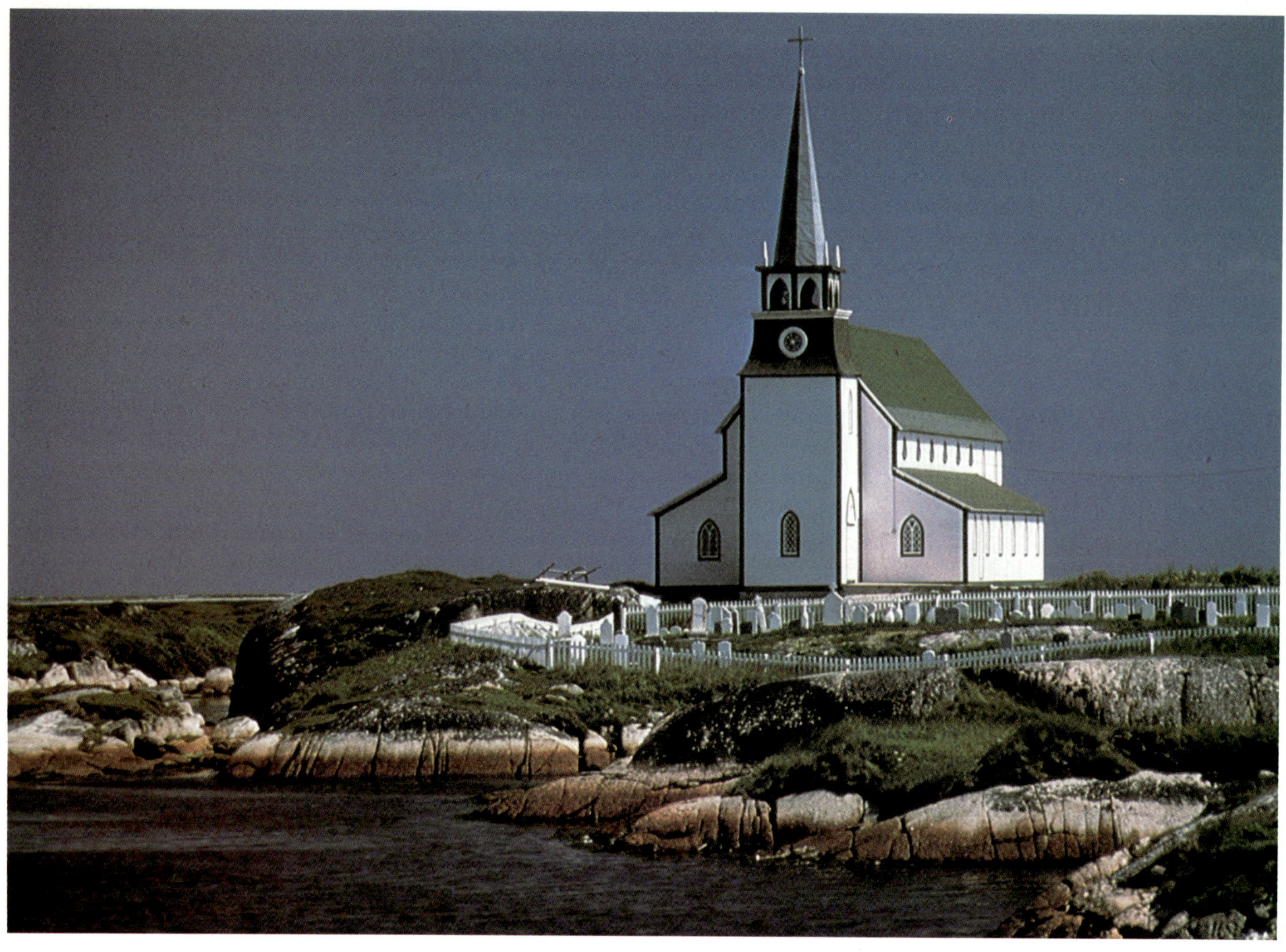

26-1 Church; Newton, Newfoundland
Religious buildings are the most noticeable buildings in many communities across Canada. Note the clean, upright lines of this church in its coastal setting of Newton, Newfoundland.

26. Architecture

Architecture combines art and engineering to plan buildings. Canadians have always needed protection from the climate. An *architect* draws plans for any type of building, such as a home, a church, a store or an office. These plans include the outside appearance and the division of the space inside. The drawings are very precise and give details such as the location of rooms, doors, windows and stairs. In addition, drawings that have linear perspective are sometimes prepared (perhaps with the aid of a computer) to see how a building will look. A scale model of the building is often made to show it as a three-dimensional structure. The architect must also plan for things such as parking and heating.

In early Canada the builders were their own architects. They adapted styles and ideas from Europe, using the materials that were available locally. For example, many early builders in Canada, particularly in Québec, designed and constructed buildings based on the French traditions of the seventeenth century. Materials for these buildings were the limestone and wood found in the area. These buildings were elegant, simple rectangles, often with symmetrical windows.

Homes based on English designs were constructed of local materials too: wood in the Maritimes, and stone in other parts of Canada. A popular English style was called Georgian. It had symmetrical proportions, with windows evenly placed and a central door. This style used overhanging eaves and decorative columns called

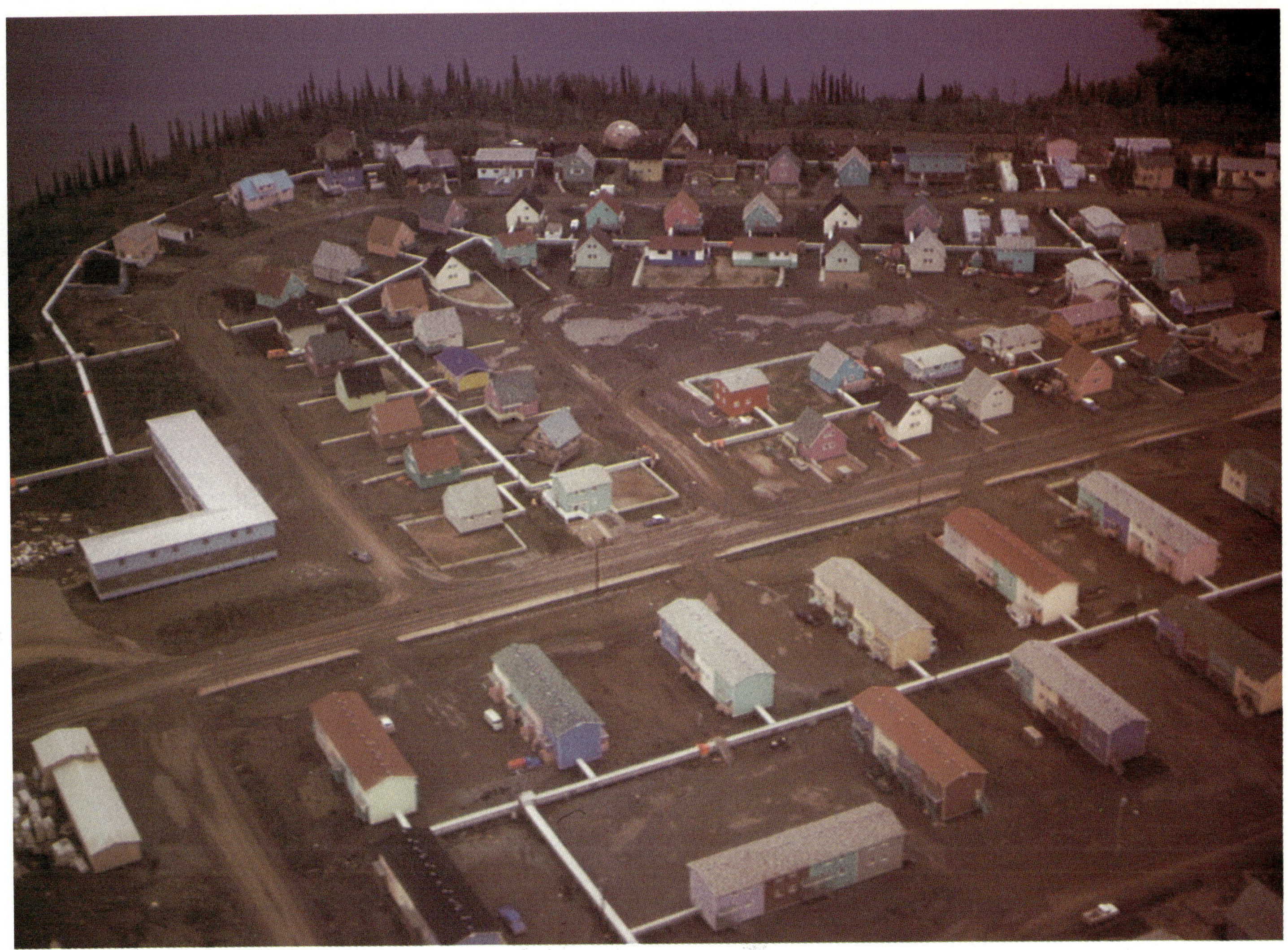

26-2 Residential area (aerial view), Inuvik, N.W.T.
The environment plays an important role in architectural design. Here, in Inuvik above the Arctic Circle, a corridor contains utility pipes. This is referred to as a "utilidor." Permafrost in Inuvik makes it impossible to bury water lines, as is usual further south.

pilasters. Classic temple architecture based on ideas from the Greeks and Romans was used for important buildings such as churches. This style symbolized beauty for many people in the eighteenth century.

Professional architects began to influence Canadian architecture in the mid-nineteenth century. European style was still important. At this time there was a Gothic revival for public buildings. Ideas from the Middle Ages were copied. This style can be seen in the plans for the Houses of Parliament as well as in university buildings and churches. Sharp upward lines gave an air of importance to these structures. Towers, spires, turrets and arches were other common features. These public buildings were made from stone and brick.

After 1930, designs became simpler and more practical. Local materials were used less. Manufactured materials, glass, steel and concrete, were used more and more. The use of elevators allowed architects to design high-rise buildings.

Each area of Canada has its own distinctive architecture. Special thought, for example, has been given to building design because of the climate in various parts of the country. Buildings in Vancouver use glass and wood in a way that is right for the mild climate. In other areas of Canada where the winter is more severe, underground complexes have been designed. In downtown Montreal, people can walk comfortably from building to building along underground corridors regardless of the weather. Here, the function of the building is more important than the architectural appearance. A similar design idea, but built above ground, is the enclosed shopping mall. In these buildings, both the function and the visual appearance are important.

When looking at architecture, think about the three-dimensional design of the building, its basic exterior shape, and the colour, texture and nature of the materials used. A well-designed building should display balance and unity. It should be attractive and interesting to look at. It should also be pleasant to be in!

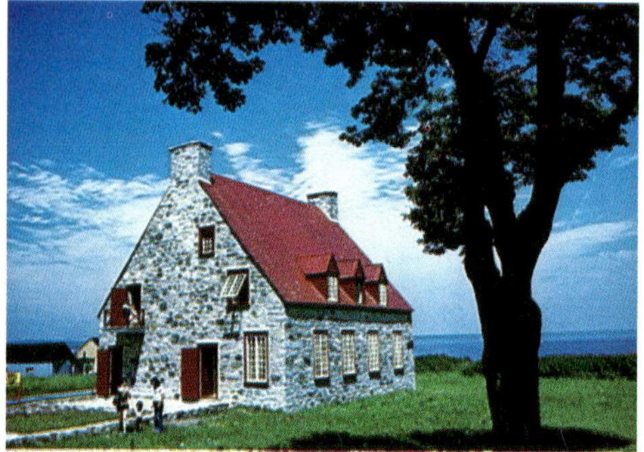

26-3 Stone farmhouse, Québec
The rectangle has been the basic architectural shape for houses in Canada since the early settlers arrived in New France.

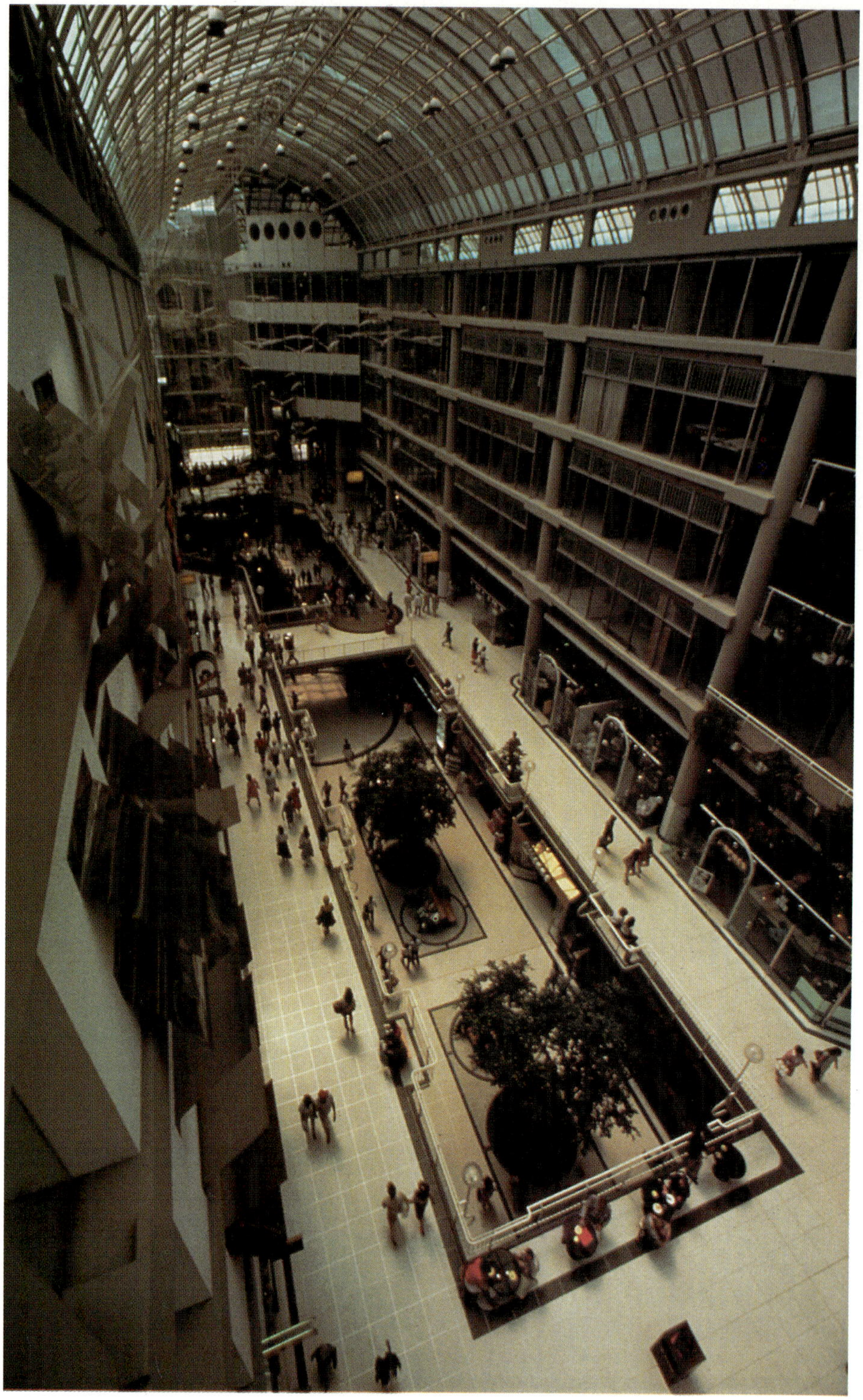

26-4 Eaton Centre (interior), Toronto, Ontario
Enclosing space for public use is not a new role for the architect. However, modern technology and materials have produced exciting achievements in designs for public use. The Eaton Centre in Toronto is a dramatic example.

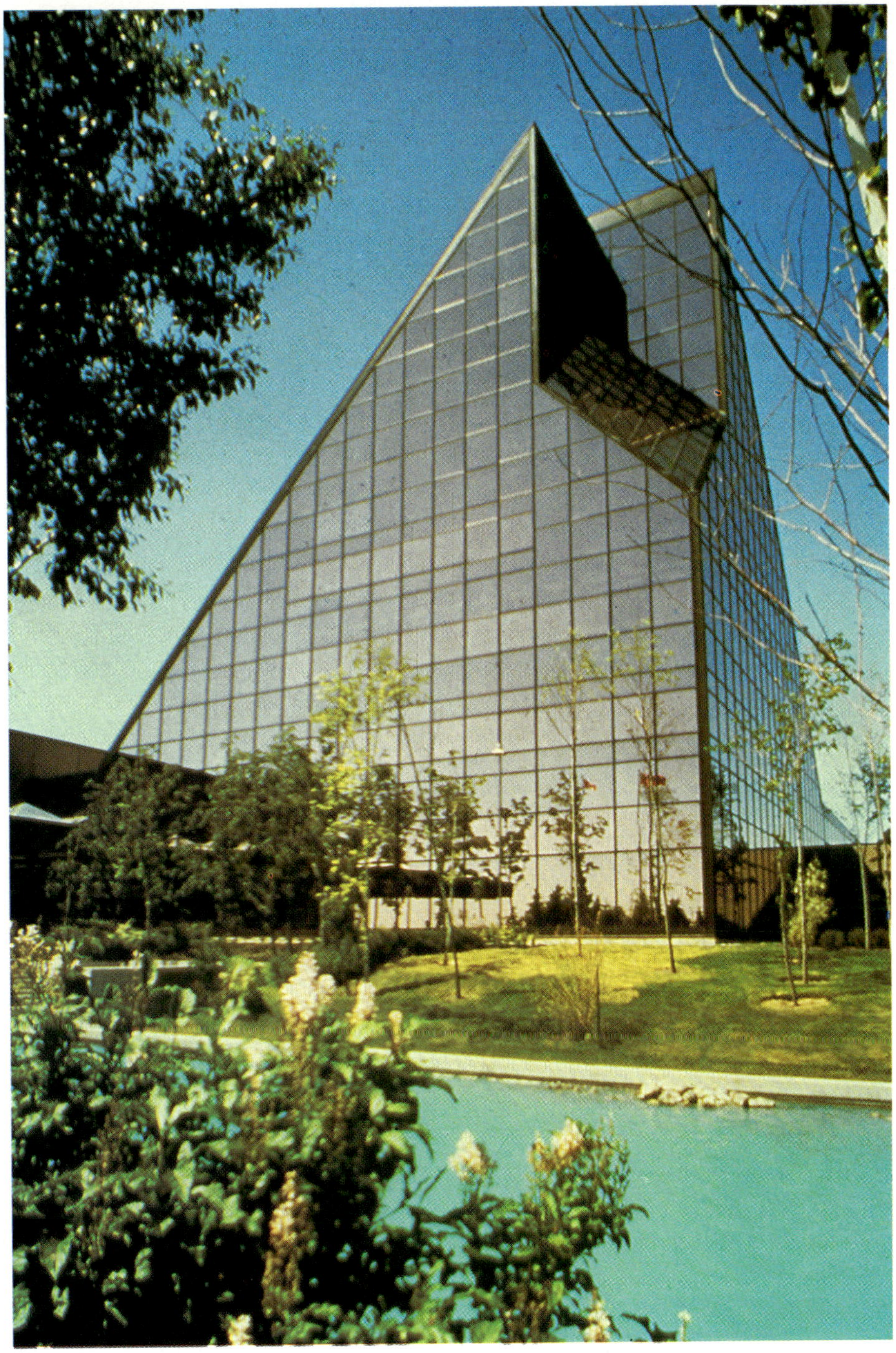

Look Again

- Do you think the utilidor in 26-2 is attractive? Or do you think it is merely functional?

- You are a pioneer farmer in Québec, sitting inside the house you built (26-3). Outside, the howling wind is driving the snow against the windows. What features of the house make it good protection?
- What improvements might you plan to make?

- You have the plans for building the Winnipeg Mint (26-5), but your only building material is wood. What problems do you foresee?

- Buildings that are designed for a specific use may well reflect that use in the design. For example, you may feel that the appearance of the Newfoundland church reflects traditional Christian ideas. Its clean white and green colour suggests purity; its plainness suggests simplicity; the vertical lines suggest uprightness; the spire that stands above the rest of the building honours a God who is greater than the people who come to worship. Try to relate design and ideas to other buildings.
- What does the design of the Eaton Centre (26-4) say to you about the importance of shopping?
- What does the design of the B.C. parliament buildings say to you about the government?

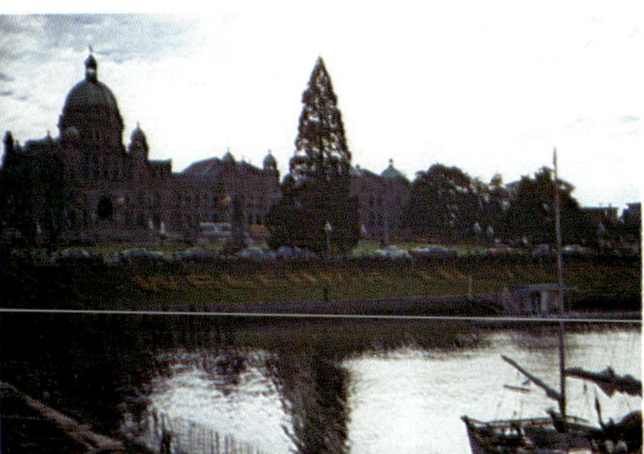

26-5 The Mint, Winnipeg, Manitoba
The Winnipeg Mint uses light and space in a modern exterior design.

26-6 Parliament Buildings, Victoria, B.C.
Symmetrical balance has been used in the British Columbia parliament buildings in Victoria. A natural inner harbour provides a unique setting.

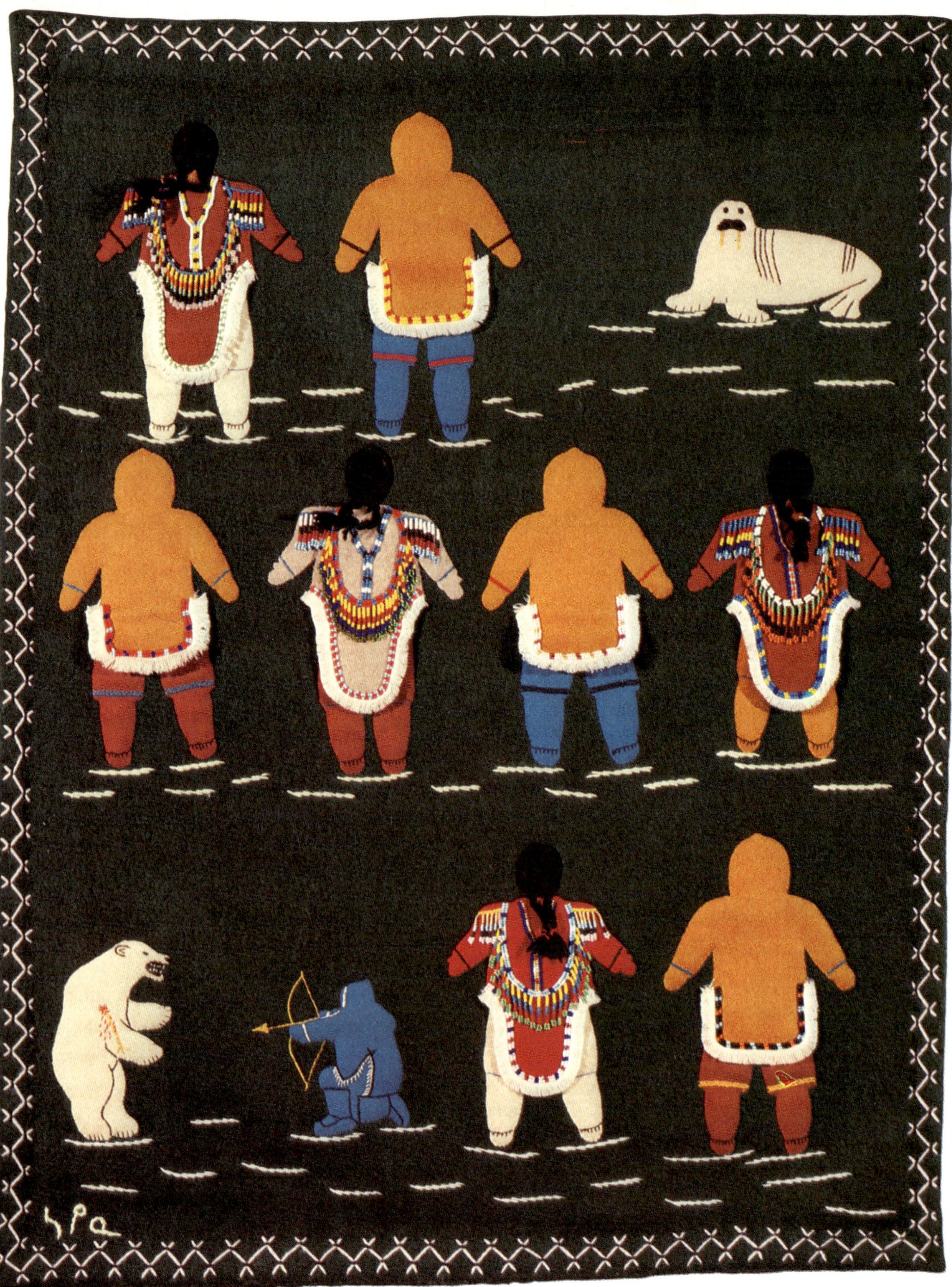

27. Crafts

Most of the products that Canadians use today have been mass-produced with the aid of machinery. In the past, most products had to be made by hand or with the aid of simple tools. The people who crafted products had to be highly skilled, for they were often responsible for making their products from start to finish. Sometimes, they were also responsible for the design. Today, many people enjoy *crafts* as a hobby. Often they follow traditional patterns or bought designs. Other people design their own craftwork. This section looks at the work of some of the *artisans* who design objects that are visually appealing and who make objects to very high standards. The focus is on a small range of crafts: fabrics and textiles, ceramics, metals and gemstones, glass and wood.

Fabric crafts are both useful and decorative. They generally fall into one of two major categories. One is *fabric construction*, which includes weaving and knotting of material. The other is surface decoration on fabric.

Weaving frequently demands the use of a loom. Very simply described, a loom holds a series of threads called the warp. A second series of threads is woven through the warp. This series is called the weft. Most woven fabrics are relatively smooth and flat and can be sewn into a variety of different items. A weaving can also be made with fibres, such as cotton, fleece or goat hair, that have not been spun into thread. This type of fabric construction generally produces an interesting, uneven surface, and the fabric is used mainly as decorative wall-hangings. *Braiding*, such as in the folk art of ceintures fléchées or "arrow sashes," is another technique for fabric construction. This method involved fine wool braided into traditional patterns and worn as sashes or belts.

Another traditional method of construction that is both useful and decorative is *knotting*. Originally, knotting was used by the sailors on the three-masted whaling ships. They used their nautical skill with ropes and knots to make decorative patterns. The square knot and the half hitch are the same knots used today for decorative and useful constructions.

Another part of fabric and textile crafts concerns surface design. This area includes *batik*, *tie dye*, painting on fabric, silkscreening, *appliqué* and *stitchery*. The emphasis in design in dyeing and painting is on colour and pattern. For example, batik is a technique of applying wax to selected areas of fabric so that the dye cannot penetrate those areas. The fabric may be waxed and dipped several times so that several colours are built up from the lightest to the darkest. The wax can be applied with great precision, and very fine effects are possible. Tie dye involves colour, too. Cloth is tied with string in various places and dipped into the dyes. The dye cannot penetrate the cloth that is covered by the tightly wound

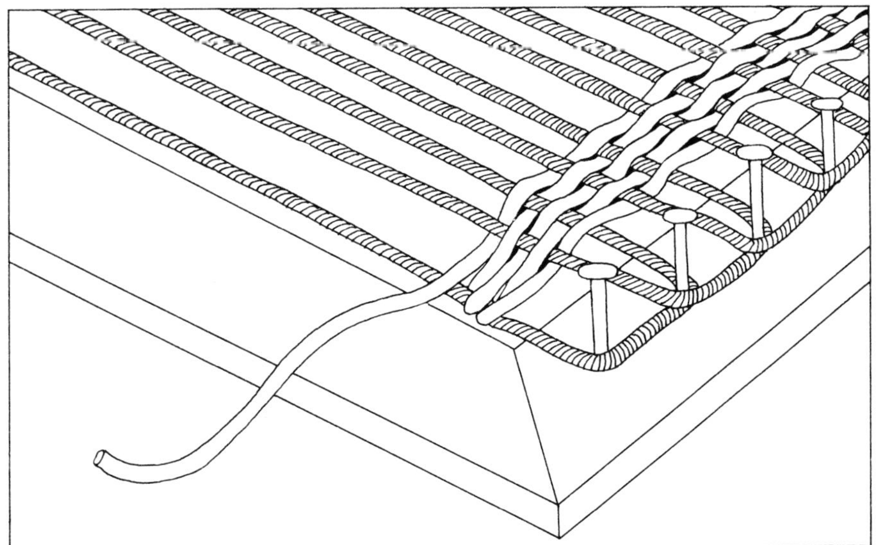

A simple loom for weaving can be made from a wooden frame. The warp is strung from nails at either end. The weft threads are interwoven to make the pattern.

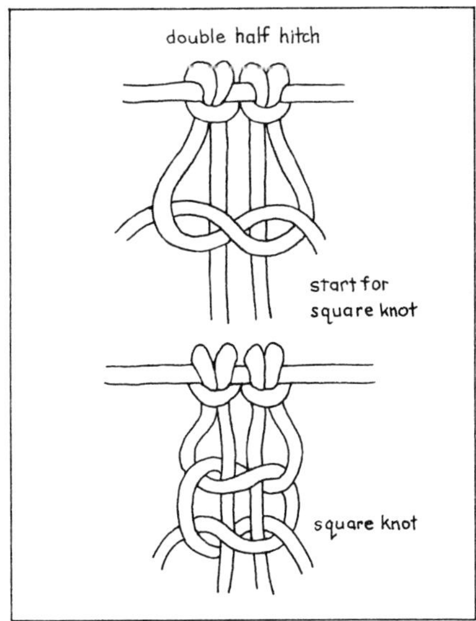

Two basic knots are the double half hitch and the square knot. Patterns can be created by repeating these kinds of knots.

27-1 Tapestry, Alice Akammuk (left) Surface decoration is seen in this wall hanging by Alice Akammuk from Eskimo Point, N.W.T. Each figure is trimmed in beadwork.

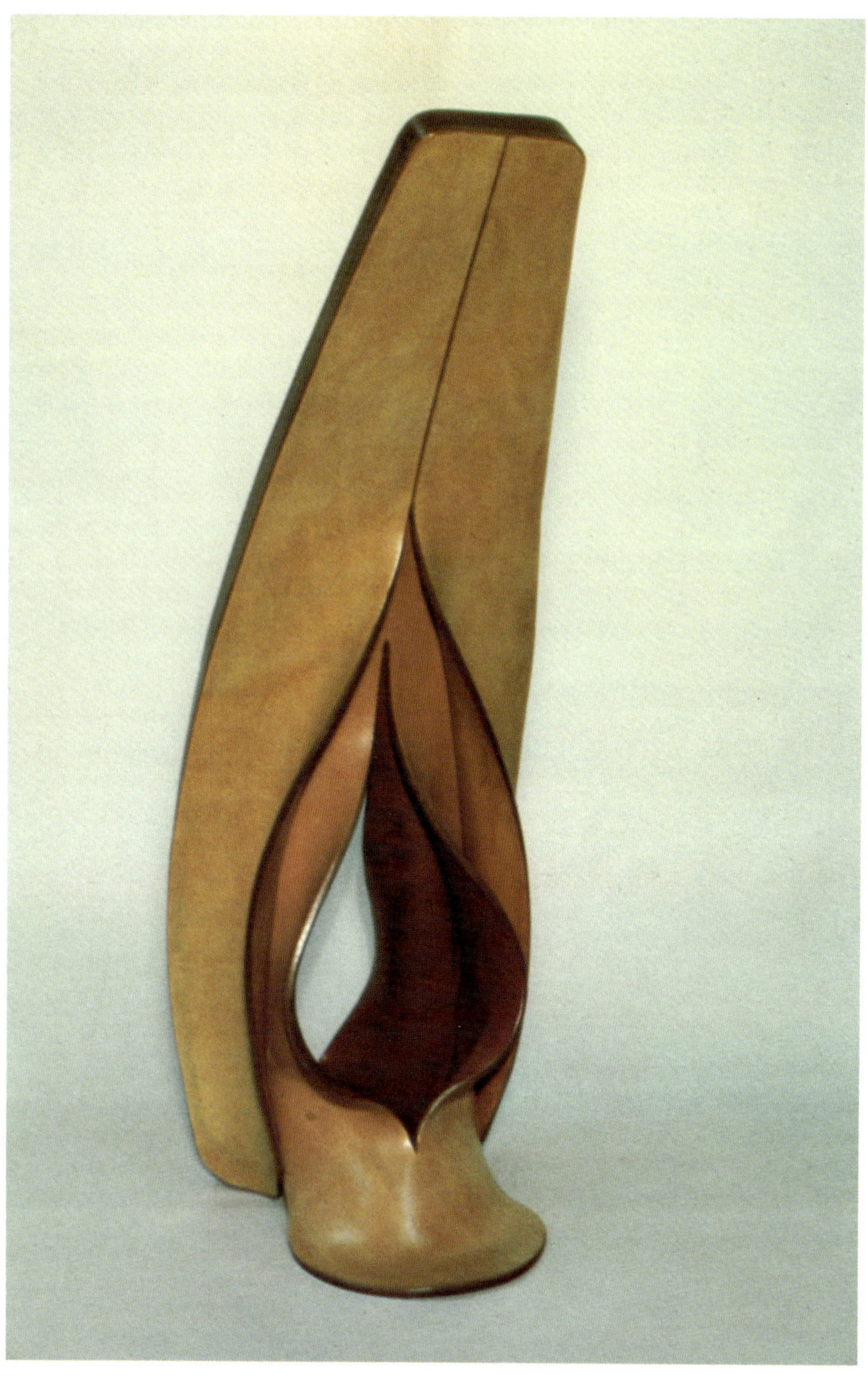

27-2 Leather sculpture, Rex Lingwood
Although many useful items are made from leather, Rex Lingwood creates three-dimensional sculptures by bending, folding or twisting the leather.

string. The process continues until an interesting pattern has been made. Painting and printing on fabric such as silk is a specialized use of these two familiar techniques. The fabric is then made into useful items such as clothing. Other fabrics are decorated with appliqué or stitchery in traditional patterns.

For example, the Inuit use decorative stitches worked on to the ground fabric to achieve distinctive patterns. Appliqué involves sewing fabric on to the ground fabric in pure design or in pictures. Banners and wall-hangings are two examples of the craft that displays stitchery and appliqué.

Ceramics as a craft involves forming clay into useful and decorative objects. The basic material used in ceramics is clay. A knowledge of design as well as of the physical properties of basic clay bodies is essential in this craft. Basic clay bodies are *earthenware*, *stoneware*, and *porcelain*. You probably have seen some pieces in each clay. For example, earthenware is usually used in basic handbuilding in school; porcelain is used for fine china. Stoneware is often used for oven-proof dishes.

People who work in ceramics rely on their hands for shaping each piece. The first stage is always to remove the air bubbles and to mix the clay by kneading or wedging it. Handbuilding methods include making pinch forms, building coils, draping clay slabs on molds, assembling slabs in constructions and joining a series of forms together. Another method for making pottery is on a potter's wheel. This method involves centring the clay on a revolving base or wheel. The wheel may be motor-driven or foot-powered. The clay then is drawn upwards while the wheel is turning. Practice is important to keep the clay even! Some useful pieces made on the wheel are plates and mugs. Ceramic pieces are often started on the wheel and then finished with other handbuilding methods. Textures may be added by pressing or stamping the wet clay of an item with another interesting surface. After textures have been added, the ceramic piece is dried. At this point it is called *greenware*. It is

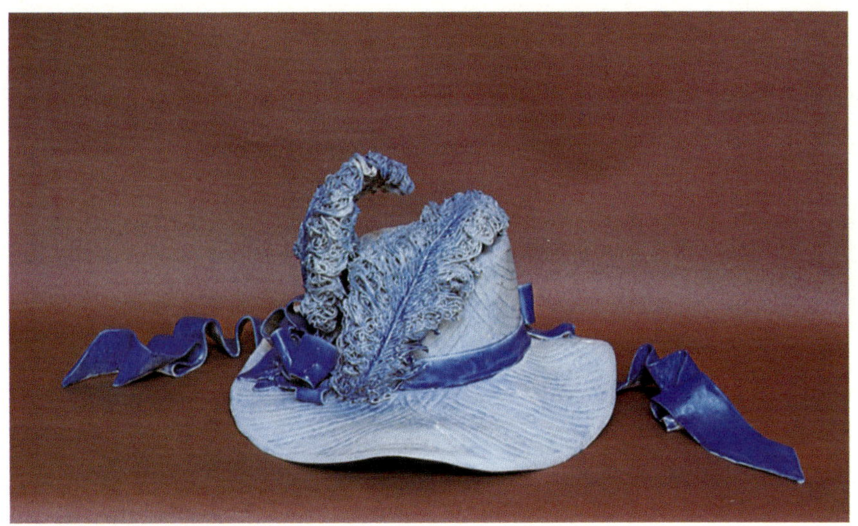

27-3 The Romantic era bonnet, 1826, Audrey Davies
Decorative ceramic work in porcelain is shown in special exhibitions. This show was called *Lost Images: 200 Years of Women's Hats in Porcelain* and based on a theme about changes in style in women's hats. This type of popular bonnet from the Romantic era (about 1826) had a high crown with a large brim and was often covered with feathers and ribbons. What kind of hat could be used as an example of today's styles?

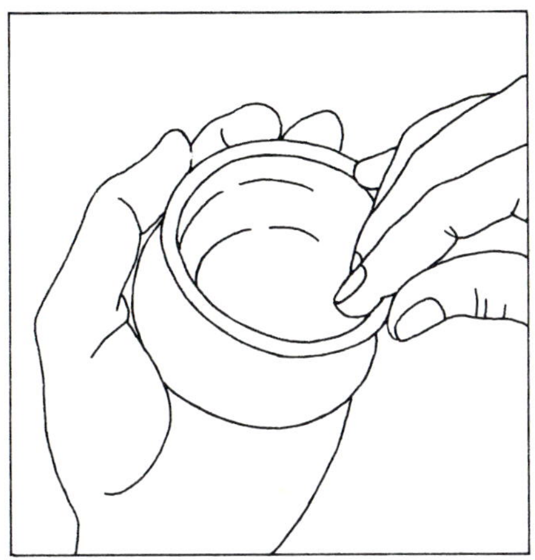

A simple, but versatile method for hand building ceramics is the pinch pot. A ball of clay is prepared and then the thumb is pressed into the centre as the sides are pinched. Several pinch pots may be made and joined together with liquid clay called slip.

A potter's wheel usually has a flat surface attached to a shaft that is operated by a small motor or by a treadle. The wheel turns continually as the pot is "thrown."

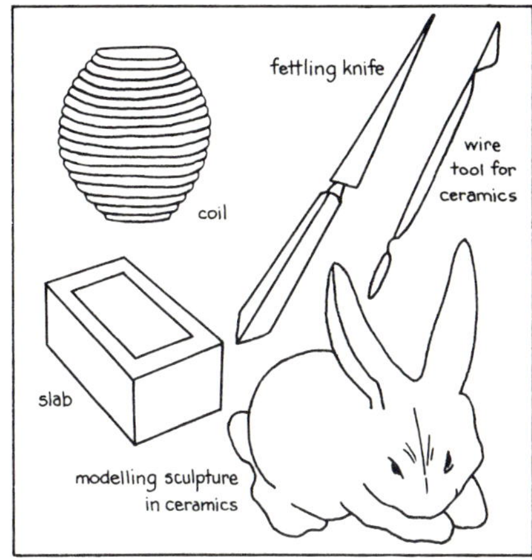

Other hand building techniques in ceramics include coil and slab construction. Clay can also be used for modelling.

then fired in a kiln. This is known as the bisque firing, and the clay piece is now called *bisqueware*. It is still porous. The final stage is to apply a glaze, which is similar to a thin layer of glass. The glaze both seals and decorates the piece. It is fired once more. Ceramic pieces may be made as useful containers such as vases, three-dimensional sculpture such as figures or animals, and relief sculpture such as decorative wall plaques.

For centuries, things have been made for personal adornment. Some are made from precious metal such as gold and silver. Others are made from bone, ivory, wood, stone, seeds and shells. Today, plastics are used too. Materials may be cut or carved. Others are fused, soldered or glued on to a base, such as metal or wood. Many different skills are required. Awareness of colour, shape and texture is important. As always, imagination on the part of the individual artisan is vital in creating beautiful jewellery.

Glass is made mainly of silicon oxide but may also contain some other oxides. By varying the amounts of different oxides, different kinds of glass can be made. All glass is liquid when heated and cools to a hard solid. These properties allow the artisan to work in either of two areas. One

YOU AND YOUR SEARCH FOR MEANING IN ART

28. Subject Matter in Art

Subject matter in art is, quite simply, what the artist has chosen to represent. The artist's choice of subject is often your first clue to the artist's message. Knowing the source of the subject matter can add more clues. For example, one artist may paint a country scene while looking directly at it. Another may recall a childhood scene from memory. A science fiction illustration may come directly from the artist's imagination.

Subject matter in art often focuses on the real world: people, places or objects. They may be easy to recognize or they may be distorted. Sometimes, a work of art may consist of lines, shapes, or colours with no obvious subject.

It is important to learn to recognize different subjects for what they are. When you look at a work of art, practise describing the subject matter. The following pages explain some of the terms artists frequently use to describe their own subject matter.

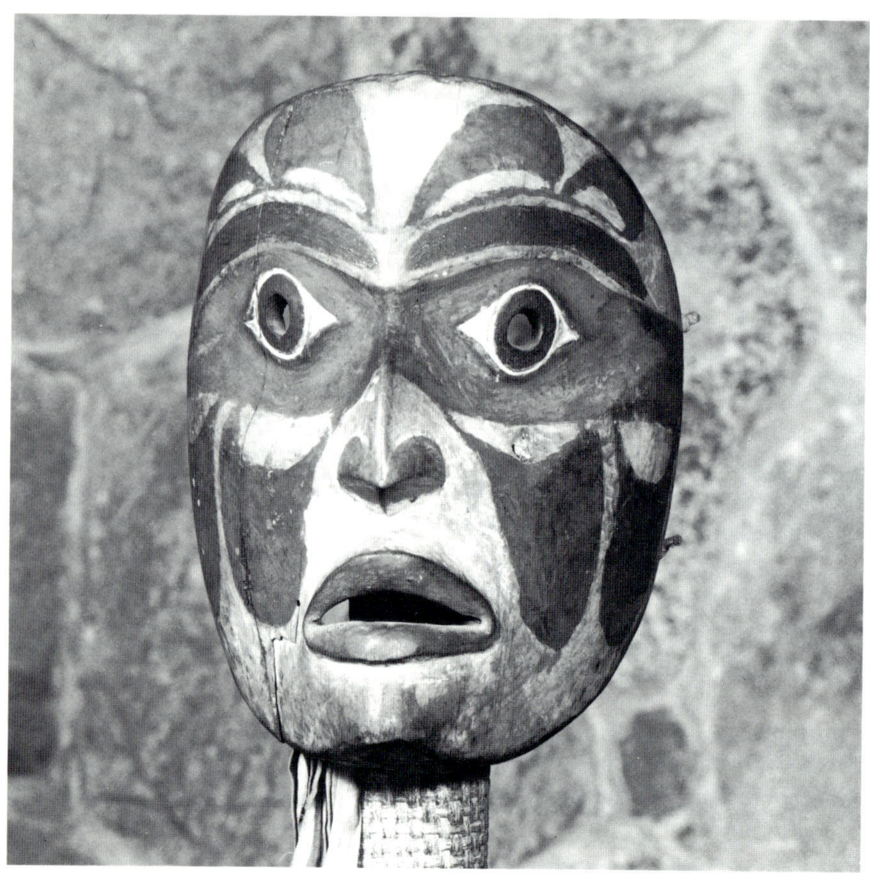

29-1 *Human Face Mask*, unknown (Tsimshian)
Figurative art has taken many forms. Can you feel the power of this West Coast Indian mask? For what purpose do you suppose it was created?

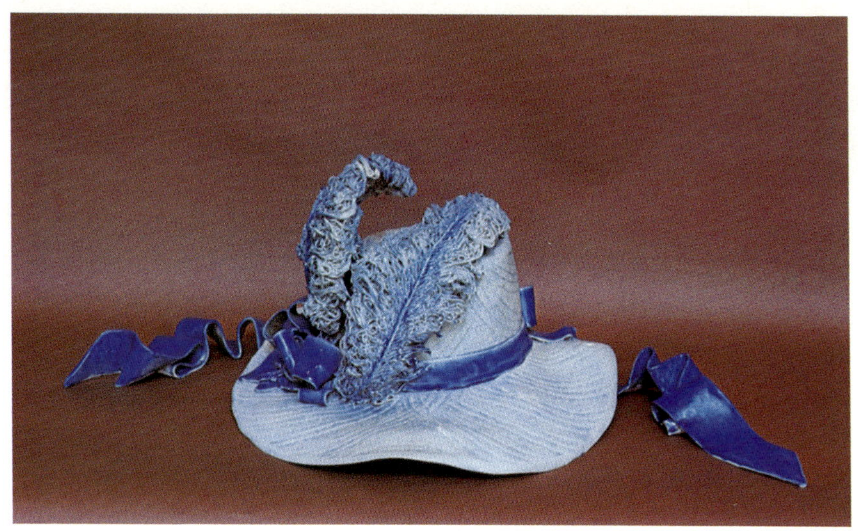

27-3 The Romantic era bonnet, 1826, Audrey Davies
Decorative ceramic work in porcelain is shown in special exhibitions. This show was called *Lost Images: 200 Years of Women's Hats in Porcelain* and based on a theme about changes in style in women's hats. This type of popular bonnet from the Romantic era (about 1826) had a high crown with a large brim and was often covered with feathers and ribbons. What kind of hat could be used as an example of today's styles?

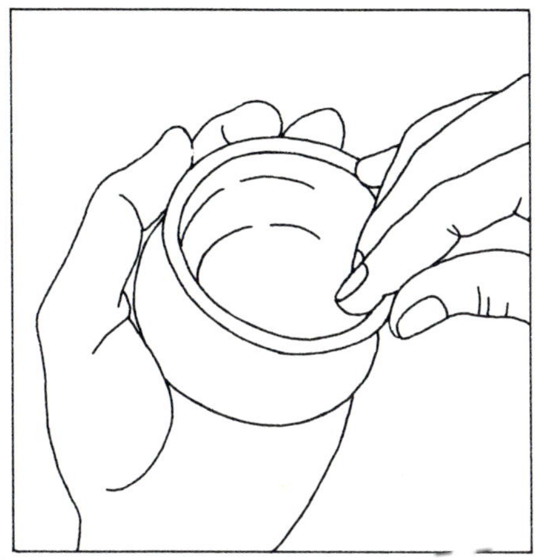

A simple, but versatile method for hand building ceramics is the pinch pot. A ball of clay is prepared and then the thumb is pressed into the centre as the sides are pinched. Several pinch pots may be made and joined together with liquid clay called slip.

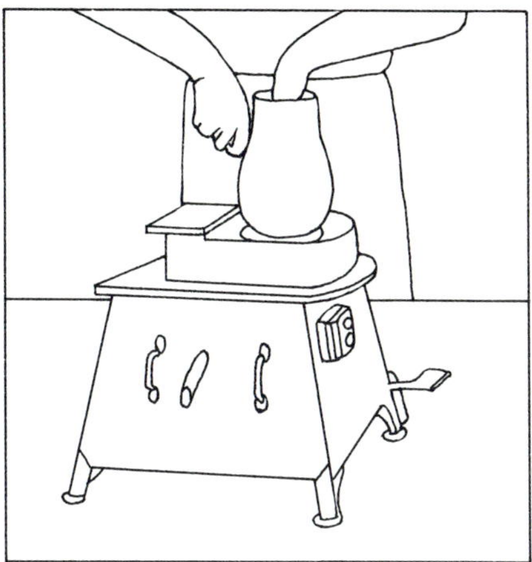

A potter's wheel usually has a flat surface attached to a shaft that is operated by a small motor or by a treadle. The wheel turns continually as the pot is "thrown."

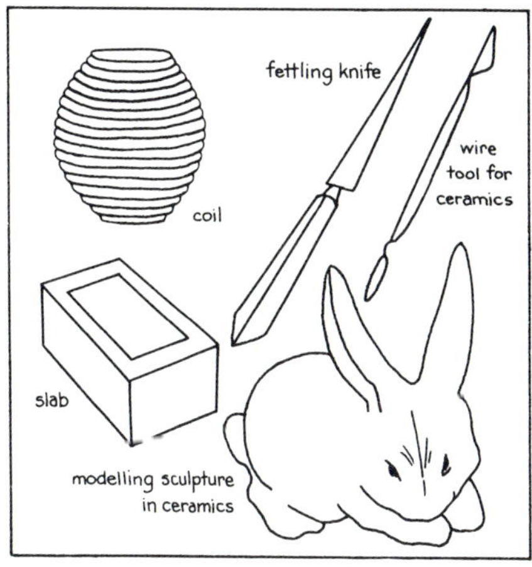

Other hand building techniques in ceramics include coil and slab construction. Clay can also be used for modelling.

then fired in a kiln. This is known as the bisque firing, and the clay piece is now called *bisqueware*. It is still porous. The final stage is to apply a glaze, which is similar to a thin layer of glass. The glaze both seals and decorates the piece. It is fired once more. Ceramic pieces may be made as useful containers such as vases, three-dimensional sculpture such as figures or animals, and relief sculpture such as decorative wall plaques.

For centuries, things have been made for personal adornment. Some are made from precious metal such as gold and silver. Others are made from bone, ivory, wood, stone, seeds and shells. Today, plastics are used too. Materials may be cut or carved. Others are fused, soldered or glued on to a base, such as metal or wood. Many different skills are required. Awareness of colour, shape and texture is important. As always, imagination on the part of the individual artisan is vital in creating beautiful jewellery.

Glass is made mainly of silicon oxide but may also contain some other oxides. By varying the amounts of different oxides, different kinds of glass can be made. All glass is liquid when heated and cools to a hard solid. These properties allow the artisan to work in either of two areas. One is *hot glass*, such as glass blowing and casting molten glass. Useful containers and decorative sculptures can be made. Colours can be produced in the hot glass by adding metallic oxides, such as cobalt to produce blue. The other area for the artisan is working with *cold glass*. This method includes decorating vases, containers and plates by etching patterns and pictures into the surface of the glass. It is also possible to carve glass and to laminate or join pieces together. For example, stained glass is often cut into pieces and joined together to form beautiful windows or lamp shades. Colour as well as shape are two important design concepts used in working with glass. The artisan needs to think carefully about the purpose of the piece, its form and the limitations of the materials.

Wood, like the other materials in this section, allows for individual and original expression. Useful and sculptural pieces may be made. Carving is one technique used when working with wood. Another is assembling. Although some wood is imported, many artisans use wood native to Canada, such as maple and pine. Each wood has its own characteristics. For example, the sugar maple is a cocoa brown colour. It is hard to carve. It has an even texture and a fine grain. Pine is light brown, soft and easy to carve. As with the other crafts a knowledge of design concepts is necessary. Balance, shape and texture are keys to successful designs in wood. Furniture, for example, must be visually pleasing and highly functional.

Look for the use of special skills and individual expression in craft designs.

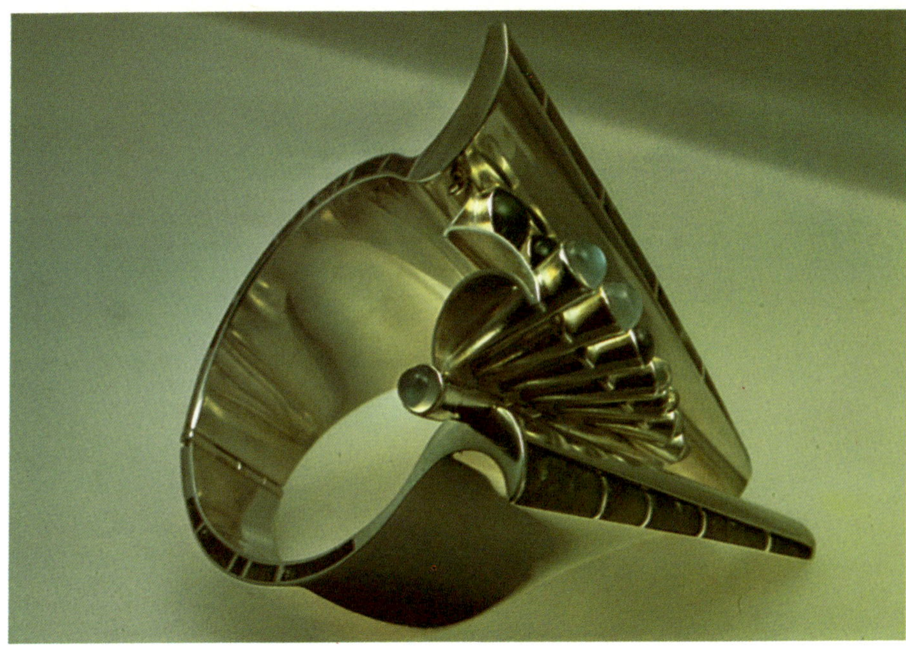

27-4 Bracelet, Lois Betteridge
This bracelet uses cabochon moonstone and British Columbia jade. Notice the effect of the curves as your eye travels around the important areas of the bracelet.

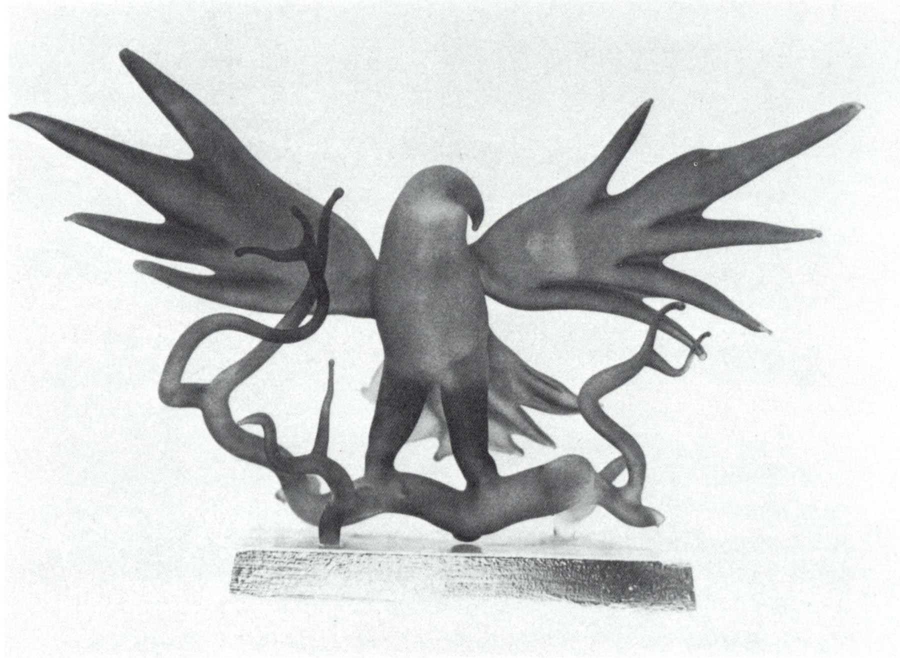

27-5 *Hawk* (etched borosilicate glass), Len Chodirker
Winnipeg artisan, Len Chodirker, creates sculpture in glass. Light adds to the delicate effect of the etched glass, creating subtle changes in value. The piece measures approximately 20 cm x 30 cm.

27-6 Chair, Michael Fortune
Michael Fortune designs functional wood furniture. The designs are unusual but always visually pleasing.

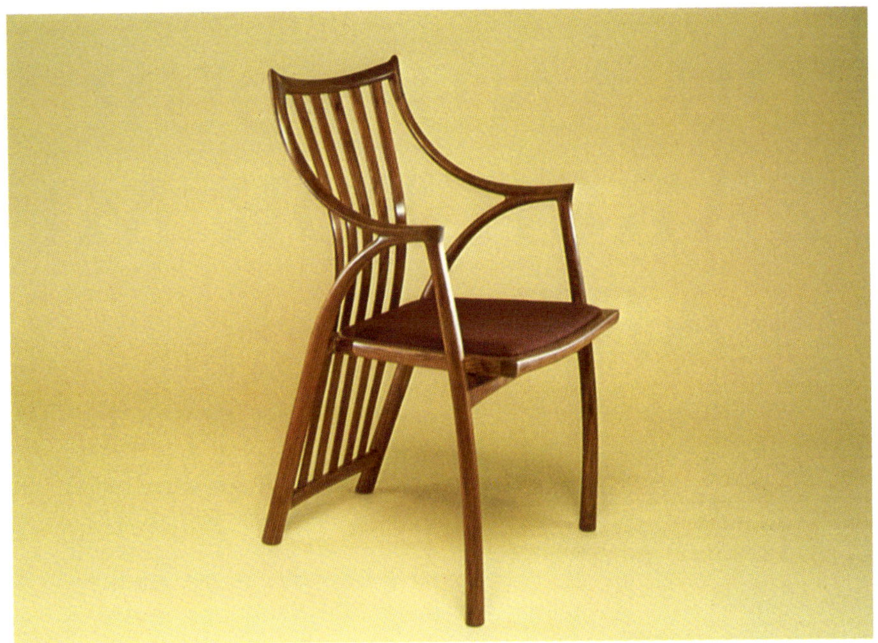

Look Again

- Some people talk about "art" and "craft" as two separate things. Try to decide for yourself the relationship between the two, by answering the following questions. Then answer the last two questions.
- Compare the hawk in 27-5 with the drawing 20-3. Which type of artwork do you think requires more skill? Which requires a better sense of design?
- Compare the tapestry (27-1) with the print (22-1).

- Audrey Davies' hat (27-3) has been shown in an exhibition. Think about the sort of person who made actual hats like this one in 1826. Was that person an artist? Why or why not? That person was quite likely a woman who had learned to sew as a child. She used her sewing skills to get a job making expensive hats for rich people. She and her client might design the hat to match a particular outfit. Then she would shape the hat and stitch it by hand. She probably earned very little money.

- It is possible to buy a simple, factory-made chair similar to your school chair for a lot less money than the price of Michael Fortune's chair (27-6). Both are equally comfortable to sit on. Which chair would you choose? Why?

- Quite often, the title of a work of art gives a clue as to its message. Neither the leather sculpture (27-2) nor the bracelet (27-4) has a title. Can you think of a title for either piece? Explain why you think a title is or is not necessary.

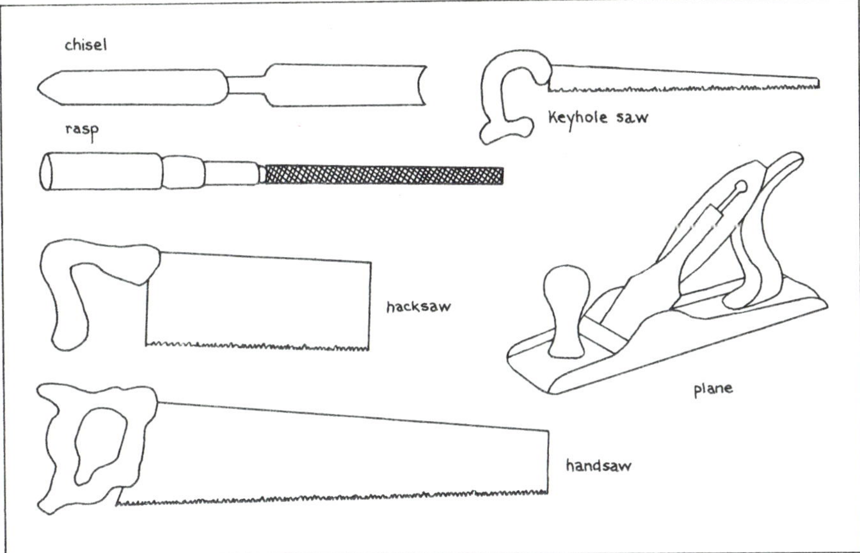

Chisels, rasps, planes and saws are some of the tools used in woodworking.

- What special gifts do the artist and the artisan share?
- Is the person who goes out into the woods to paint on a Sunday afternoon more of an artist than the person who designs and makes clothes?

- Of all the forms of art that you have studied so far, which do you most enjoy? Try to explain why. Ask yourself questions such as, do I like handling the material? Do I like the finished product?

YOU AND YOUR SEARCH FOR MEANING IN ART

28. Subject Matter in Art

Subject matter in art is, quite simply, what the artist has chosen to represent. The artist's choice of subject is often your first clue to the artist's message. Knowing the source of the subject matter can add more clues. For example, one artist may paint a country scene while looking directly at it. Another may recall a childhood scene from memory. A science fiction illustration may come directly from the artist's imagination.

Subject matter in art often focuses on the real world: people, places or objects. They may be easy to recognize or they may be distorted. Sometimes, a work of art may consist of lines, shapes, or colours with no obvious subject.

It is important to learn to recognize different subjects for what they are. When you look at a work of art, practise describing the subject matter. The following pages explain some of the terms artists frequently use to describe their own subject matter.

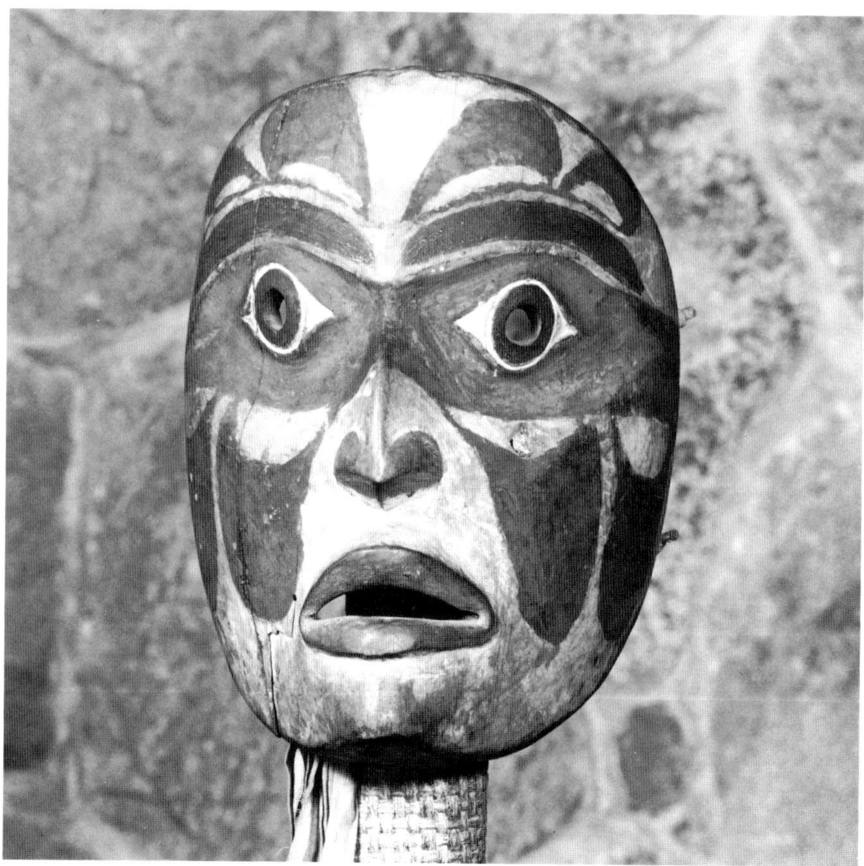

29-1 *Human Face Mask*, unknown (Tsimshian)
Figurative art has taken many forms. Can you feel the power of this West Coast Indian mask? For what purpose do you suppose it was created?

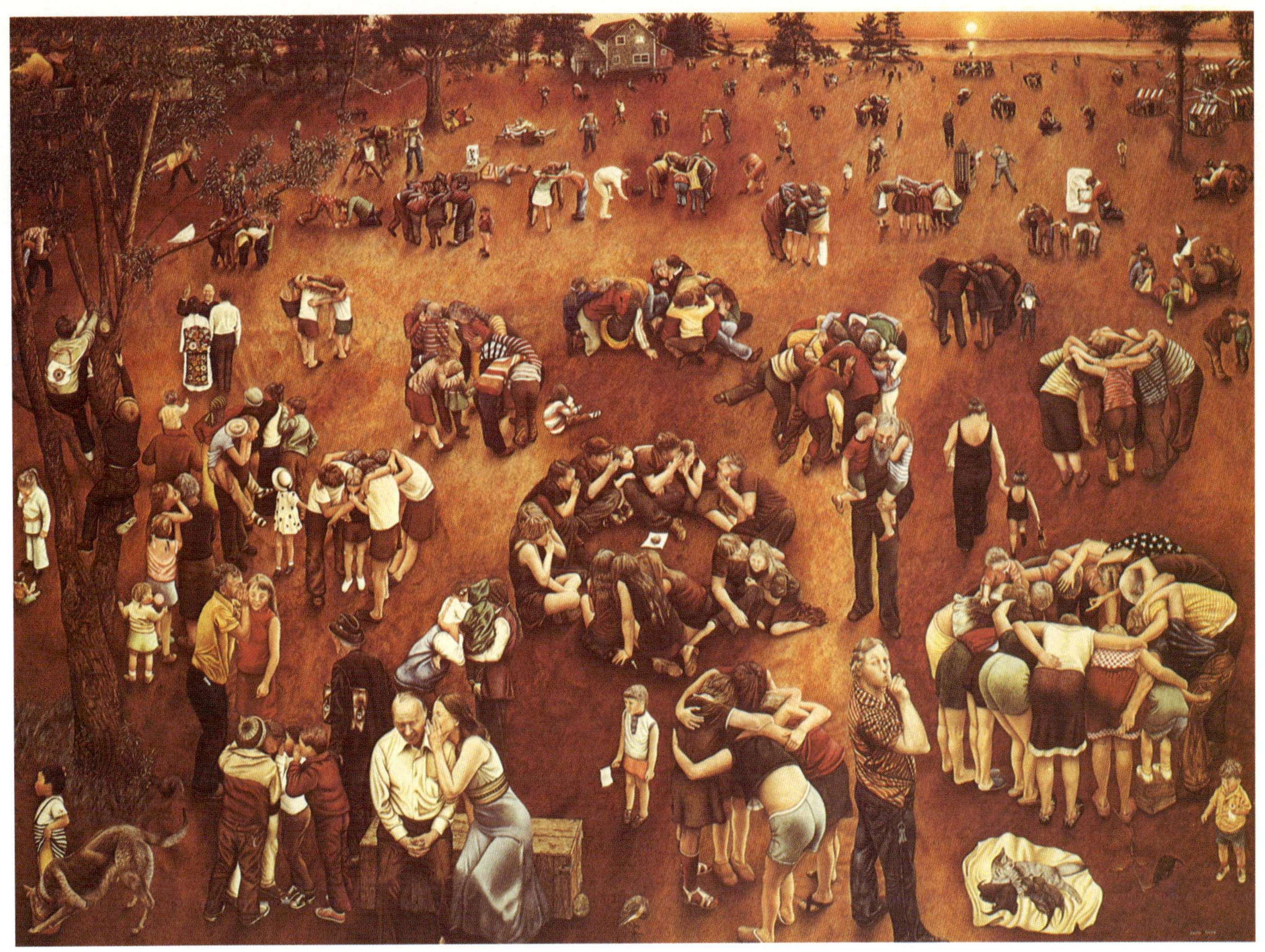

29-2 *Secrets*, **Jeremy Smith**
Jeremy Smith's *Secrets* is one of the most exciting figure compositions ever attempted by a Canadian painter.

29. People: Figurative Art

Art that focuses on images of people is called *figurative art*. This word may be used to refer to art that represents a crowd of people, a few people, or even just one person. Figurative art that shows a close-up of a person's face is called a *portrait*. Sculptural portraits are called *busts*.

When you look at figurative art, it is helpful to ask yourself some very simple questions. How many people do you see? Are they men or women, grown-ups or children? What are they doing? Can you guess the relationship between them? Where are the people shown to be? What mood are the people in? Does the artist tell you in the title of the work who these people are? Answering questions such as these will provide you with a good basic description of figurative art.

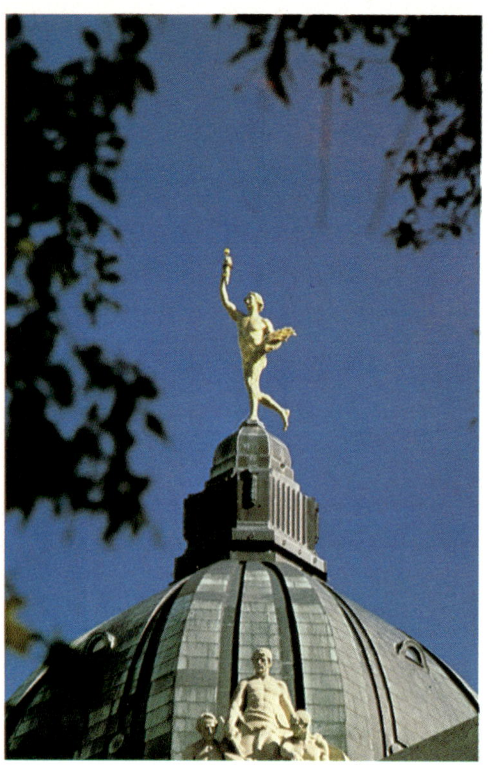

29-3 ***The Golden Boy*****, Manitoba Legislature, Winnipeg**
People frequently use art work to represent ideals or values. This sculpture on the dome of the provincial government building in Winnipeg is a famous landmark in Manitoba. *The Golden Boy* holds a sheaf of wheat in his left hand and a torch in his right. He faces north, representing the spirit of prosperity advancing towards new frontiers.

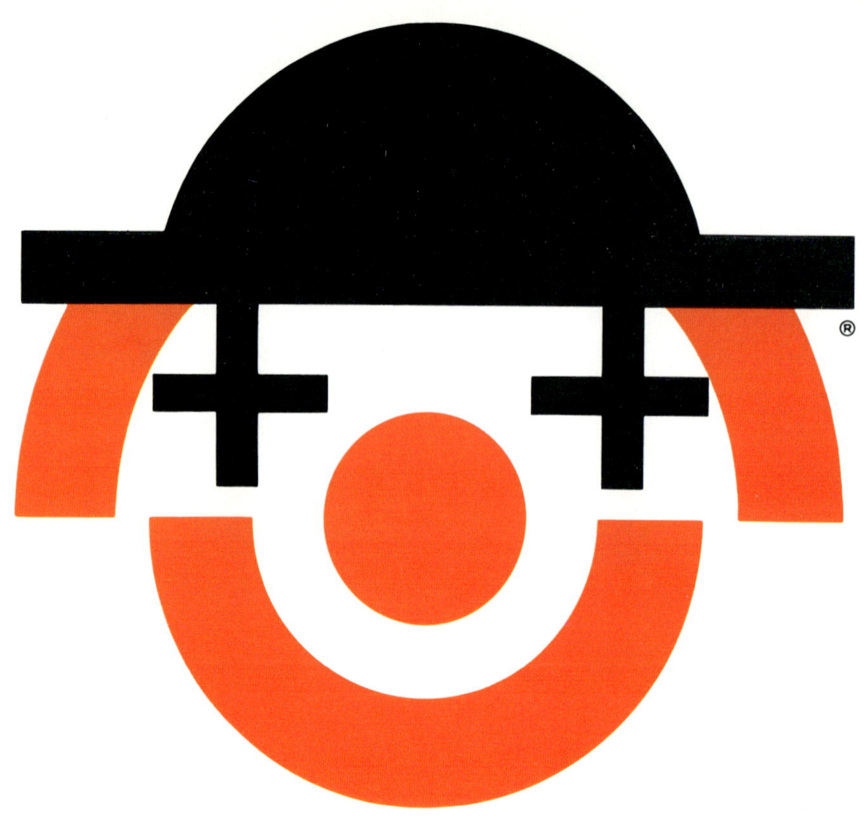

29-4 ***Conklin Clown*****, Canada's Conklin Shows**
The human face has been simplified in the familiar logo for Canada's Conklin Shows, the carnival people.

Look Again

- If you had to join the people in Jeremy Smith's *Secrets* (29-2), to whom would you go and speak?
- Why would you choose this person or group and not the others?
- Think about the times that you tried to join a crowd of strangers – at school, at a party, or at a club. Does this picture remind you in any way of what that occasion looked like? Does it remind you of how you felt?

- Compare this multi-figure painting to Tom McNeely's multi-figure illustration for the Canadian Amateur Swimming Association (24-3). What is the purpose of each? What is the message for the viewer?

- The Conklin Clown and the Tsimshian mask are both based on the human face. In what ways are they similar? Different?
- Describe the expression on the mask and the one on the clown.
- How has the artist of each created that expression?

- Compare *The Golden Boy* (29-3) with *Louis Riel* (4-2). Describe the following:
  – the visual appearance of each statue
  – the person shown in each statue
  – how you think each person feels
- Now try the same comparison between *The Golden Boy* and the *Olympic Torch Runner* (16-3).

30. The Environment: Landscape

The environment is another theme for subject matter. A piece of art that depicts the physical world is called *landscape*. This word seems particularly suitable for the natural environment with its farmland, prairies, mountains, lakes and forests. Variations of the word are used to describe other types of places. The words *cityscape* and *seascape* are common examples. It is easy to tell the type of scene that each refers to.

When you look at a landscape, be careful to notice what you think the artist has tried to emphasize. It may be the objects in the scene itself, or it may be something more general, such as the weather or the light. Describing what it is that you see may be easier if you start up close and work back. *Foreground*, *middle ground* and *background* are common divisions in landscape art.

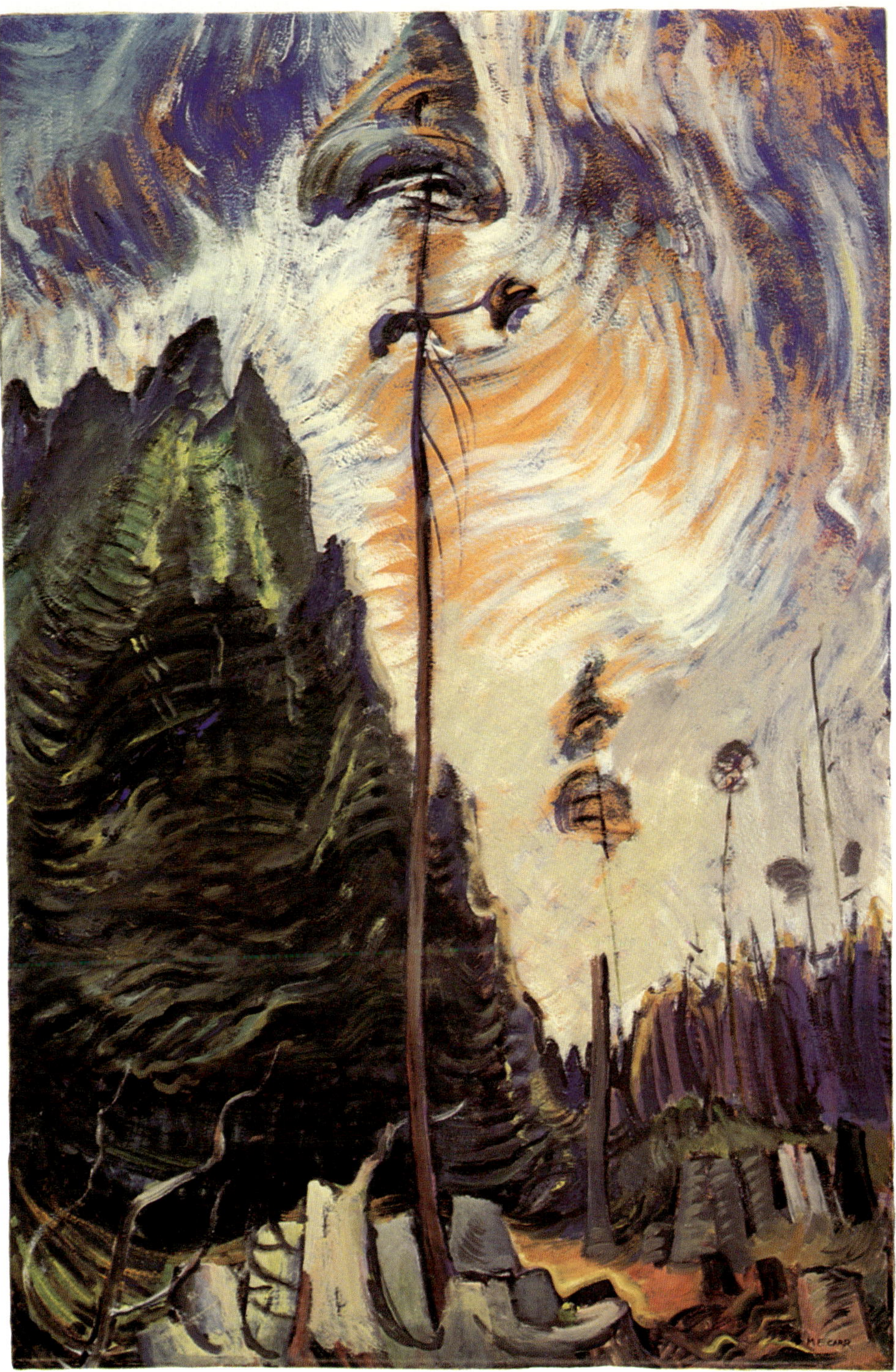

30-1 ***Edge of the Forest*****, Emily Carr**
Emily Carr from the Canadian West Coast was fascinated with the forest. She showed the lush forests of coastal British Columbia as swirling forms. Notice how the element of space is used to create a feeling of distance in her landscape.

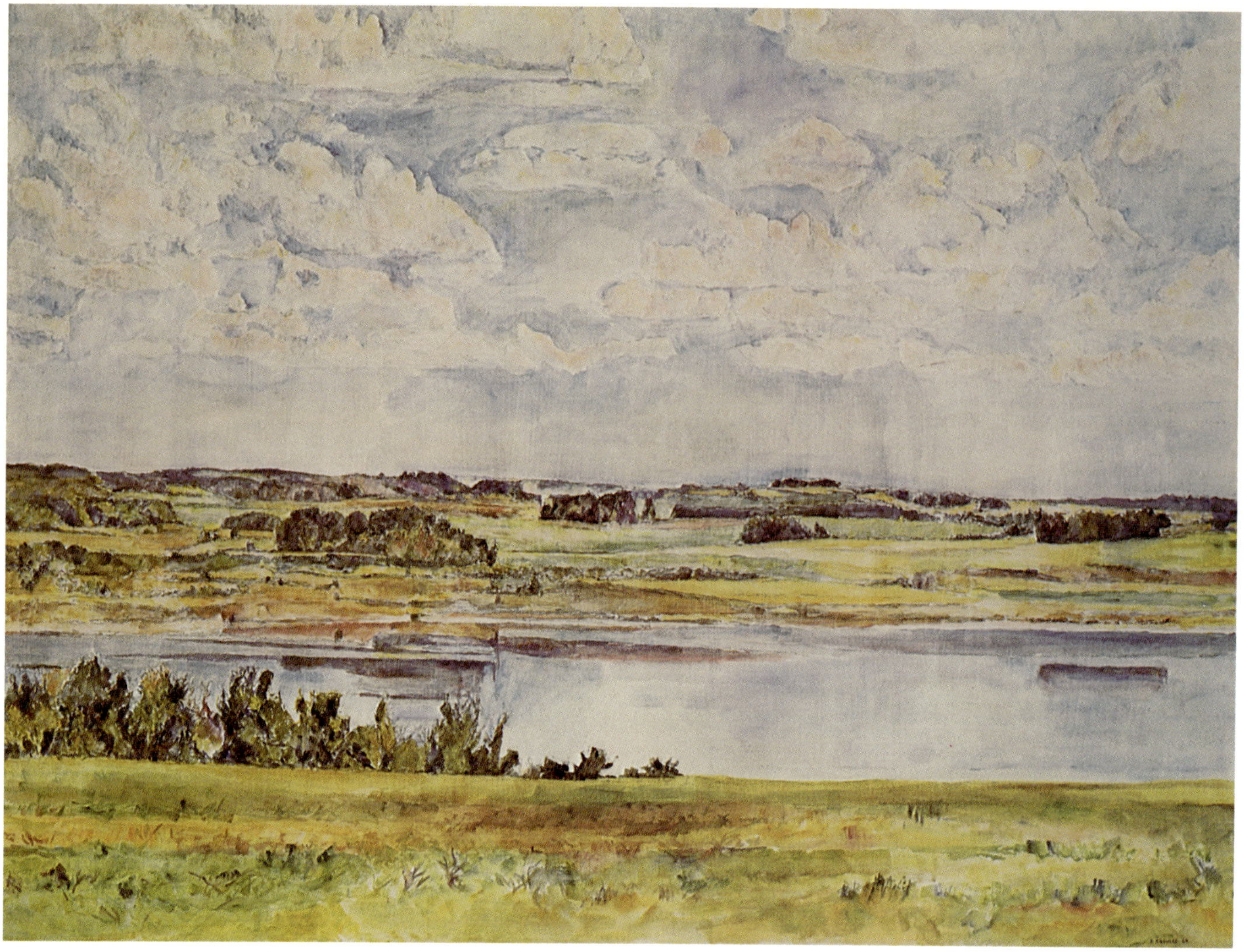

30-2 ***Summer Day*****, Dorothy Knowles**
Some landscape artists today simplify and distort what they see as they interpret the land. Notice how Dorothy Knowles of the prairies stresses sunlight on the landscape in *Summer Day*.

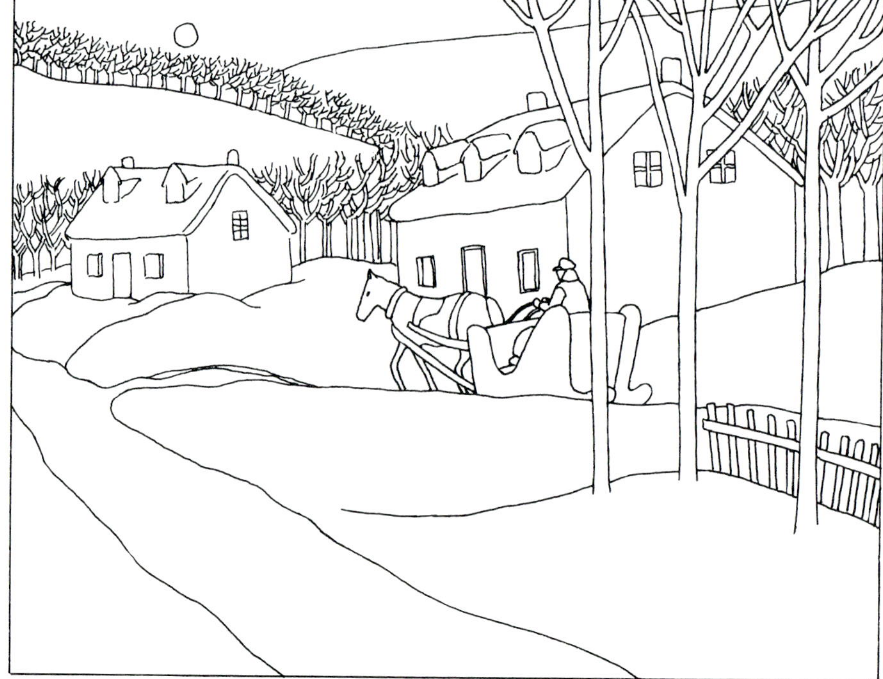

Objects close to the lower edge are in the foreground. Near the centre is the middle ground, and in the distance or upper part is the background.

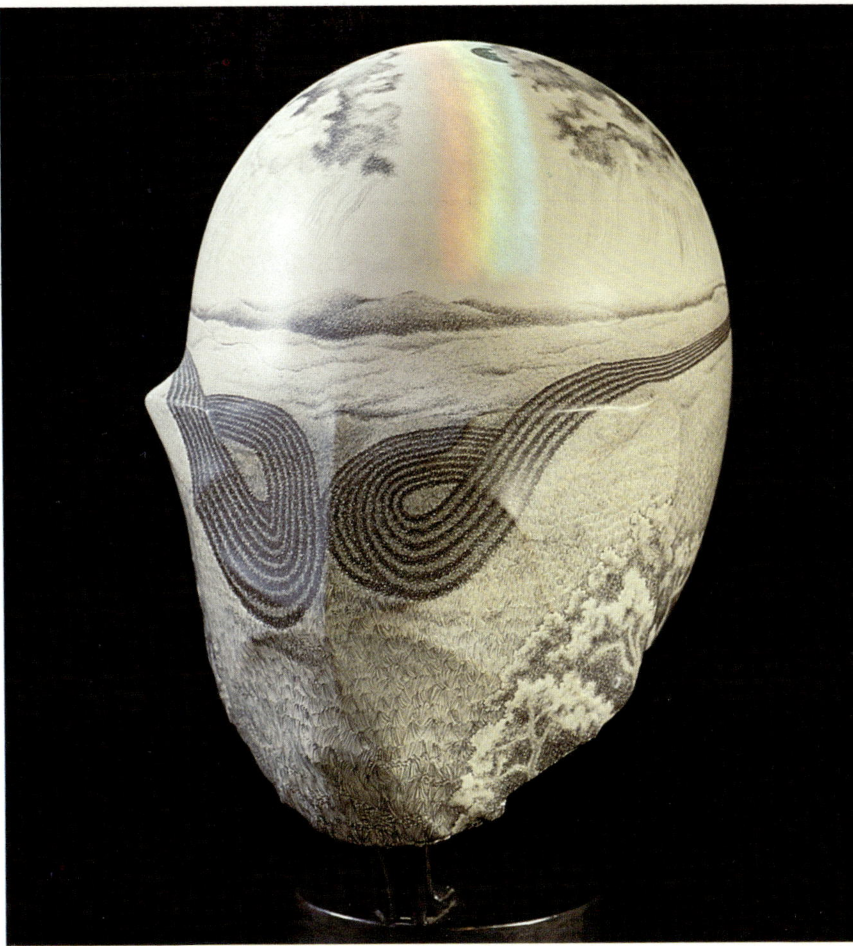

30-3 ***Rainbow Mask*****, Don Proch**
Manitoba artist Don Proch has combined both figurative and landscape subject matter in his *Rainbow Mask*.

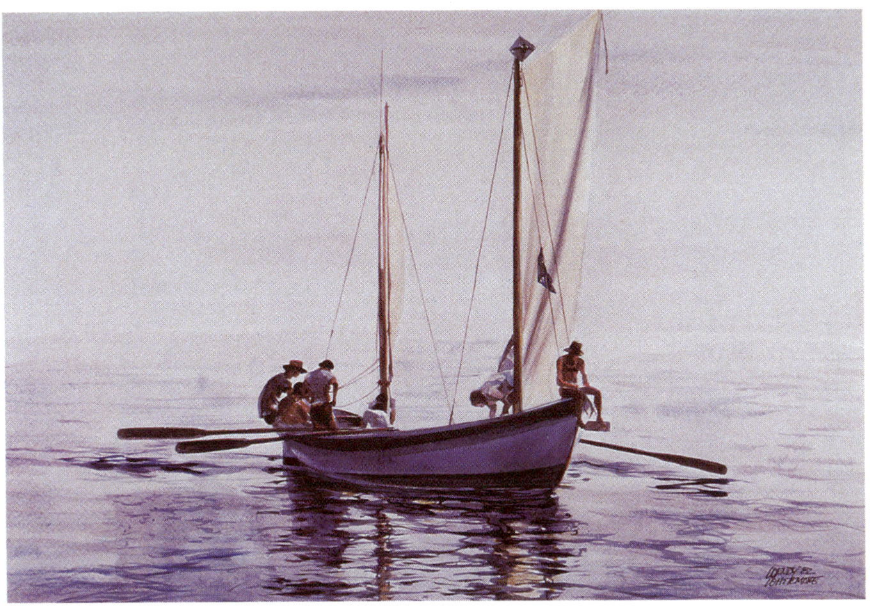

30-4 ***At Sea Illustration*****, Wendy Whitemore**
While your attention is focused on the boat and figures in Wendy Whitemore's illustration, a calm sea provides a peaceful mood.

Look Again

- You are standing on the edge of the forest (30-1). Will you go in, or not? Describe what it is like inside the forest.

- Art can cause the viewer to experience certain feelings. If you were a weather forecaster for Environment Canada, what would be your description of the weather depicted by Dorothy Knowles in *Summer Day*?
- How might the same landscape look on a winter day?
- How is the element of space used?

- Imagine you can put on the rainbow mask. What thoughts come to your mind? What do you see?
- What do you suppose Don Proch is saying about a person's relationship to the prairie landscape in this mask?

- Seascapes and landscapes often use the weather to reflect a mood. Describe a landscape that would give a peaceful mood, like what you feel when you look at Wendy Whitemore's *At Sea Illustration*.
- Where do you suppose this illustration might be used?

- Can you separate the foreground from the middle ground and the background in the landscapes represented here?

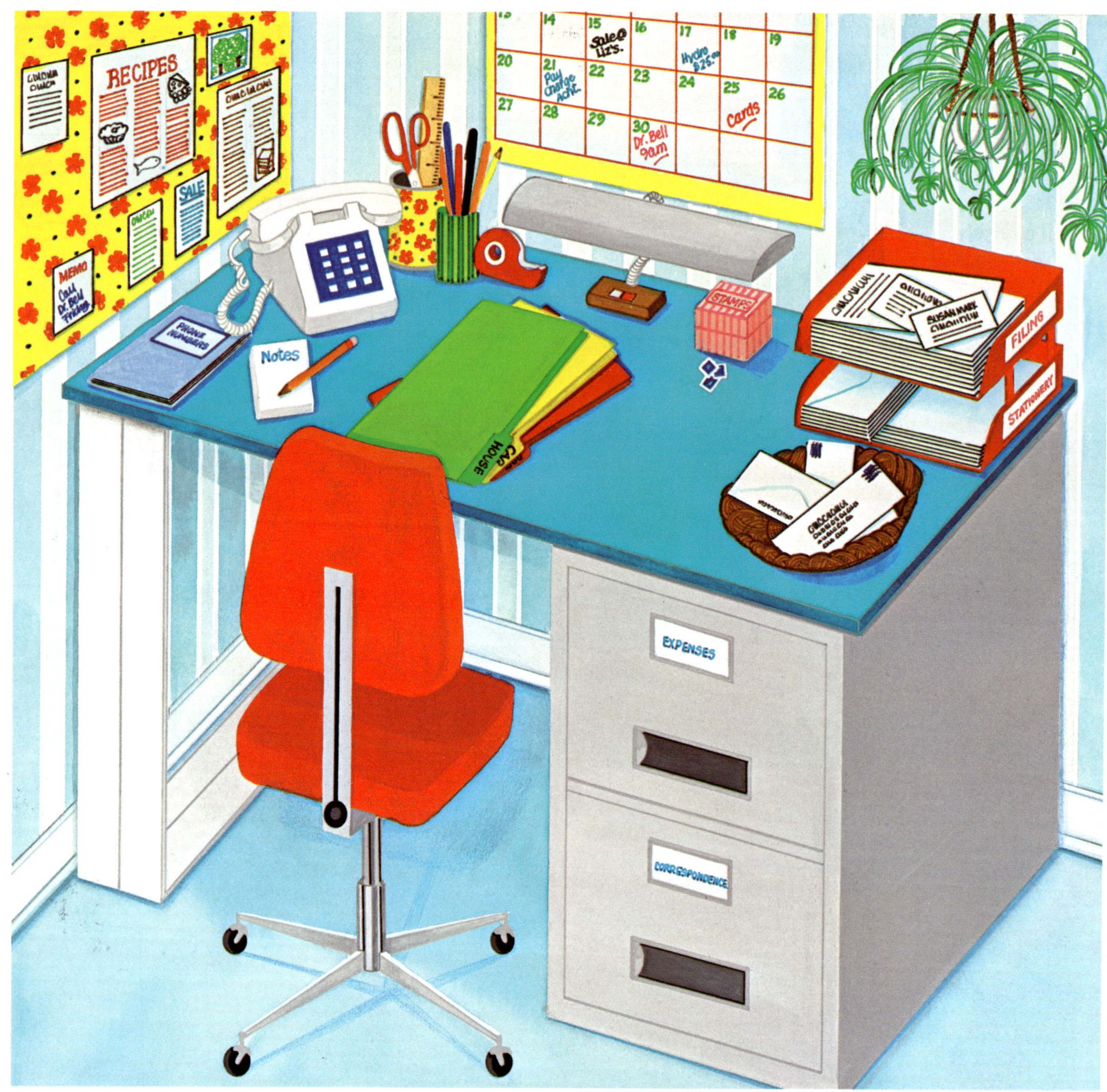

31-1 *Plan your own office*, Susan Mark
Objects from the real world are seen on this carefully organized desk presented by commercial illustrator, Susan Mark. Notice how she has used perspective to help you see objects as they are grouped together on the top of the desk.

31. Things: Still Life

Works of art that take objects as their subject matter are referred to as *still life*. The artist selects and arranges the objects very carefully. The objects may be chosen because they all relate to the same theme. For example, toys may represent memories of childhood; other objects may recall a favourite hobby.

When looking at still life art, first look at the objects individually, and then try to see them as a group of objects. Are they objects that you would likely find together in the real world, or has the artist made an unusual grouping? What is the theme? Do you associate the objects with any special theme?

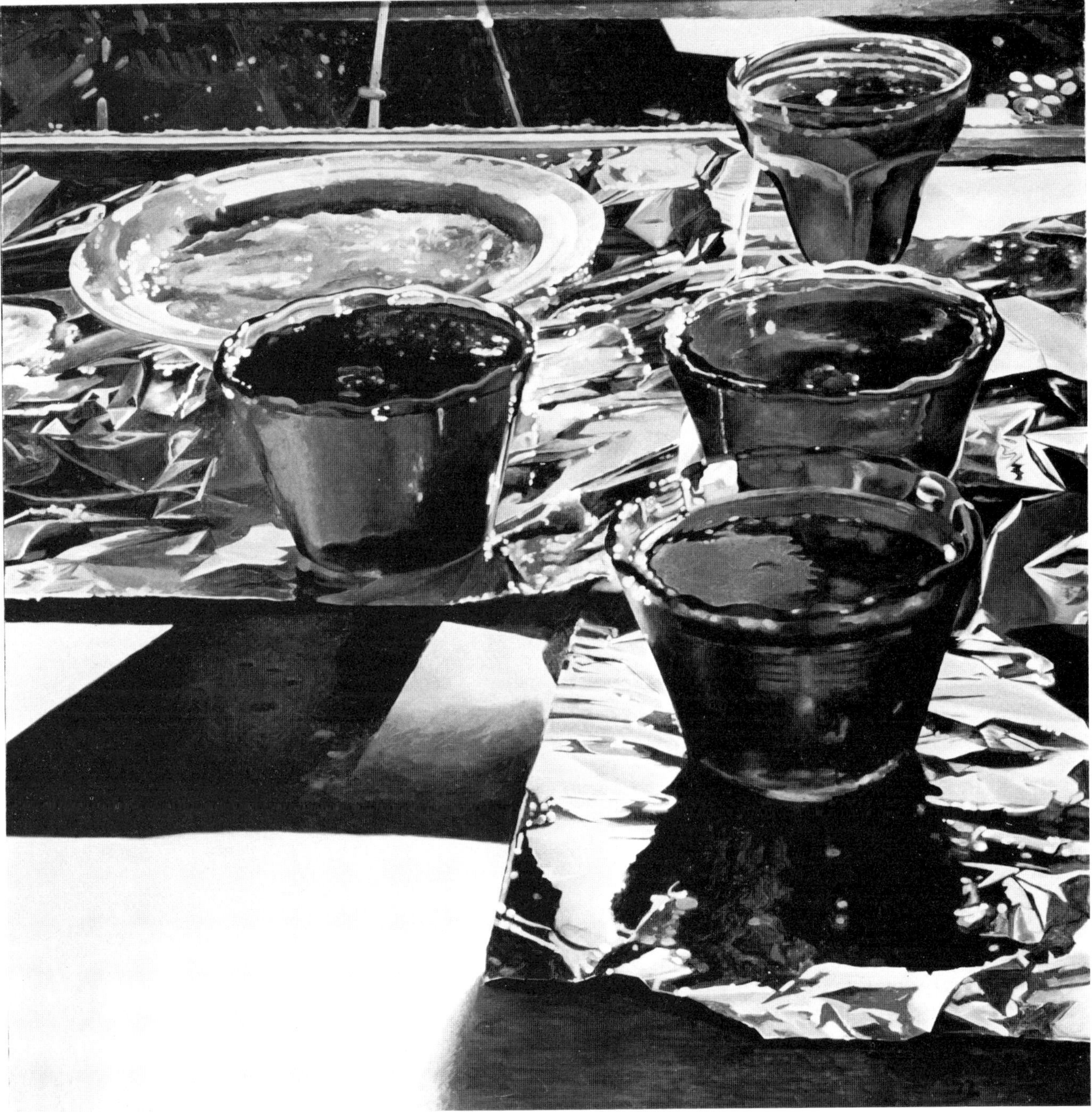

31-2 *Red Currant Jelly*, **Mary Pratt**
Everyday things can be the subject matter of art. Look at the arrangement of colours, shapes and textures.

Look Again

- What three objects would you select from the desk to make an interesting drawing emphasizing texture?
- Describe what this desk would look like if a disorganized person worked here.
- What interesting objects could you organize and sketch to show the place where you work?

- Mary Pratt chooses subjects that people see and use every day. What groups of objects are common in your kitchen or bedroom?
- Try to imagine a story behind her still life objects.

- What objects would you choose to represent the kind of person you are?

32. Special Subject Matter

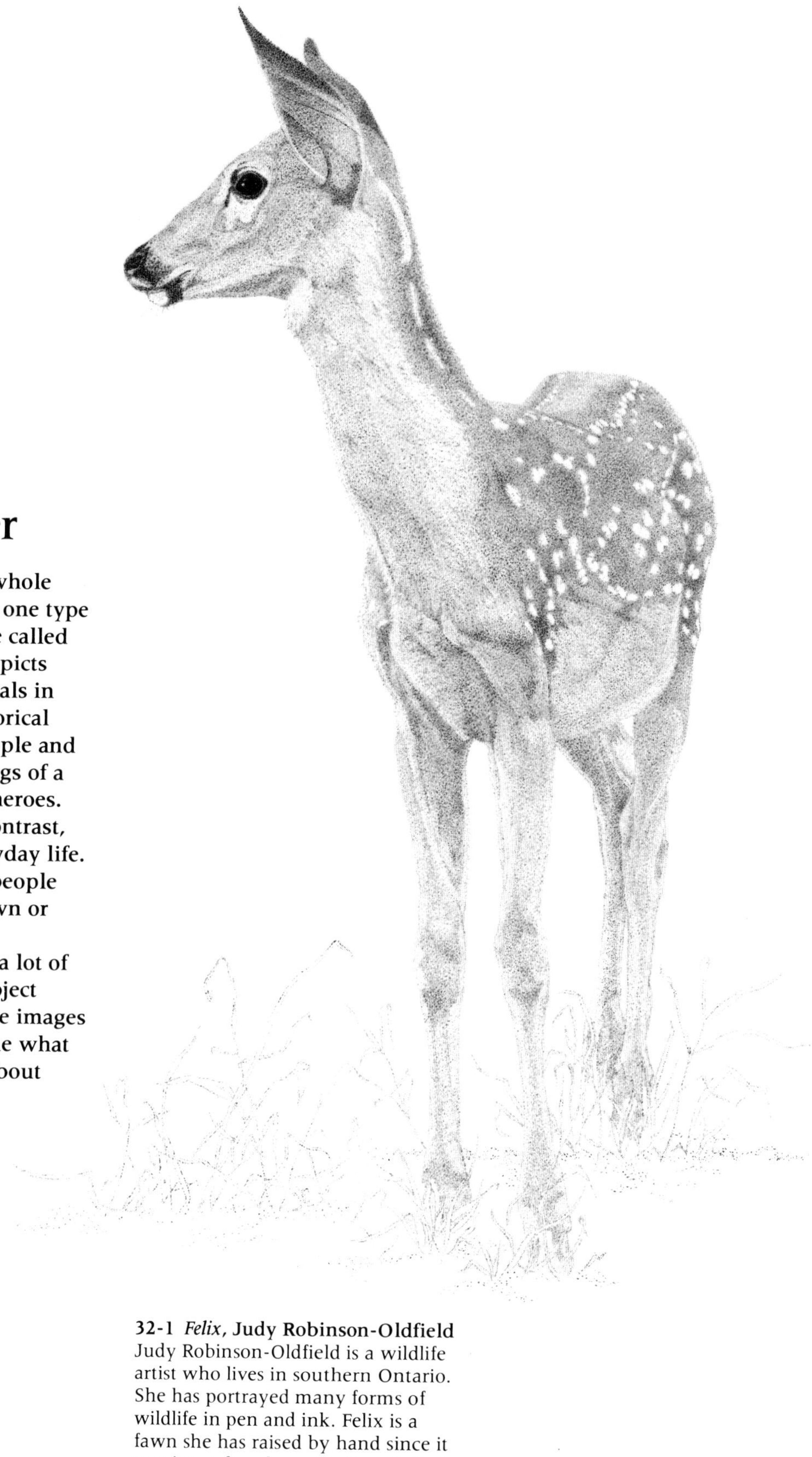

Some artists spend their whole careers working with just one type of subject matter. They are called specialists. Wildlife art depicts birds, fish and other animals in their natural habitat. Historical subject matter records people and events. It includes paintings of a nation's leaders and war heroes. *Genre* subject matter, by contrast, deals with people in everyday life. Examples are pictures of people at work and at play, in town or country settings.

The specialist artist has a lot of concern for the chosen subject matter. Look at the way the images are presented. Try to decide what the artist is trying to say about them.

32-1 *Felix*, **Judy Robinson-Oldfield**
Judy Robinson-Oldfield is a wildlife artist who lives in southern Ontario. She has portrayed many forms of wildlife in pen and ink. Felix is a fawn she has raised by hand since it was just a few days old. Here Felix is portrayed in a dot technique referred to as pointillism.

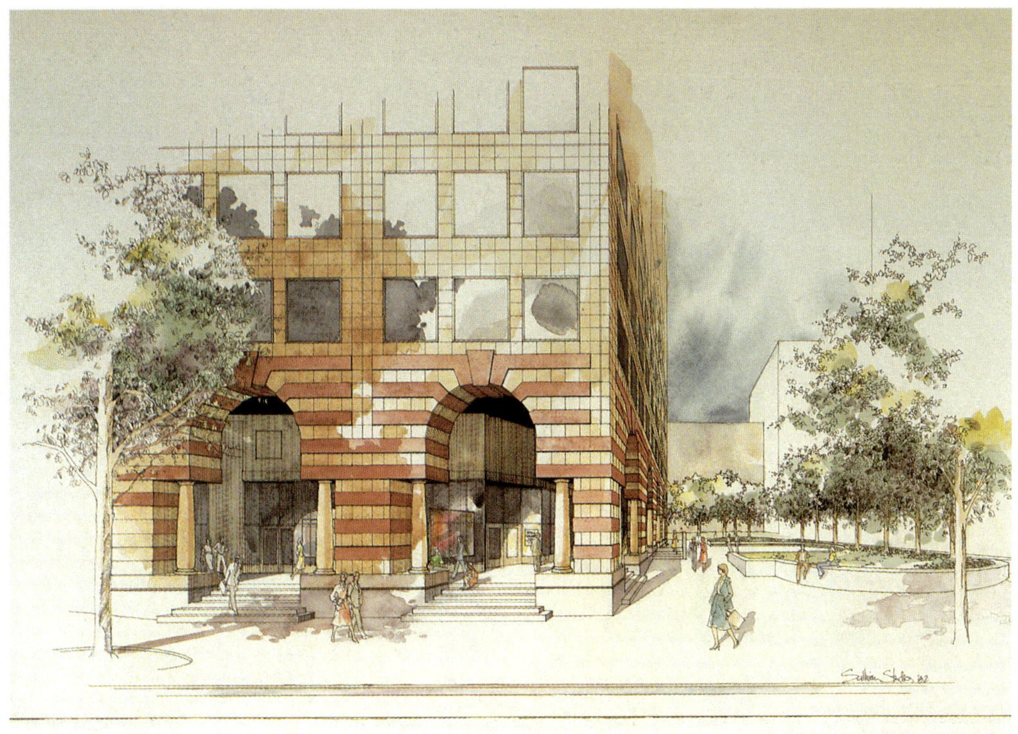

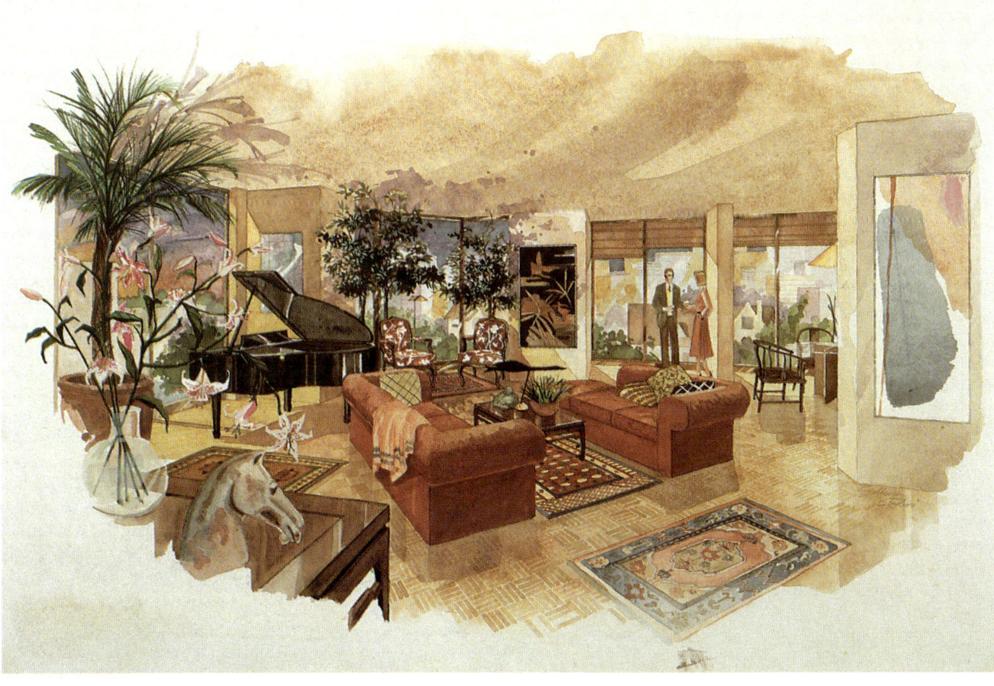

32-2 Architectural illustration, Judy Hulme and Fran Moore
Commercial artists often specialize. Illustrators Judy Hulme and Fran Moore specialize in architectural illustration.

Look Again

- Compare the fawn picture (32-1) with the photo of Felix in Chapter 2. What differences do you see?
- If you have a special pet, think about how you would draw it. What would you emphasize that would not show up in a photo?
- What do you think is the purpose of the architectural drawings? Are they to help the builder? The buyer? Give reasons for your answer.
- Fashion illustrators are also specialists. Compare the purpose of 24-1 with 32-2.
- Although the subject matter is different, what similarities do you see between the wildlife composition and the architectural illustration?

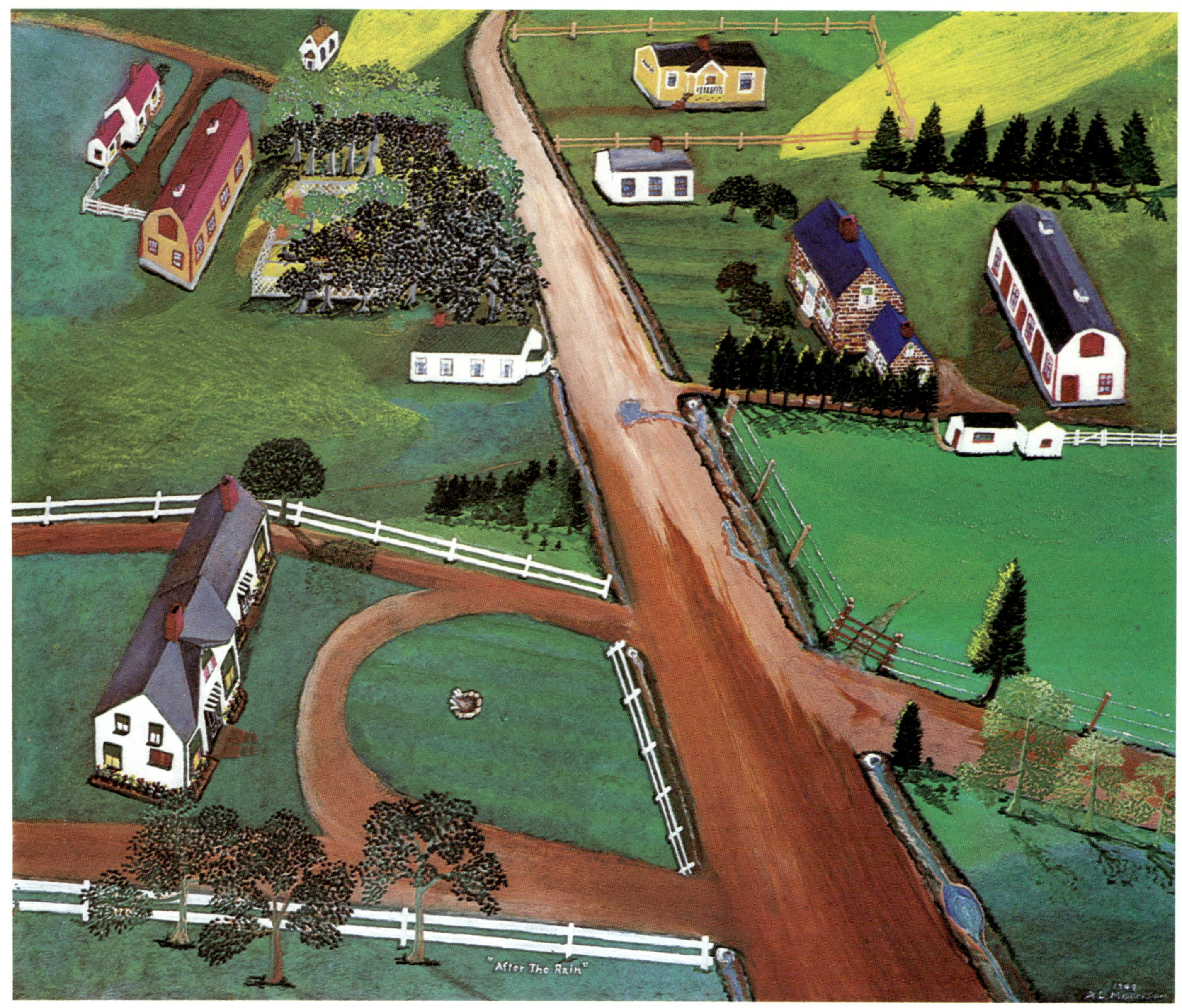

33-1 *After the Rain*, **Alfred L. Morrison**
Alfred L. Morrison is a folk artist from Prince Edward Island. He does not have formal training as an artist. He portrays the history and community life of Prince Edward Island.

33. Style in Art: Personal Style

Today, the word *style* is used in a variety of ways. For example, you hear of hair styles, styles of cars and clothing, and stylish occasions. Some people are described as having style.

An artist is said to have personal style. It is similar to a person's handwriting. It is the special way the artist uses the elements of design and organizes them in a work of art. It is also the artist's own way of using a medium – paint, or fabric or clay. The artist's style also affects the way the subject matter is portrayed. There are as many styles as there are artists. Personal style is part of the way that each artist puts a personal message into each piece of art.

Understanding an artist's style is somewhat like getting to know a new person. Some styles, like people, may seem easier to understand and accept than others. You need to look at several works of art by the same artist to see the style. Also, finding out about the artist's life and what the artist feels is helpful in getting to know an artist's style. Above all, avoid making snap judgements.

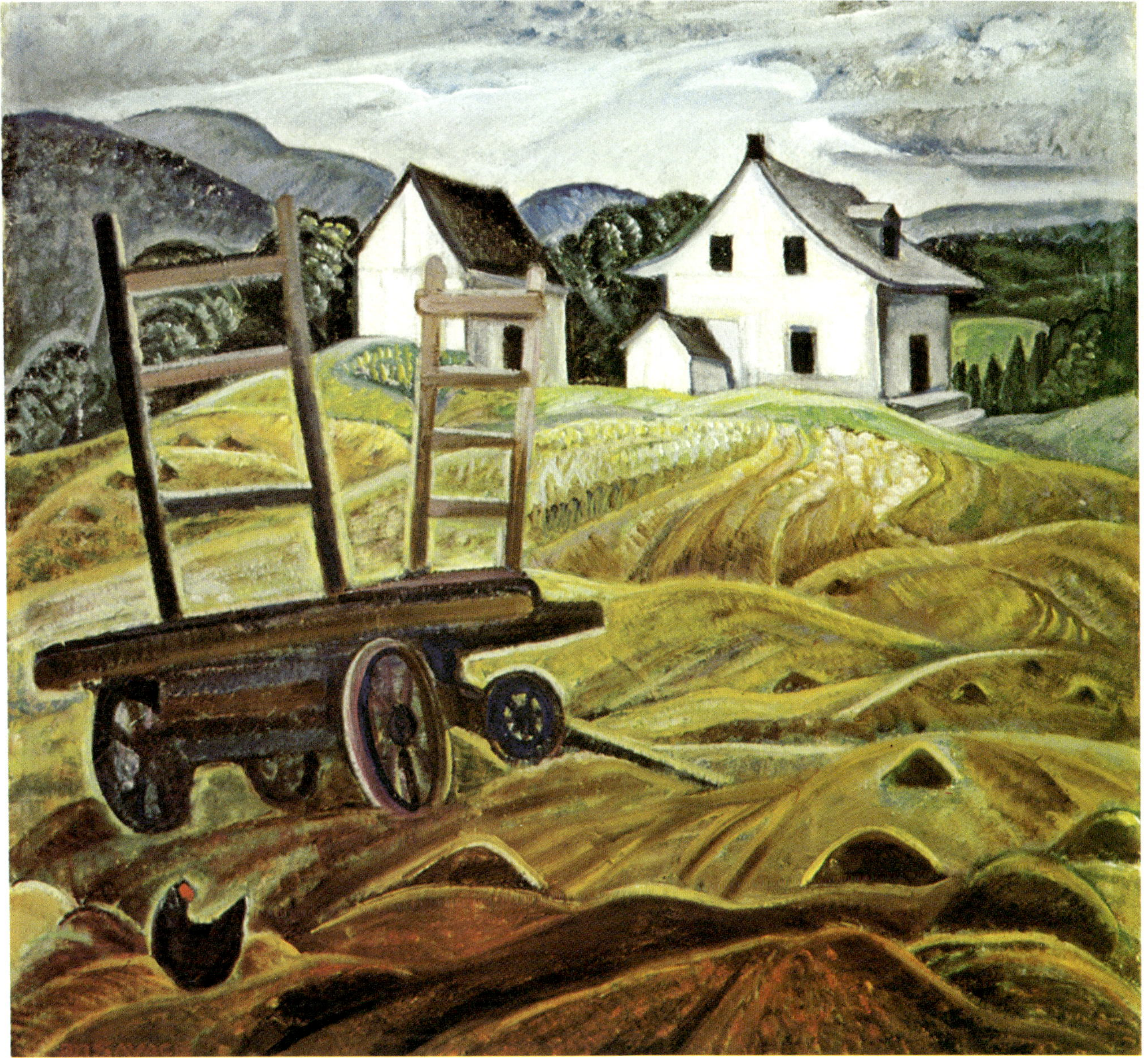

33-2 ***After Rain*****, Anne Savage**
Anne Savage was an art teacher in Ottawa during the years that Canada's famous Group of Seven were painting. Artists often become art instructors in order to make a living.

Look Again

- What sorts of words describe style? For example, try to find words that describe your handwriting. Ask another student in your class to suggest some more words.
- What words would you use to describe Alfred Morrison's style?

- Anne Savage was a close friend of A.Y. Jackson, a member of the Group of Seven. It is common for friends to influence each other. What similarities can you discover between Anne Savage's style and the style of A.Y. Jackson? Look back at Jackson's *Barns* (13-3).

- The same subject can be interpreted in many ways. The artist's personal style works with the subject matter to determine what the final message will be. Compare how Anne Savage and Alfred L. Morrison have interpreted the theme *After the Rain*.
- In each case, how does the picture show that it has been raining?
- How does each picture show that the rain has stopped?

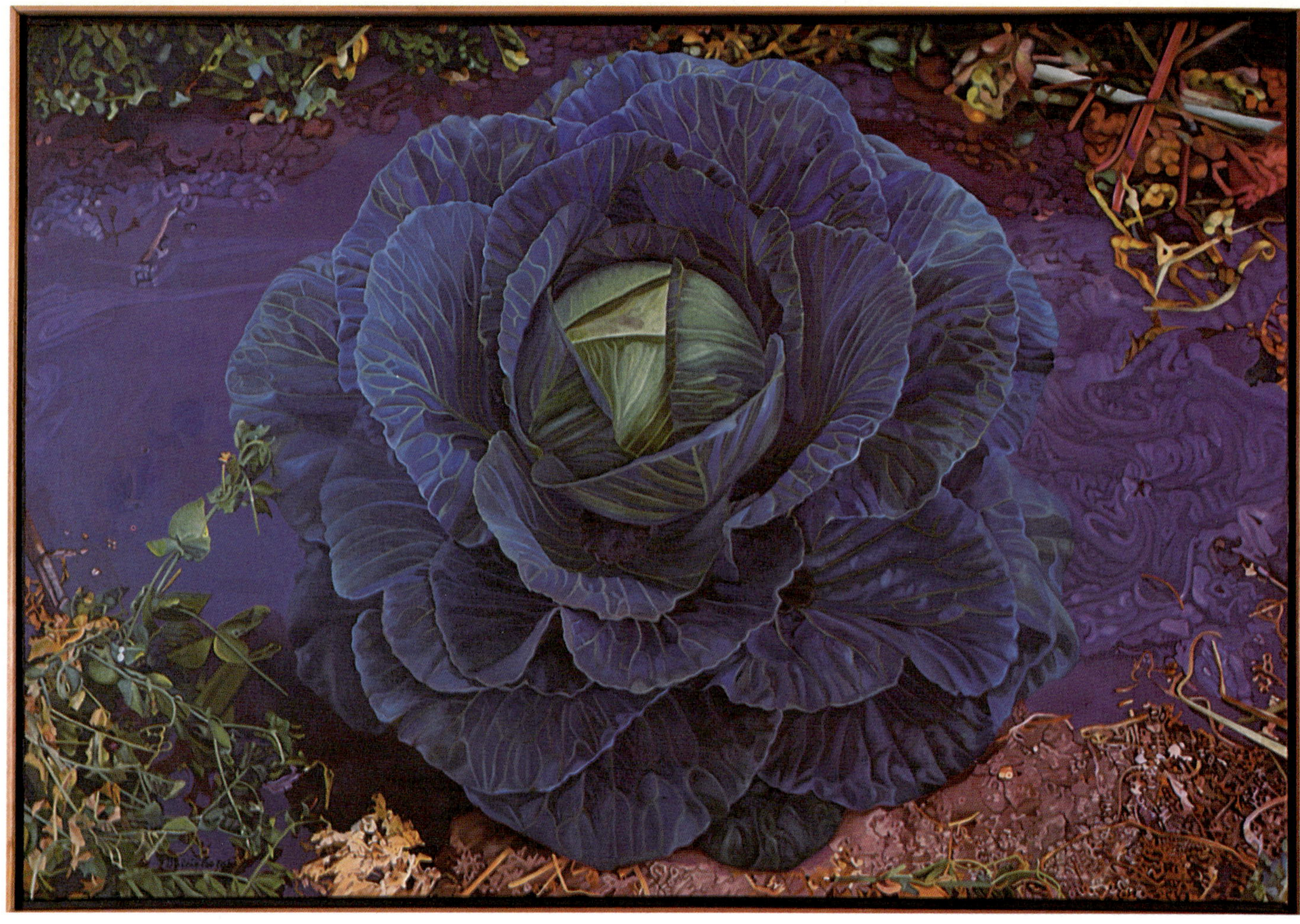

34-1 *Cabbage*, **Dulcie Foo Fat**
A recognizable image (the cabbage) makes Dulcie Foo Fat's painting representational in style.

34. Categories of Style

Although each artist has a personal style, it is possible to group art into categories of style. There are several ways of doing so.

One way is by *culture*. For example, native Indian sculpture is different from Inuit sculpture. Both styles are quite unlike that of the statues found in French Canadian churches, for example.

Another way is by *historical period*. The styles of pioneer homes are often quite different from the styles of new homes designed today. Advertising art from the early part of this century may seem quaint compared with modern advertisements. Of course, sometimes old styles become popular once again. You can probably think of styles in clothing that have been revived.

Yet another way is by other features of the art itself – by function or the type of message.

However, it is helpful to begin with one simple classification that is based on appearance. Art may be representational or non-representational.

Look Again

- What style categories are commonly referred to in clothing? In cars? In eating places? In haircuts? In footwear?

- Find examples of different cultural styles in the art in this book. Choose a word that best describes each style.

- Look at the pictures in Chapter 26. Which building most resembles the parliament buildings in Ottawa?
- What sort of style is this? (Read through Chapter 26 if you are not sure.)

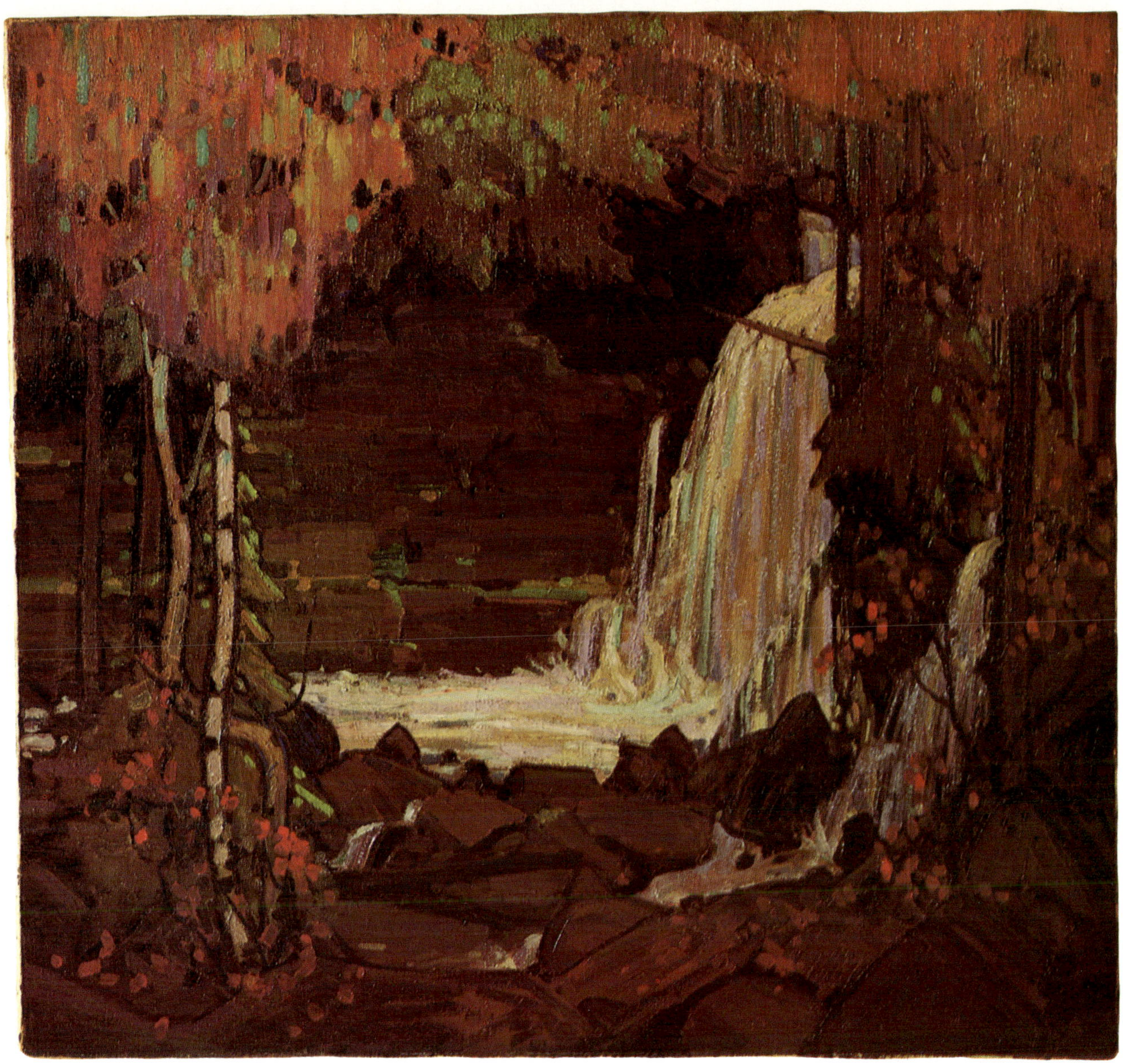

35-1 *Woodland Waterfall*, Thomas John (Tom) Thomson

The development of the camera in the mid-1800s freed the artist from the need to portray the world realistically. Early in the 20th century Tom Thomson and the Group of Seven attempted to develop a style of painting that suited the Canadian landscape. Notice the emphasis on colour and light, the absence of detail and the presence of visible brush strokes. (This style was borrowed in part from a group of French artists known as the Impressionists.)

35. Representational Styles

When you look at a work of art for the first time, you often try to recognize something in it. *Representational art* contains recognizable images of the real world. They may be trees, people or buildings. Some art is very realistic. Other artists may purposely distort or simplify things to give the subject special meaning. They may make them prettier or uglier than they really are.

When you see a work of art that is representational, look carefully at the artist's style. Think about how the artist's choice of line, shape, colour, value or texture has affected the meaning of the subject matter that you see. Does the artist's style focus your attention on a particular aspect of the subject matter? How has the artist's style and choice of subject matter worked together to communicate a message to you?

35-2 *Good Friday*, **Christopher Pratt**
Some artists in the Atlantic provinces have become famous for realism. Christopher Pratt's style shows a real world that could be anywhere, anytime. This special effect is called High Realism.

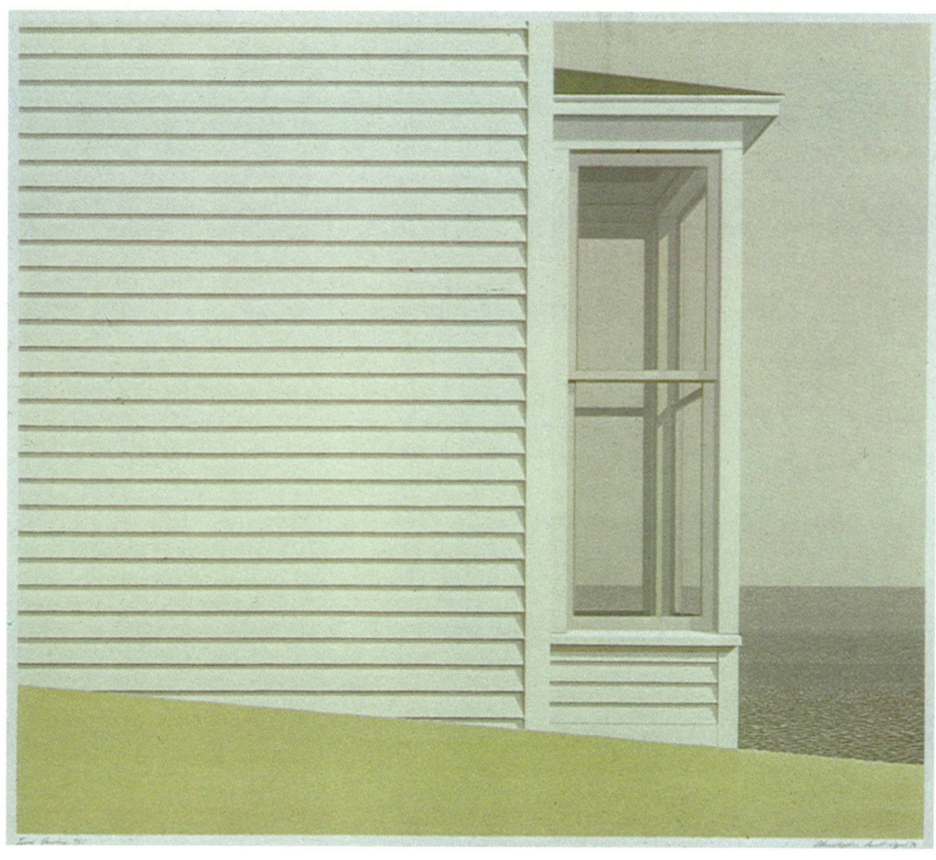

Look Again

- Try to imagine the landscape that Tom Thomson must have been looking at when he painted *Woodland Waterfall* (35-1). In what ways is his painting not realistic?
- What does the painting show that a photo would not show?
- If the colours were changed, how might your feelings about the painting change?

- Find out more about the style of the Group of Seven.
- What words would you choose to describe their style?

- The building in Christopher Pratt's painting is clearly recognizable – but the picture is called *Good Friday*. What would you put in a picture called *Good Friday*?

- Christopher Pratt was a student of Alex Colville at Mount Allison University in New Brunswick. Compare Pratt's style to that of Colville as seen in Chapter 15.

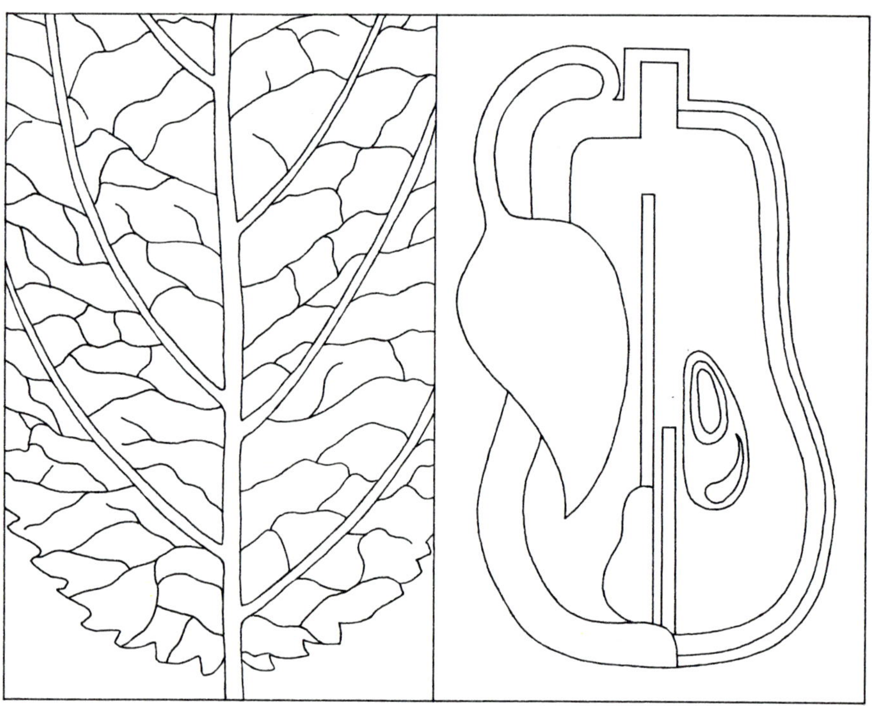

Although based on natural objects, it is possible to see how a representational drawing can be purposely distorted or simplified.

36. Non-representational Styles

Non-representational art does not offer recognizable images. Works of this kind can be puzzling. Learn to think of them in a different way. How has the artist used the elements of design – line, shape, colour, value, space and texture? Does the art work suggest a feeling or an emotion? Does the work of art suggest that the artist's method was spontaneous and quick or slow and precise? What special clues does the title of the art work add to its meaning or intent? Answers to questions such as these will guide your response to non-representational styles.

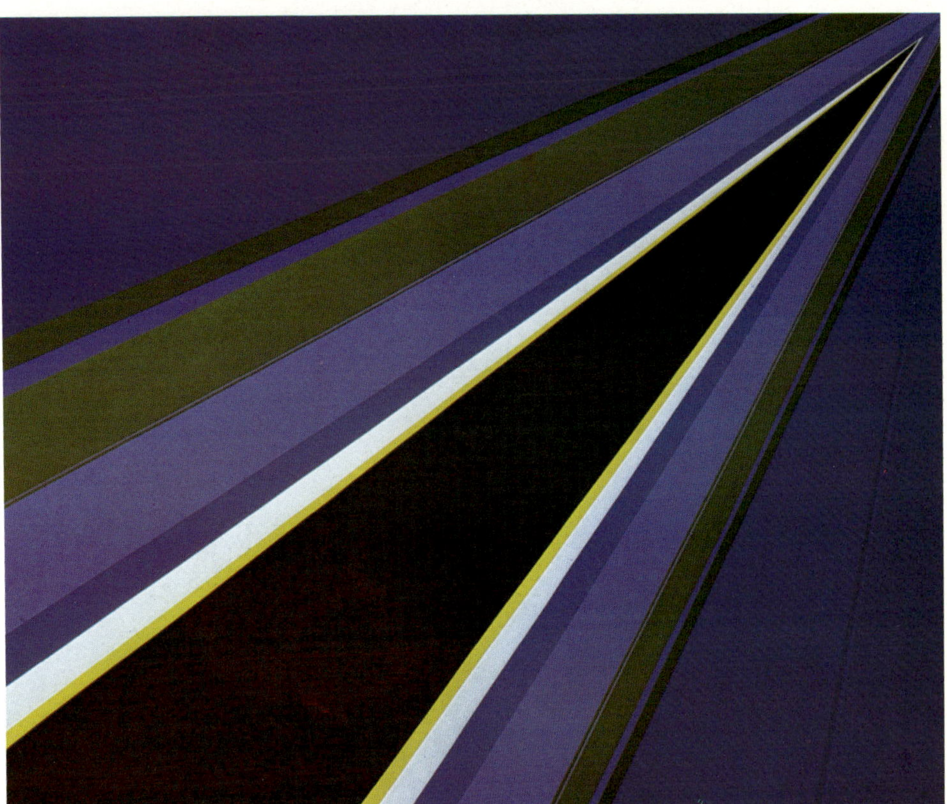

36-1 *Irdu*, **Rita Letendre**
Artists of Québec were among the pioneers of non-representational art in Canada. Rita Letendre, born in Drummondville, Québec, follows this tradition. Wedge-shaped images create cool movement.

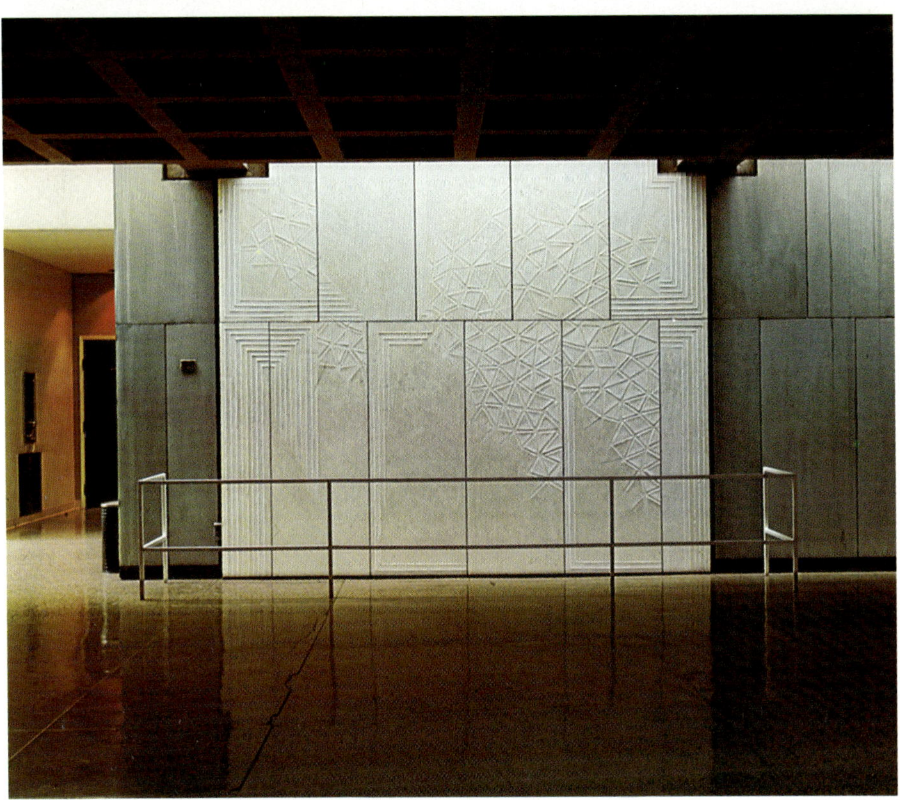

36-2 ***White Mural*, Ron Bloore**
Practise looking at non-representational art. Here is Ron Bloore's *White Mural* as displayed in the Confederation Centre of the Arts in Charlottetown, P.E.I. Look for subtle effects in value and texture in a seemingly plain work of art.

Look Again

- What are the relationships of the colours used in Rita Letendre's *Irdu*?
- Think of your own title for this work of art. Choose a title that expresses an idea, not the name of an object.

- How would the use of brilliant reds and yellows change the effect of Ron Bloore's *White Mural*? Describe what mood it has in white. What mood would it have in red?
- How would a change in texture affect the mood? Imagine the mural if it were all plain or all patterned.

YOU AND YOUR RESPONSE TO ART

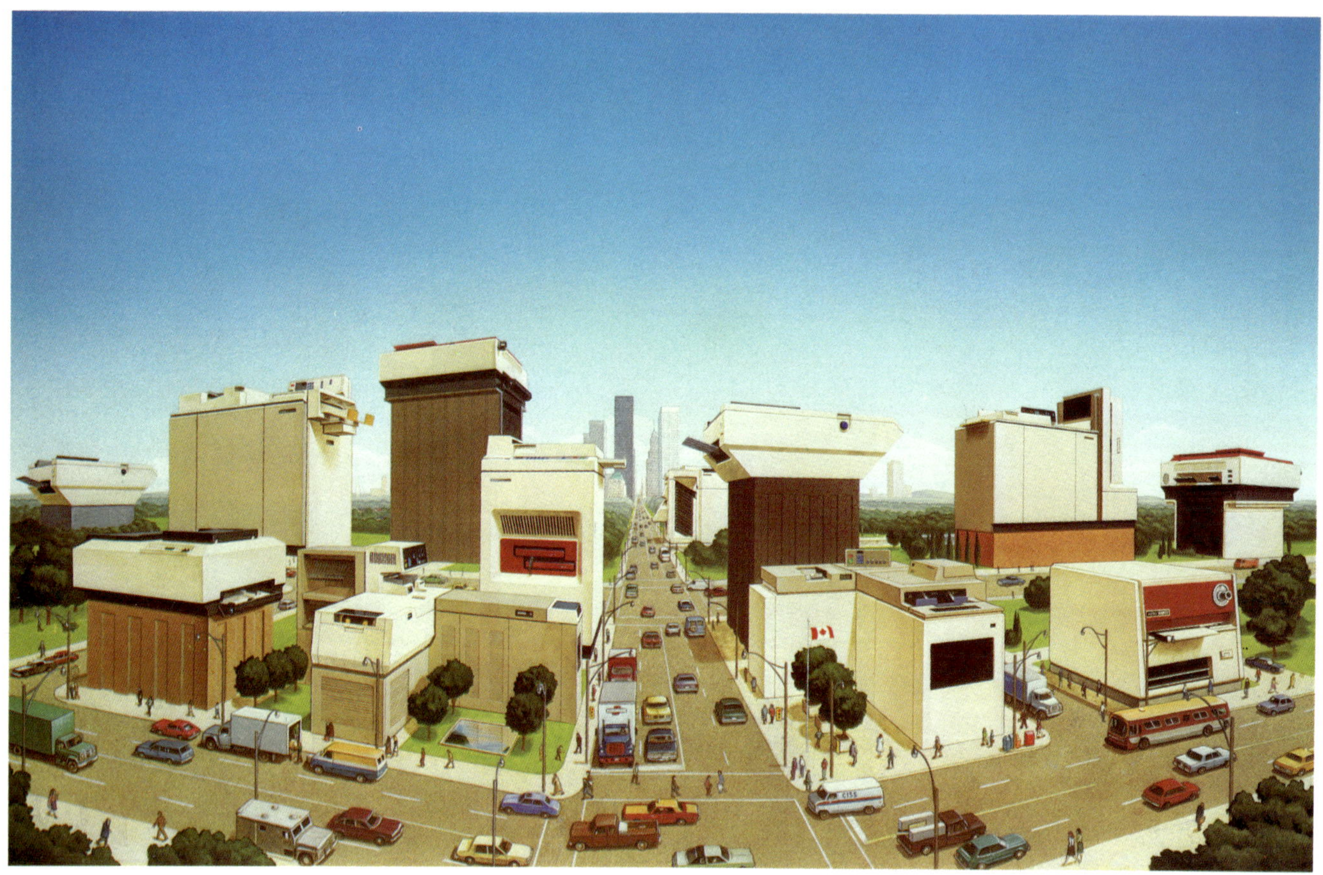

37-1 *Cityscape: Photocopy Machines*, **Julius Ciss**
This illustration done by Julius Ciss for Xerox surprises the viewer. You suddenly discover that what appears as a cityscape has copiers as its buildings. An illustrator can make the artist's message fun to discover.

37. Discovering the Artist's Message

So what is art all about? It is a visual language made up of many parts. This book has shown you many forms of art. You have seen how the elements and principles of design are the words and grammar of the visual language of art. You have learned about some materials that artists use. Also, you have seen how subject matter and style together suggest the meaning of the work of art. Each of these topics has been dealt with individually like the pieces of a puzzle. As you fit the pieces together, you begin to discover the artist's message.

However, there is never one right answer to the question – what does this piece of art mean? Sometimes the title gives a clue. Sometimes the message is hard to find. Sometimes different people see different messages. Great art may offer a new meaning each time you look at it.

Questions:

- What is the artist saying to you about cities and about copiers in 37-1?
- How does the message of this picture differ from the message in Harris' *Mount Lefroy* (38-1)?

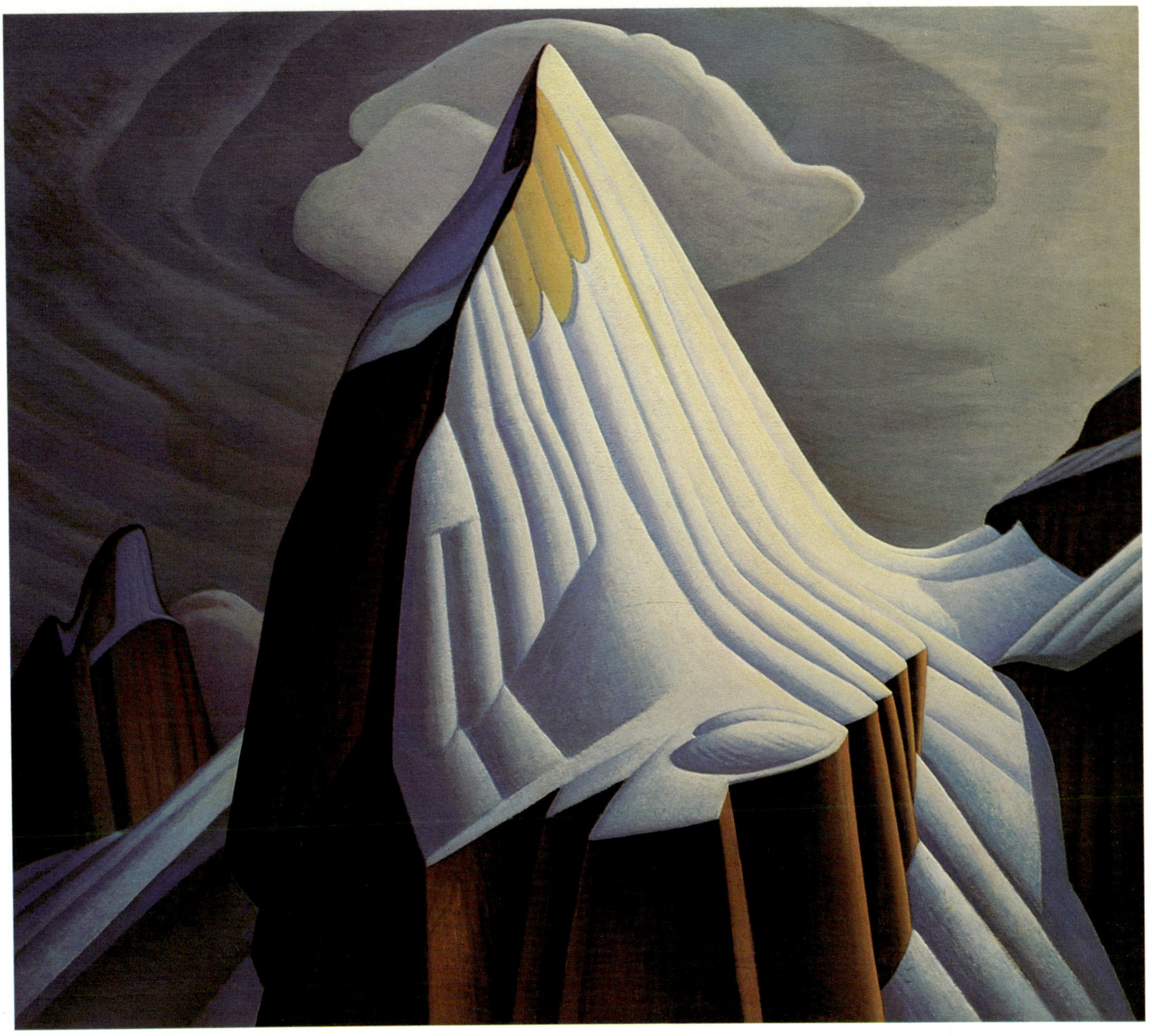

38-1 *Mount Lefroy*, Lawren Harris
Great art allows for the discovery of new meaning with each viewing. Lawren Harris was among the first Canadians to explore, simplify and distort his subject matter.

38. The Value of Art

No book or art teacher can teach you what art to like. Just as an artist's style is personal, so too is the value that you place on the art that you see. Know the difference between good art and the art that you happen to like. There may only be a few works that you like among the many that you recognize as good art. The works that you do not like are not necessarily poor art.

Before you dismiss a work of art, ask yourself if there is anything good about it. For example, is it well designed? Have the materials been handled well? Is it effective in conveying its message? You may still not like it, but you may begin to appreciate it.

Look Again

- How has Lawren Harris made this painting more than just a picture of a mountain?
- What new meaning does Harris' style add to *Mount Lefroy*?

39. Towards Greater Discoveries

Recall the images that you value. How might they differ from those preferred by your parents? Your friends? Remember that responses to art are as personal as the act of creating art. People differ and are influenced in many ways.

Find out about a particular artist whose work you like.
How does knowledge of the artist's values and life experiences affect the messages that you receive through art?
How does the environment of the artist influence the art work created?

Research the cultural background of a favourite artist.
How is the message of the work of art affected as you learn more about the culture in which it was created?

Think of the person you are and the things that you like.
Do you think you will always like the same art that you like now? Why or why not?

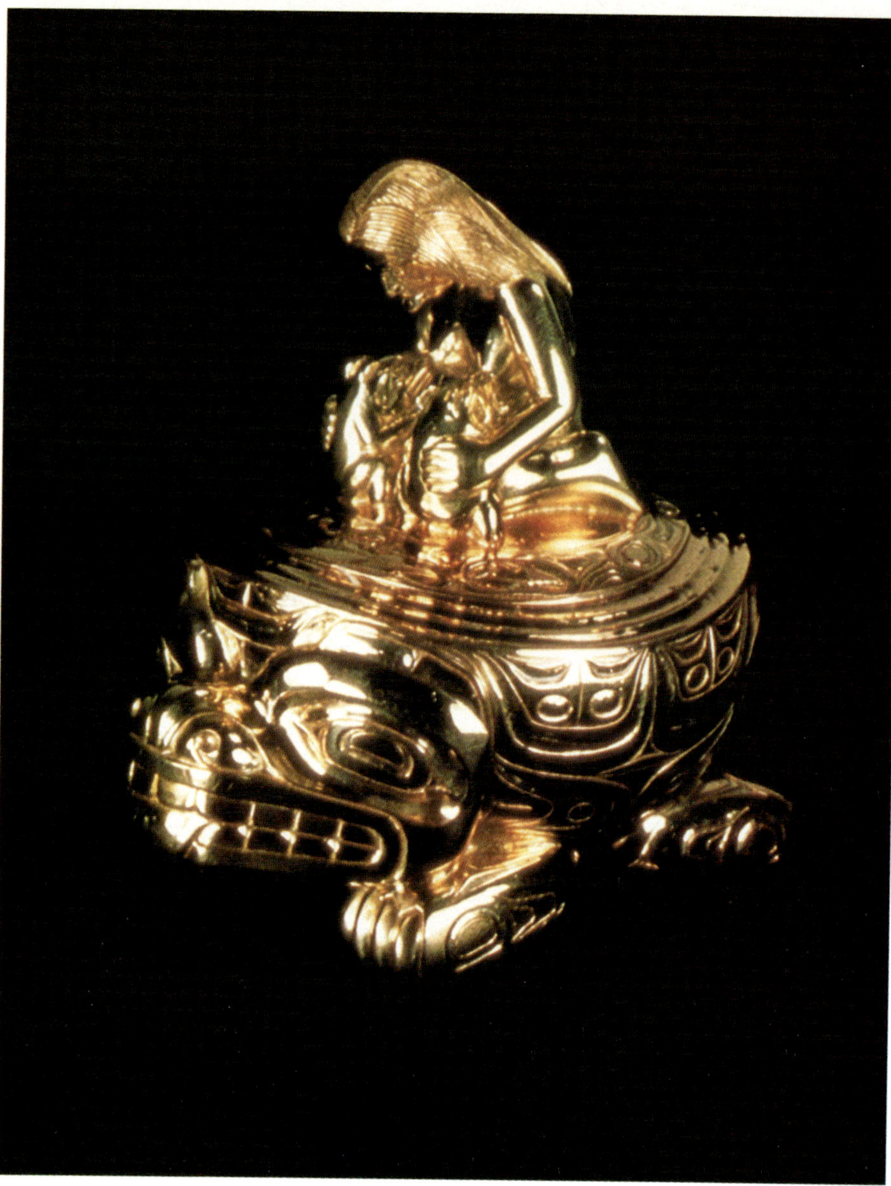

39-1 *Box: Haida Myth of Bear Mother,*
Bill Reid
Here British Columbia artist Bill Reid has created a stunning image in the form of a gold box. It portrays the Haida legend of a beautiful young girl who mates with a bear.

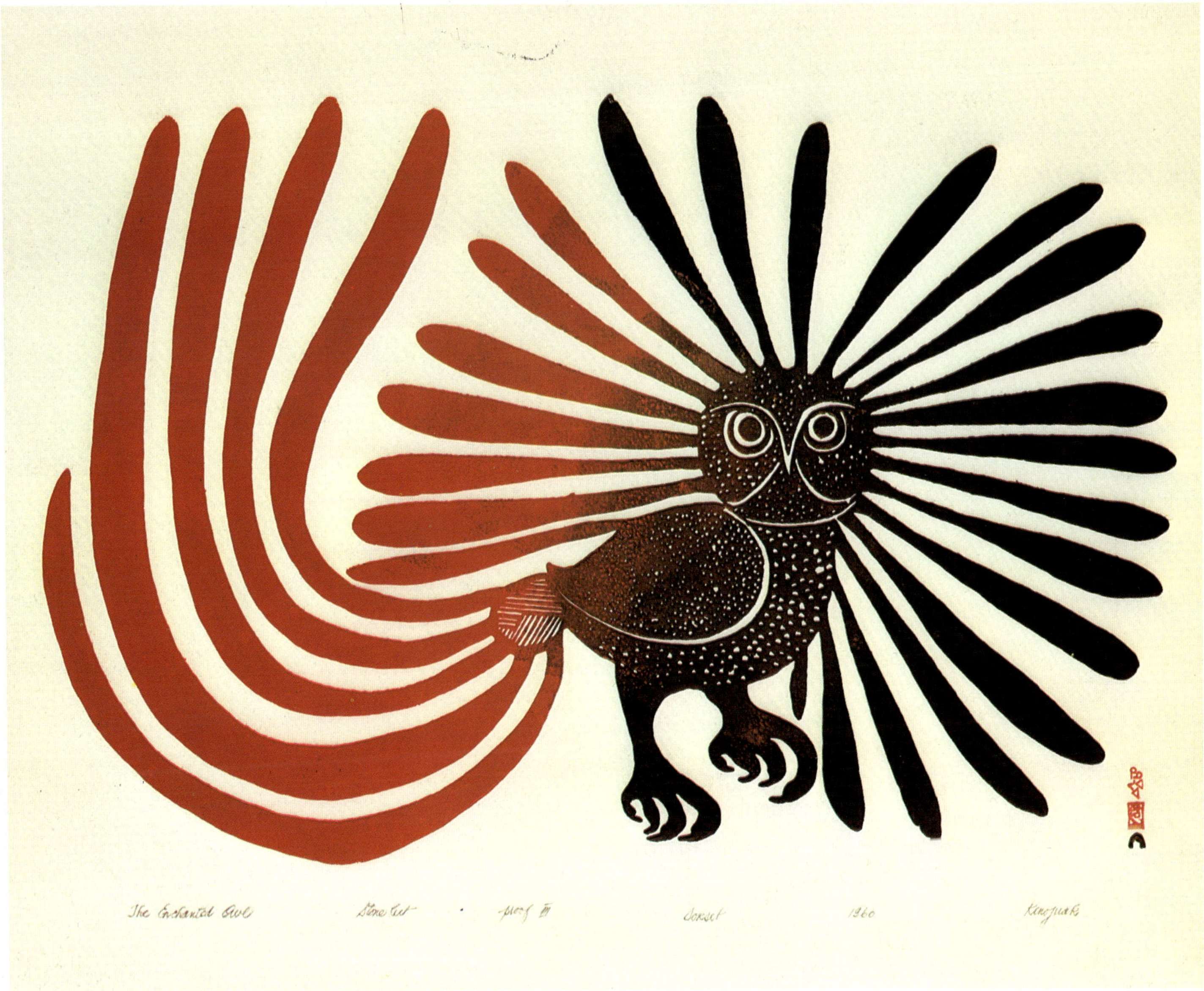

39-2 ***Enchanted Owl*****, Kenojuak**
Enchanted Owl is a famous image created in print form by Inuit artist Kenojuak. It has even appeared on postage stamps.

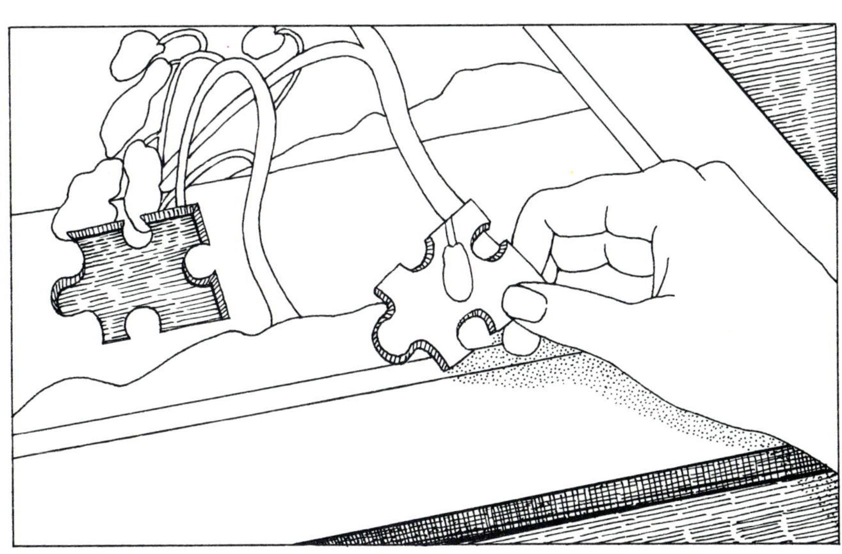

There are many separate clues to discovering the message in each work of art you see. Put all the clues – elements and principles, medium, subject matter, style – together for an answer.

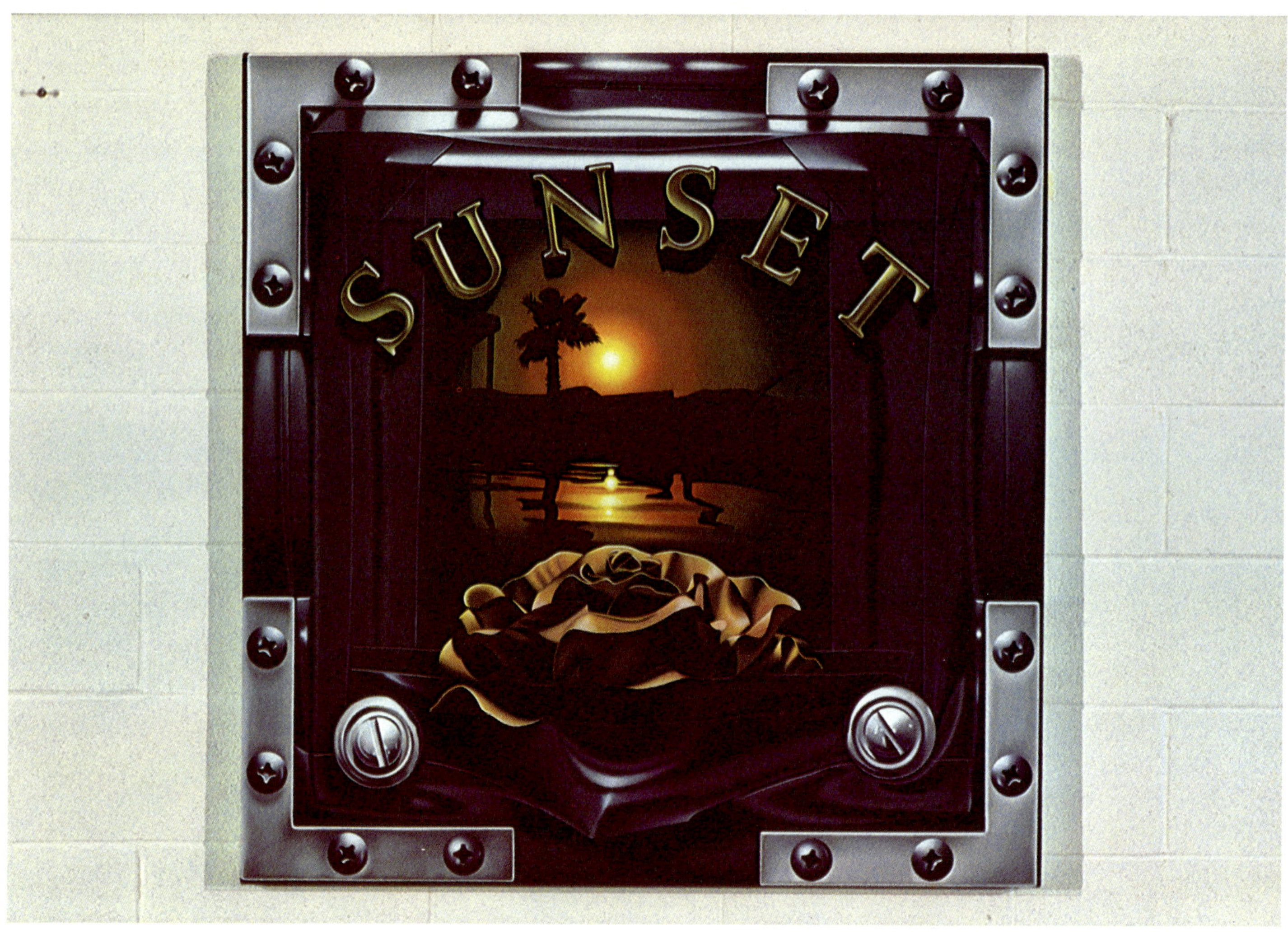

39-3 *Sunset*, **John Hall**
The artist's message is a personal expression. John Hall's *Sunset* is not like any sunset you will see in nature.

Look Again

- In Kenojuak's *Enchanted Owl* (39-2), what elements of design make the image powerful?
- Where is the point of dominance?
- How has movement added impact?

- John Hall's *Sunset* is an unusual one. Carefully examine this work of art. What effects do you expect from a sunset?
- What surprises does this work of art bring?

- Look at art carefully. First, identify what you see. Then look for the relationships between the elements in it. Decide what purpose it was made for. Try to find its message.

Credits

The authors are deeply grateful to all the artists and artisans, the galleries, the museums, the design agencies and all other contributors whose wonderful cooperation made the completion of this book possible. If any acknowledgement or credit has been inadvertently omitted, the authors would appreciate being informed about it so a correction can be written into subsequent editions.

1-1 Ontario Ministry of Tourism and Recreation; **1-2** John H. Murray, Toronto, Ontario; **1-3** Alberta Public Affairs Bureau; **1-4** Travel Manitoba; **2-1** Maryann Kovalski (illustration); **2-2** B. Bennett; **2-3** Frank Robinson; **3-1** Norval Morrisseau, 1931- (Ojibwa), c. 1978, acrylic on canvas, 208.3 × 127.0 cm, The McMichael Canadian Collection, Purchase 1979, 1979.6; **3-2** C.S.E.A. Canadian Young People's Art Collection; **3-3** Frauke Voss and The Ontario Crafts Council; **4-1** Illustration by Cliff Kearns; **4-2** Wascana Centre Authority; **5-1** Marcel Barbeau, 1925- Canadian, *Bas de fleuve*, Liquitex on canvas,50.8 × 152.4 cm, The National Gallery of Canada, Ottawa; **5-2** Designer: Robert Burns; **6-1** B. Bennett; **6-2** John H. Murray, Toronto, Ontario; **6-3** Ontario Ministry of Tourism and Recreation; **6-4** B. Bennett; **6-5** John H. Murray, Toronto, Ontario; **6-6** Alberta Public Affairs Bureau; **8-1** C.S.E.A. Canadian Young People's Art Collection; **8-2** Catherine Burgess and The Canada Council Art Bank; **8-3** © Wendy Whitemore, Illustrator and Designer; **9-1** John H. Murray, Toronto, Ontario; **9-2** Dura Glide Slide developed by Paris Playground Equipment Ltd., Don Curtis, President, Photo: Ken Banks; **9-3** C.S.E.A. Canadian Young People's Art Collection; **9-4** Niviaksiak, 1959, stencil on paper, 59.7 × 44.6 cm, The McMichael Canadian Collection. Purchased with funds donated by the Canadian Dental Association, 1973.9; **10-1** Alberta Public Affairs Bureau; **10-2** Judith Dingle and The Ontario Crafts Council, *Orange Becoming Red Series #2*, 1980, cottons, hand-quilted, 137 × 137 cm; **10-3** C.S.E.A. Canadian Young People's Art Collection; **10-4** Robert Jekyll and The Ontario Crafts Council; **11-1** Samon, whalebone, sinew horn, 11.7 × 19.2 × 6.6 cm, The McMichael Canadian Collection, Purchase 1973, 1981.106.10; **11-2** Cynthia Root and The Ontario Crafts Council; **11-3** John H. Murray, Toronto, Ontario; **12-1** Ivan Eyre; **12-2** Promotion Services Department of Development, Government of Newfoundland and Labrador; **12-3** Molly Bobak and The Canada Council Art Bank; **12-4** Colette Whiten, Carmen Lamanna Gallery and The Canada Council Art Bank; **13-1** 1981, wood sculpture. Installed at the Macdonald Stewart Art Centre, Guelph, Ontario, Edward A. Turvey; **13-2** Ontario Ministry of Tourism and Recreation; **13-3** A.Y. Jackson, Canadian, 1882-1974, c. 1926, 81.6 × 102.1 cm, oil on canvas, Art Gallery of Ontario, Toronto. Gift from Reuben and Kate Leonard Canadian Fund, 1926; **14-1** Alexandra Haeseker and The Canada Council Art Bank; **15-1** C.S.E.A. Canadian Young People's Art Collection; **15-2** Alexander David Colville, Canadian, 1920- , 1952, tempera on board, 80.7 × 60.3 cm, The National Gallery of Canada, Ottawa; **15-3** Taffi Rosen; **16-1** Ontario Ministry of Tourism and Recreation; **16-2** Rita Letendre and The Canada Council Art Bank; **16-3** Illustration; Fred Oakley of Art and Design Studios Ltd., Client: Loblaws Limited; **17-1** Wanda Koop, Photo: William Eakin, Winnipeg, Manitoba; **17-2** Marion Spanjerdt and The Ontario Crafts Council; **17-3** Marion Spanjerdt and The Ontario Crafts Council; **18-1** Emily Carr, Canadian, 1871-1945, 1929, oil on canvas, 108.6 × 68.9 cm, Art Gallery of Ontario, Toronto. Bequest of Charles S. Band, 1970; **18-2** Duffy Wilson, 1925- (Tuscarora), 1975, steatite, 14.0 × 11.0 cm, The McMichael Canadian Collection. Purchase 1975, 1975.51; **20-1** Gary Olson and Galerie Dresdnere (Collection of Richard Selfridge, Edmonton, Alberta); **20-2** Jack Humphrey, Canadian, 1901- , 1957, watercolour, 36.8 × 54.6 cm, The National Gallery of Canada, Ottawa; **20-3** Illustration, Ted Larson; **20-4** Carol H. Fraser and The Canada Council Art Bank; **21-1** Nita O. Forrest and The Canada Council Art Bank; **21-2** *Mount Jacobsen #2*, 1974/75, acrylic on canvas, 287.7 × 367.5 cm, Collection of The Winnipeg Art Gallery. Donated by the Women's Committee. G-76-5. Photo: Ernest Mayer, The Winnipeg Art Gallery; **21-3** Watercolour, 28.8 × 38.6 cm, Collection of the Edmonton Art Gallery. Purchased with funds donated by Builder's Contract Management; **22-1** Pitseolak, 1904-1967 (Cape Dorset), 1967, stone cut and stencil on paper, 39.8 × 55.5 cm, The McMichael Canadian Collection. By Exchange, 1973, 1973.13.2; **22-2** Lauréat Marois; **22-3** University of Guelph Collection/Macdonald Stewart Art Centre, Guelph, Ontario. Gift of the Class of 1956, Macdonald Institute, in memory of Dr. M. Isabel Irwin, 1978; **23-1** John H. Murray, Toronto, Ontario; **23-2** Annemarie Schmid Esler; **23-3** Frances Loring, Canadian, 1887-1968, 1928, bronze, H: 58.4 cm, Art Gallery of Ontario, Toronto. Gift of the Canadian National Exhibition Association, 1966; **23-4** Michael Hayden and The Canada Council Art Bank; **24-1** Sheila McGraw; **24-2** Paul Griffin, Sheridan Computer Graphics Labs; **24-3** Tom McNeely, designer and illustrator, commissioned by Imperial Oil Limited on behalf of the Canadian Amateur Swimming Association; **25-1** Photograph by Barbara Astman. Courtesy The Sable-Castelli Gallery, Toronto; **25-2** Sam Tata and The Canada Council Art Bank; **25-3** Ontario Ministry of Tourism and Recreation; **25-4** Ellie Forrest; **26-1** Promotion Services Department of Development, Government of Newfoundland and Labrador; **26-2** John H. Murray, Toronto, Ontario; **26-3** Direction générale du tourisme, Québec; **26-4** Ontario Ministry of Tourism and Recreation; **26-5** Travel Manitoba; **26-6** John H. Murray, Toronto, Ontario; **27-1** Photo courtesy of the Arctic Trading Company, Churchill and the Tetrad Design Group, Winnipeg, Manitoba; **27-2** Rex Lingwood and the Ontario Crafts Council; **27-3** *Porcelain bonnet Romantic era, 1826* by Audrey Davies from the collection *Lost Images: 200 Years of Women's Hats in Porcelain*, Ontario Crafts Council; **27-4** Lois Betteridge and the Ontario Crafts Council, Photo: Keith Betteridge; **27-5** Len Chodirker; **27-6** Michael Fortune and the Ontario Crafts Council; **29-1** Wood and paint,

22.0 × 16.8 × 12.8 cm, The McMichael Canadian Collection. Gift of Mr. A.Y. Jackson, 1969.28; **29-2** Courtesy of the Mira Godard Gallery, Toronto, Ontario; **29-3** Travel Manitoba; **29-4** Conklin & Garrett Limited; **30-1** Emily Carr, 1871-1945, c. 1935, oil on paper, 86.7 × 58.4 cm, The McMichael Canadian Collection. Gift of Dr. and Mrs. J. Murray Speirs, 1969.20; **30-2** Dorothy Knowles, 1969, acrylic on canvas, 142.2 × 184.4 cm, Collection of the Edmonton Art Gallery. Purchased in 1972 with funds donated by the Women's Society; **30-3** Glenbow Museum, Calgary, Alberta; **30-4** Wendy Whitemore, Illustrator and Designer; **31-1** Susan Mark, Design and Illustration; *Canadian Living Magazine*; **31-2** Mary Pratt, 1935- , Canadian, 1972, oil on board, 44.5 × 44.5 cm, The National Gallery of Canada, Ottawa; **32-1** Judy Robinson-Oldfield; **32-2** Sullivan Studios Inc., 51 Buliver St., 3rd Floor, Toronto, Ontario M5T 1A1; **33-1** A.L. Morrison, Libby Oughton Publisher, Ragweed Press, Charlottetown, P.E.I.; **33-2** Anne Douglas Savage, 1897-1971, Canadian, c. 1942, oil on canvas, 76.8 × 101.6 cm, The National Gallery of Canada, Ottawa; **34-1** Dulcie Foo Fat, *Cabbage*, 1974, oil on canvas, 97 × 143 cm, Collection of the Government of Alberta; **35-1** Thomas John (Tom) Thomson, 1877-1917, c. 1916, oil on canvas 121.9 × 132.5 cm, The McMichael Canadian Collection. Purchase 1977 with funds donated by the W. Garfield Weston Foundation, 1977.48; **35-2** Christopher Pratt and the Canada Council Art Bank; **36-1** Rita Letendre and the Canada Council Art Bank; **36-2** Confederation Centre of the Arts, Charlottetown, P.E.I.; **37-1** Julius Ciss Illustration Inc.; **38-1** Lawren Harris, 1885-1970, 1930, oil on canvas, 133.5 × 153.5 cm, The McMichael Canadian Collection. Purchase 1975, 1975.7; **39-1** National Museum of Man, National Museums of Canada, Neg. #S73-1115; **39-2** Kenojuak, 1927- (Cape Dorset), 1960, stone cut on paper, 58.2 × 65.7 cm, The McMichael Canadian Collection. Purchase 1979, 1979.10.1; **39-3** John Hall and the Canada Council Art Bank.

For further information concerning the C.S.E.A. Canadian Young People's Art Collection contact

Dr. Margaret Travis
Director, C.S.E.A. Canadian Young People's Art Collection
Faculty of Education
University of Victoria
P.O. Box 1700
VICTORIA, B.C.
V8W 2Y2

Glossary

acrylic paint – water-based, polymer pigments, which dry quickly to a waterproof surface.

additive method – a way of making sculpture by adding material, as in the construction method.

analogous colours – neighbouring colours on the colour wheel, such as green, blue-green and blue.

applied arts – forms of art such as the graphic arts or crafts used for practical purposes.

appliqué – a technique of fabric decoration that involves stitching materials such as cloth or beads on to the fabric.

architect – a person who designs and draws up the plans for buildings.

architecture – a form of art that includes the planning, designing, and construction of buildings for public and private use.

artisan – a person skilled in a craft or trade; a craftsperson.

asymmetrical balance – balance in which the parts are not equal in size, but produce a balanced visual effect; also called informal balance.

background – the part of a picture that is or appears to be farthest from the viewer.

balance – refers to a principle of design used to develop a pleasing harmony of the various elements in a design or painting. See also radial balance, symmetrical or formal balance, and asymmetrical or informal balance.

batik – dip and dyeing technique that uses wax to block out areas that are not supposed to take the colour of the dye.

bisqueware – ceramic clay that has been fired once in the kiln and not yet glazed.

braiding – the interweaving of three or more strands of hair, rope, fabric or other materials.

bust – a piece of sculpture representing the head, shoulders and upper chest of a person.

casting method – a sculptural technique in which a liquid, often hot metal or plaster, is allowed to harden in a mold.

ceramics – a process in which clay is fired to a permanent state. It is used to make many objects such as decorative sculpture, jewellery and dishes.

cityscape – a view of buildings and streets, used as subject matter in art.

colour – an element of design.

colour wheel – an arrangement of the hues, with each one opposite its complementary colour or hue.

cold glass method – a technique of carving or etching designs into cold, hard glass.

commercial art – art that is made specially to promote business.

complementary colours – opposite colours on the colour wheel. For example, red and green, blue and orange, purple and yellow.

compositional movement – part of a principle of design; used to direct the viewer's gaze.

computer graphics – art or design produced with the aid of a computer.

contrast – often refers to dark and light or other differences used to create strong feelings in a work of art.

construction method – the joining together of materials to produce sculpture.

cool colours – colours suggesting coolness; green, blue, purple.

crafts – forms of art including textiles, woodworking and jewellery.

cultural period – a time-span often recognizable by specific styles used by a society in art and architecture.

dominance – a principle of design that involves making part of a work stand out from the rest.

drawing – a form of art that involves sketching or outlining with tools such as pencils, conté crayons, or pens.

earthenware – a basic clay body used in ceramics.

elaboration – something that is worked out with great care; to elaborate a work of art is to add details to it.

fabric construction – one part of fabric crafts; it includes weaving and knitting.

figurative art – art that depicts people.

fine arts – forms of art including painting, drawing, sculpture and architecture.

foreground – the area in a picture appearing closest to the viewer.

formal balance – same as symmetrical balance; parts are balanced visually.

genre – a style of painting showing ordinary daily life.

graphic arts – includes drawing, painting, photography; also engraving, etching, lithography; often used to refer to art used for business purposes.

greenware – ceramic work that is dry but has not been fired to a permanent state in a kiln.

historical period – a particular time span of history; for example, the Victorian era.

hot glass method – a technique of creating containers or sculptures with glass that is in a liquid state; includes glass blowing.

hue – refers to pure pigment; the name of a colour, such as red.

illustration – a picture, diagram or design used to explain or decorate something.

informal balance – same as asymmetrical balance; the parts are not equal in size but produce a balanced visual effect.

intaglio – a method of making prints, in which the paper takes the ink that has been pressed into grooves made in the printing plate.

intermediate colours – see tertiary colours.

intensity – the brightness or dullness of a colour.

knotting – a technique of fabric construction.

landscape – a view of the scenery on land, often used as subject matter in art.

layout – the plan or arrangement used by an artist for a design, such as a poster.

lettering – letters drawn, painted or stamped; often used in a layout.

line – the path that a dot makes as it moves; line is one of the elements of design.

linear perspective – a formal system in drawing, used to give the illusion of depth or distance.

lithography – a type of printmaking involving transferring an image on to paper from a flat surface such as limestone or metal.

media – substances, such as paint, chalk, wood, or ink used by artists.

middle ground – the area in a picture appearing between the foreground and the background.

movement – a principle of design. See

compositional movement or physical movement.

neutrals – having little or no colour, such as grey.

non-representational art – art that does not offer recognizable images.

oil paints – permanent, slow-drying paints that are mixed with varnish, turpentine and linseed oil.

painting – a form of art that involves applying paint to a prepared surface.

photography – a form of art in which images are produced on film by using a camera.

physical movement – action such as running or swimming as shown in a picture.

picture plane – the flat surface on which an artist creates the picture; also refers to depicting advancing and receding space.

porcelain – a hard, white clay body that is fired at very high temperatures to produce fine, almost transparent objects.

portrait – a picture or painting of a person.

primary colours – three basic colours that can be mixed together to make any other colour; red, blue and yellow are the three basic hues.

principles of design – guides used by the artist to create unity in a work of art.

printmaking – a process by which more than one copy of a picture is pulled from a printing block. See also intaglio, lithography, relief printmaking, serigraph, stenciling.

radial balance – refers to design elements organized around a central point.

relief – the projection of figures and forms from a flat surface. See also relief printmaking and relief sculpture.

relief printmaking – the process of making prints from linoleum, metal or stone that has been carved away, leaving a raised surface.

relief sculpture – the process of carving a sculpture into a flat piece of wood or stone; a raised surface can also be made by adding on materials, such as ceramic clay.

repetition – the repeated use of an element or motif to create a sense of movement.

representational art – art that contains recognizable images of the real world.

sculpture – a three-dimensional work of art molded, carved or constructed out of materials such as plaster, ceramics, wood or stone.

sculpture-in-the-round – sculpture that looks complete from any angle.

seascape – a view of ocean scenery, often used as subject matter in art.

secondary colours – orange, purple and green, which are made by mixing two primary colours together.

serigraph – an original colour print produced by the silkscreen process

shade – a variety of a hue, produced by adding black.

shape – an element of design. The outward contour or outline; the form of a person or thing.

silkscreen – a form of printmaking in which ink is forced through a screen of silk or similar material that is prepared as a stencil.

space – an element of design used to describe distance, depth and perspective. Refers also to interior and exterior architectural design.

stenciling – a form of printmaking in which paint or ink is forced through holes cut in a paper or metal stencil on to paper or another surface.

still-life – art in which objects are the subject matter.

stitchery – part of the textile crafts, using decorative stitches with a variety of threads and yarns.

stoneware – a hard, porous clay body used in ceramics that is fired at a temperature higher than that for earthenware but lower than that for porcelain.

style – a personal way of working. Also refers to a group of artists whose works have similar aspects in the use of design or materials.

subject matter – the person, object or idea represented.

subtractive method – a way of making sculpture by taking away some of the materials, as in the carved method.

symmetrical balance – balance in which the parts are visually equal; also called formal balance.

tempera paints – water-based paints that can also be mixed with egg or some similar substance.

tertiary or intermediate colours – colours that are made by mixing one primary and one secondary colour.

texture – surface feel or quality; i.e., rough or smooth.

three-dimensional – having length, width and depth.

tie dye – a textile dyeing technique that uses ties to prevent parts of the fabric taking dye when dipped in the dye bath.

tint – a variety of a hue produced by adding white.

two-dimensional – having only length and width.

typography – the art or process of printing with type to produce material such as posters, advertisements or books.

unity – refers to a principle of design in which all parts of a composition or sculpture appear to work together.

value – the element of design having to do with degrees of lightness and darkness.

variety – a principle of design; repeating elements using changes in the patterns.

volume – a shape having three dimensions.

warm colours – colours suggesting warmth; yellow, orange and red.

watercolour paints – pigments that are mixed with water to produce clear, transparent colours.

weaving – the interlacing of threads or yarns to make a fabric, usually done on a loom.

Index